# ON BEING A MACHINE
## Volume 1
## Formal Aspects of Artificial Intelligence

**ELLIS HORWOOD SERIES IN ARTIFICIAL INTELLIGENCE FOUNDATIONS AND CONCEPTS**
*Series Editor:* Dr AJIT NARAYANAN, Head of Computer Science, University of Exeter

**ARTIFICIAL INTELLIGENCE AND INTELLIGENT SYSTEMS: The Implications***
D. ANDERSON

**AI AND PHILOSOPHY OF LANGUAGE***
B. CARR

**ON BEING A MACHINE, Volume 1**
**ON BEING A MACHINE, Volume 2***
A. NARAYANAN

**CAN MACHINES THINK FOR US?**
D. STEIN

**ARTIFICIAL INTELLIGENCE: A Handbook of Professionalism**
B. WHITBY

* *In preparation*

# ON BEING
# A MACHINE
## Volume 1
## Formal Aspects of
## Artificial Intelligence

AJIT NARAYANAN, B.Sc., Ph.D.
Department of Computer Science
University of Exeter

**ELLIS HORWOOD LIMITED**
Publishers · Chichester

Halsted Press: a division of
**JOHN WILEY & SONS**
New York · Chichester · Brisbane · Toronto

First published in 1988 by
**ELLIS HORWOOD LIMITED**
Market Cross House, Cooper Street,
Chichester, West Sussex, PO19 1EB, England
*The publisher's colophon is reproduced from James Gillison's drawing of the ancient Market Cross, Chichester.*

**Distributors:**

*Australia and New Zealand:*
JACARANDA WILEY LIMITED
GPO Box 859, Brisbane, Queensland 4001, Australia

*Canada:*
JOHN WILEY & SONS CANADA LIMITED
22 Worcester Road, Rexdale, Ontario, Canada

*Europe and Africa:*
JOHN WILEY & SONS LIMITED
Baffins Lane, Chichester, West Sussex, England

*North and South America and the rest of the world:*
Halsted Press: a division of
JOHN WILEY & SONS
605 Third Avenue, New York, NY 10158, USA

*South-East Asia*
JOHN WILEY & SONS (SEA) PTE LIMITED
37 Jalan Pemimpin # 05–04
Block B, Union Industrial Building, Singapore 2057

*Indian Subcontinent*
WILEY EASTERN LIMITED
4835/24 Ansari Road
Daryaganj, New Delhi 110002, India

© **1988 A. Narayanan/Ellis Horwood Limited**

**British Library Cataloguing in Publication Data**
Narayanan, Ajit
On being a machine. —
(Ellis Horwood series in artificial intelligence foundations and concepts)
Vol. 1: Formal aspects of artificial intelligence
1. Artificial intelligence
I. Title
006.3
**Library of Congress Card No.** 88–23020

ISBN 0–85312–957–6 (Ellis Horwood Limited)
ISBN 0–470–21235–7 (Halsted Press)

Typeset in Times by Ellis Horwood Limited
Printed in Great Britain by Hartnolls, Bodmin

# Contents

*This book is dedicated to Ravi and Belinda*

# Preface

There is a central thesis that runs throughout these two volumes and which will surface from time to time, especially in the second volume where the thesis will be explored in some depth. The thesis, very briefly, is this: artificial intelligence (AI), despite considerable advances in its techniques, tools and applications, has not developed significantly as far as its theoretical and philosophical aspects are concerned, because from the very beginning AI has been miscategorized by theoreticians, philosophers, and even AI researchers. The cause of the miscategorization can be traced back partly to not only Turing's seminal paper (discussed in some detail in Chapter 1) but also the roots of computer science (Chapter 2) as well as the roots of formal philosophy (Chapters 3 and 4). On the computational side, by allowing itself to be tied in with formal computer science from the very beginning, AI has necessarily, and therefore not surprisingly, been constrained in its theoretical power: all the formal limitations that apply to computer science apply to AI. On the philosophical side, by allowing itself to be tied in with formal developments in philosophy, especially in the areas of logic and semantics, AI has necessarily, and therefore again not surprisingly, been constrained in its philosophical power: all the limitations that apply to formal philosophy apply to AI. That, at least, is the thesis.

The traditional answers given by AI researchers to these constraints have been either to accept the formal constraints and work within them, or to side-step the constraints through the use of non-formal theories, which leads to a weakening of their arguments in the eyes of the formalists. The idea of *overcoming* the formal constraints of computer science and philosophy, and of identifying the manner by which such constraints are overcome with a methodology and subject matter of AI proper, has not been seriously explored. The main aim of these two volumes is precisely to explore how the formal constraints can be overcome, and to examine the claim that such an endeavour characterizes the essential methodology of AI.

The conclusion will be that, in AI, it is perfectly possible and highly desirable that formal theories be augmented by non-formal, yet rigorous, models and approaches. The main constraint on the power of AI has been the accepted equivalence of formality with rigour, as if one is not possible without the other. Our conclusion, it is hoped, will convince AI researchers that it is possible, and highly desirable, to have rigour, but not complete formality, in their methodology, and that once the requirement for formality is loosened AI will make significant contributions to not only theoretical computer science but also the philosophies of mind and language.

To achieve our aim, we have split the book into two volumes: the first volume deals with computational concepts and formal philosophy, whereas the second deals with recent developments in the philosophies of mind and science, and in cognitive science.

One aim of the first volume, which is mainly expository in nature, is to present as objective an account as possible of the conceptual foundations on which much of AI sits. Another is to remind ourselves of many interesting assumptions that lurk behind these formal developments. Some recent criticisms of AI which are based on such conceptual and formal foundations are examined at the end of the relevant chapters. The second volume, however, is much more critical: it will be argued that many attacks on AI disguise metaphysical and philosophical assumptions, many of which are as questionable as the claims made on behalf of AI.

Another way to describe the structure of the overall book, very roughly, is to state that the first volume deals mainly with the so-called 'Mathematical Objection', 'Lady Lovelace's Objection', and 'The Argument from the Informality of Behaviour', whereas the second deals with the 'Argument from Consciousness'. Hence, the first volume, roughly, will deal with formal aspects of AI, and the second with philosophical aspects.

As far as possible, the material presented in both volumes assumes very little knowledge of the relevant subject matter on the part of the reader. This is deliberate: some formal theoreticians may want an introduction to the recent and relevant developments in philosophy, and many philosophers may want an introduction to formal theory and to the basis of the 'Mathematical Objection', about which they may have heard much but of which they may have read little. However, the real aim for *introducing* the subject matter in this way is two-fold. Firstly, it is to remind expert formal theoreticians and philosophers that at the roots of their subject are very many definitions and assumptions which they may have forgotten about as their experise in their chosen area increases. Secondly, it is to be able to start the critical evaluation of formal methods in AI in the second volume with a clear assumption that the reader will be able to understand the more technical points as they arise.

Taken together, these two volumes present a view of machine consciousness and thought, of what it could be like to be a machine. We shall see that, if our thesis is true, it is perfectly possible to raise the question of machine consciousness within the framework of questioning what it could be like to be a machine. Turing wrote:

> According to [the 'Argument from Consciousness'], the only way by which one could be sure that a machine thinks is to be the machine and to feel oneself thinking.

As we shall show, the Argument from Consciousness (sometimes explicitly, at other times implicitly) is often central to the very many debates on whether machines can be intelligent, or can think. Hence, the best way of tackling the overall question, 'Can machines think?', may well be to ask whether it is possible to be a machine and feel oneself thinking.

Briefly, the approach we adopt in this volume for tackling this question is as follows. Chapter 1 introduces the (modern) conceptual and philosophical foundations of AI. Chapter 2 deals with computation theory and towards the end of that chapter we introduce the idea of a theory of computational intelligence, based very loosely on the Chomsky-grammar classification concept. In Chapters 2 and 3, we discuss the status of statements taken from such a theory of computational intelligence by looking at the assumptions behind the Chinese Room Argument. In Chapter 3 we examine the limitations of any theory of computational intelligence if it is expressed in formal terms. In Chapter 4, we discuss how such an intelligence theory might be justified, namely, by means of some form of intuitively appealing ascription theory.

The aim of this volume is deliberately to leave a few loose strands which will be tied together in the second (and less formal!) volume.

Finally, I need to acknowledge several people. First and foremost, Antony Galton, who patiently waded through several drafts of this volume, pointing out inaccuracies, over-generalizations, and straightforward misconceptions: I too was not immune from the crime of forgetfulness and oversimplification! His tireless efforts cannot be underestimated. I take full responsibility for whatever mistakes remain. Next, Colin Beardon, Brian Carr, Glen Langford, Steve Torrance, and Masoud Yazdani, for various comments and promptings at critical times. Also to Ravi, who patiently but eagerly typed the manuscript into the computer. And to Sue Horwood, for accepting many excuses for failing to meet deadlines.

**PART I**

# INTRODUCTION

# 1

# Introduction to the philosophy of artificial intelligence and computational philosophy

## 1.1 COMPUTATIONAL PHILOSOPHY AND THE PHILOSOPHY OF ARTIFICIAL INTELLIGENCE

Our purpose is to explore several issues which fall into the areas which we call 'Philosophy of Artificial Intelligence' and 'Computational Philosophy'. First, let us state what we mean by these terms. By 'Philosophy of Artificial Intelligence' we mean a meta-level conceptual exploration of theories, approaches, methodologies and notations of artificial intelligence (AI). For example, just as 'Philosophy of Language'

> ... consists in the attempt to analyze certain general features of language such as meaning, reference, truth, verification, speech acts, and logical necessity ... (Searle, 1971, p. 1)

and the 'Philosophy of Mind'

> ... has as its primary responsibility the *analysis* of the *concepts* of consciousness and specific mental phenomena ... (Shaffer, 1968, p. 8) (his italics)

so, by analogy, 'Philosophy of Artificial Intelligence' consists of that area of philosophy which

(1) attempts to analyse certain general features of AI, such as intelligence, knowledge representations, automated reasoning, memory organizations, language understanding, and learning; and
(2) has as its primary responsibility the analysis of the concepts of AI and specific AI phenomena.

By 'Computational Philosophy' we mean, also be analogy, that area of philosophy which

(1) attempts to analyse certain general features of computation, such as

automata theory, Turing Machines, computability, and decidability; and

(2) has as its primary responsibility the analysis of the concepts of computation and specific computational phenomena.

We shall use the term 'Computational Philosophy' to cover the Philosophy of Computation as well as to imply that we are dealing with philosophical theories that are computational in nature. One of the most striking aspects of artificial intelligence philosophizing is the appeal to various 'mind games' or 'thought experiments' involving the concept of an intelligent computer. As we shall see, such appeals can be made both to strengthen as well as to criticize the notion of machine intelligence.

The central theme that runs through this book is the attempt on our part to demonstrate the deep relationships between these two areas of philosophy and the implications that these relationships have for

(1) the concept of 'thinking, intelligent machine', and
(2) the idea that we, as human beings, are thinking, intelligent machines.

Neither (1) not (2) above presupposes that thinking, intelligent machines will, or must, be built, or that a human being *is* a thinking, intelligent machine. Rather, the aim is to provide a conceptual framework within which such ideas and concepts can be explored and evaluated so that we can come to some agreement as to what it is like, or whether there is anything that it is like or could be like, to be such a machine.

The starting point of our explorations will be Turing's paper, 'Computer machinery and intelligence', published in 1950. There are three main reasons for adopting such a starting point. Firstly, Turing himself was a computational theorist who was fascinated by the possibility of thinking machines. His paper neatly falls into the overlap area between Philosophy of AI and Computational Philosophy mentioned earlier.

Secondly, in a historical context, Turing's paper is usually considered to have laid a conceptual, and controversial, foundation stone for the discipline that was to become AI.

> In 1950, Alan Turing wrote a most prophetic and provocative article on Artificial Intelligence. (Hofstadter, 1979, p. 594)

> [The Turing Test] which he proposed in 1950 [is part of] an influential discussion of machine intelligence. (Haugeland, 1986, p. 133)

Some AI researchers believe that Turing's contribution to AI started before 1950:

> Alan Turing's great contribution was published in 1937, when he was 25. (Michie, 1982, p. 28)

> Alan Turing's influence in the development of computers and in their

possibilities as 'intelligent machines' is now well known, and he may legitimately be regarded as *the* pioneer of what is now known as Artificial Intelligence. (Hutchins, 1986, p. 26) (my italics)

So, for computational theorists, it may well be the case that Turing is best remembered for his work on an abstract mechanism called 'Turing Machine' and on 'computable functions'. As we shall see later in the book, for Turing the notions of machine intelligence, abstract machines and computable functions were closely intertwined. But it is important to return to this paper since, like many seminal papers on a subject, much myth and hearsay surround its content. By using the 1950 paper as a starting point, we effectively begin our exploration of AI concepts and theory with a blank slate.

Thirdly, since 1950 tremendous advances have been made in computational theory, AI and philosophy — advances which even Turing would have found difficult to envisage. In computational theory we had the growth of mathematical and formal linguistics. The early writings of Chomsky concerning the formal properties of grammars, and the developments in the relationships between automata and languages, to mention just a couple of areas, took place during the 1950s and early 1960s. Some of the theoretical advances were caused by the tremendous interest in machine translation during that period, especially in the United States of America. This is of relevance to us since the nature of the 'test' that Turing proposed in 1950, and which we shall carefully examine, depends heavily on the idea that a computer could converse naturally with a human. And in AI, we had an explosive growth in the development of tools, concepts, techniques and theory during the 1960s, and 1970s. Indeed, the growth has not yet stopped. The main results of this growth include new knowledge representation techniques, learning strategies, reasoning methods and implementation languages, and a variety of methodological appoaches.

Nor was philosophy immune from change during this period. Wittgenstein's *Philosophical investigations* was published, in English, in 1952, almost immediately after its appearance in German. Other philosophical works by Strawson, Grice, Searle, Quine, Dummett, Montague and Davidson also appeared during the three decades following 1950.

And so another aim of this book is to re-appraise Turing's basic argument and views in the light of this explosion in theoretical and philosophical knowledge that appeared subsequent to (and not, of course, because of!) the publication of his paper.

## 1.2 TURING'S IMITATION GAME: EXPOSITION

Let us first look at Turing's paper, 'Computing machinery and intelligence', published in the philosophical journal *Mind* in 1950. All references to that paper in this book will be taken from this original publication. This is a deliberate attempt on our part to return to the original version rather than relying on subsequent, but sometimes heavily edited, versions of the paper.

We shall work through his paper fairly carefully. Much of the misunderstanding that surrounds Turing's aims and objectives arises from a lack of detailed analysis of his paper. For the purposes of this chapter, we shall concentrate on the philosophical content of Turing's paper and leave the computational content until Chapter 2. Also, we shall try to present the information in the way that a reader in the early 1950s would understand. Hence, we shall not introduce concepts and theories which were developed after the publication of the paper. Such developments will be left to subsequent chapters.

In the paper, Turing poses the question: 'Can machines think?'. Since, he claims, the quotation contains loaded terms, he proposes a different way to approach the question. This approach is contained in 'the imitation game'. The imitation game is played between three people: a man (A), a woman (B), and an interrogator (C) of either sex. C stays in a room apart from the other two. The object of the game for the interrogator is to determine which of the other two is the man and which the woman. C is allowed to put any questions C likes to both A and B in order to come to a decision. In order that tones of voice do not help C, there should ideally be a teleprinter communication between A and B on the one hand, and C on the other. (Nowadays, we should use VDU-based communication.) Furthermore, it is A's objective to help C come to a wrong decision, whereas it is B's objective to help C come to a right decision. The best strategy for B is for her to give truthful answers, e.g. 'I am the woman'. A, of course, can also say the same. Given this scenario, Turing suggests that the question, 'Can machines think', should be replaced by another '. . . which is closely related to it' (Turing, 1950, p. 433), namely:

> 'What will happen if a machine takes the part of A in this game?' That is, will the interrogator decide wrongly as often when the game is played like this as when the game is played between a man and a woman? (Turing, 1950, p. 434)

We should at this point note that Turing is *replacing* one question with another, *related* question, on the basis that he cannot make much sense of the original question but can of the replacement. This does not mean that he considers the two questions to be *equivalent*, although some commentators have been led erroneously to this interpretation:

> . . . Turing proposes to replace the original question with another that shall be (a) essentially equivalent to it, and (b) significantly less ambiguous. It is remarkable, then, that he nowhere states the replacement question — which is, in effect, "Can a computer be programmed so as to fool human beings, with some regularity, into thinking that it is

another human being?" — in a form that allows its *equivalence to the original* to be clearly displayed and evaluated. (Halpern, 1987, p. 81) (my italics)

Turing does not, of course, provide such a demonstration of the *equivalence* of the replacement, because that is not his intention. Nor would he wish to, in case it is replied that if the first question is apparently meaningless, then, according to equivalence, so must the replacement. That is, replacing like with like is not the object of the Imitation Game.

Having proposed the test and discussed it, Turing remarks:

> The original question 'Can Machines Think?' I believe to be too meaningless to deserve discussion. Nevertheless, I believe that at the end of the century the use of words and general educated opinion will have altered so much that one will be able to speak of machines thinking without expecting to be contradicted. (Turing, 1950, p. 442)

This radical reformulation of the original question, 'Can machines think?', into the imitation game occupies only the first two pages of a 28-page article. Before going on to examine the rest of Turing's paper, let us pause for a short while to answer two immediate questions:

(1) Why, if his article is called 'Computing machinery and intelligence', is Turing concentrating on the apparently different question, 'Can machines think?'
(2) In the original formulation of the game, the roles of A, B and C are quite obvious to not only themselves but also each other. Does the same apply to the reformulated game?

Before we look at some answers to these questions, we again stress that we shall adopt a 1950 view of the Turing test and that therefore some of the material that follows in this Chapter will now seem dated.

The first question, which essentially is asking for an interpretation of the imitation game, queries why it is that Turing is treating the topics, those of machine intelligence and machine thought, as equivalent, whereas it may be better to say that machine thought is necessary for machine intelligence, i.e. without machine thought, there can be no machine intelligence, since intelligence depend on thought and thought-processes. That is, if the claim were made that someone, or something, is intelligent, then since intelligence assumes the capability of thought, it would be, quite rightly, contradictory to claim that the intelligent entity could not think. For the remainder of this chapter, however, we shall equate machine thought with machine intelligence.

Another common interpretation is this:

> [Turing's article] is really about two things. One is the quetion 'Can a machine think?' — or rather, 'Will a machine think?' (Hofstadter, 1982, p. 70)

Asking whether something *can* be the case is sometimes a different question to asking whether something *will* be the case. For instance, asking whether Exeter City *can* win the Football League Championship may lead to discussions which centre around the circumstances under which it is possible for Exeter City to win the Championship (e.g. 'If they are promoted to the First Division from the Fourth Division, first of all', 'If they buy better players'). But asking whether Exeter City *will* win the First Division Championship may lead to such answers as: 'Only if they are promoted to the First Division from the Fourth, and only if they buy better players, then yes, it is possible that Exeter City will win the Championship, but it's all very unlikely.'

There are two important points here. First, answers to the question of whether it is possible that Exeter can or will win the Championship are sometimes expressed in 'If . . .' form and sometimes in 'Only if . . .' form. This is important only in so far as we need to determine whether Turing means that the passing of the imitation game is *necessary*, or *sufficient*, for a machine to think. The second point is whether 'can' implies *possibility* only, whereas 'will' implies *actuality*, and therefore whether it is the possibility of machine thought, or the actuality of machine thought, that Turing had in mind.

Let us adopt a simple propositional logic approach to these questions, as a way of starting the debate. Although the much more powerful first-order predicate calculus had been developed almost fifty years prior to 1950 (by Russell and Whitehead), we shall not use it here. Instead, our aim is to introduce some simple concepts in causal and logical theory.

If C1 is

'Machine X *passes* the imitation game'

and E1 is

'Machine X *thinks*'

what does the imitation game tell us about the relationship between C1 and E1? Also, If C2 is

'Machine X *can* pass the imitation game'

and E2 is

'Machine X *can* think'

what sort of relationship holds between C2 and E2? We shall examine two sorts of relationships that can occur between the Cs and Es above: causal and logical.

If we say that C causes E, we usually mean more than C preceding E, since it is quite possible that at a certain moment in time a cat miaows and that at a following moment in time, on the other side of the world, a dog barks, but the first does not cause the second. Instead, let us look at the notions of 'necessary condition' and 'sufficient condition'.

If C is *necessary* for E, what we usually mean is that in our experience, in order for E to occur, C needs to occur, i.e. without C, E never occurs.

C is usually said to be *sufficient* for E if whenever C occurs, E occurs, i.e. if E does not occur, then nor does C.

The British philosopher, John Stuart Mill, defined 'cause' as a sufficient condition. That is, for an event to occur, there will be many conditions, e.g. 'For Exeter City to win the Championship, they will need to buy better players, be promoted to the First Division, . . .' When all the necessary conditions are fulfilled or present, the event occurs:

> The real Cause is the whole of these antecedents . . . (Mill, 1843)

In most cases, however, the list of necessary conditions will run to hundreds, if not thousands, but for Mill, despite the lengthy list of conditions that may need to be identified and to occur before a sufficient cause exists, this is the only *scientific* way to proceed. For instance, determining through experimentation that a proposed cause is not, in fact, a cause is still part of the scientific process.

The logical connection between C and E must not be confused with the scientific one described above. The notion of logical necessity is a relationship between statements or propositions, rather than events. Usually, this sort of relationhsip is brought out by the concept of inference and logical deduction: 'If p implies q and p is the case, then q must be the case.' That is, if the argument is valid and the premiss true, then the conclusion must be true.

The point we wish to make here is that reinterpreting the question, 'Can a machine think?', as 'Will a machine think?', could lead to a causal interpretation being placed on the imitation game, whereas a logical interpretation may be the one required. As we shall see when we discuss the objections of other writers to Turing's proposal, there is much confusion concerning which of these interpretations should be placed on his reformulation.

In the context of Turing's paper, which provides a conceptual framework within which to pose a reformulation of the original question, it is more consistent to assume that, when Turing asks

> What will happen when a machine takes the part of A [the man] in the game? Will the interrogator decide wrongly as often when the game is played like this as he does when the game is played between a man and a woman? (Turing, 1950, p. 434)

what Turing has uppermost in mind is the *logical* interpretation, although a causal approach may not have been dismissed by him. Let us look at the causal interpretations first. Remember that C1 is 'Machine X passes the imitation game' and E1 is 'Machine X thinks'. What sort of causal relationship holds between C1 and E1?

(1) The necessary condition interpretation would claim that a negative answer to the question, 'Will the interrogator decide wrongly as often when the game is played like this as he does when the game is played between a man and a women?', would mean a negative answer to the question of machine thought. The underlying form of this interpretation is 'If not-C1 then not-E1', i.e.

> S1: If machine X does not pass the imitation game
>     then it does not think.

That is, if your answer is negative (not-C1), then you have answered the question of whether machines can think negatively (not-E1), or, perhaps better put,

> S1': If machine X thinks, then it passes the imitation game

The passing of the imitation game then becomes one necessary condition for the actuality of machine thought, but there may well be others. The totality of such necessary condition could, in certain circumstances, lead to such an actuality, but it may be unclear how many such conditions need to be identified and to occur.

(2) The sufficient condition interpretation would claim that an affirmative answer is sufficient for machine thought. That is, if you say that you can imagine the interrogator making as many any misidentifications in the reformulated game as before, then you are saying 'If C1 then E1'. That is

> S2: If machine X passes the imitation game then it thinks

or

> S2': If machine X doesn't think, then it doesn't pass the
>      imitation game.

One of the problems with Turing's paper is that both interpretations are possible, which in turn lead to a third causal interpretation.

(3) The successful passing of the imitation game is both a necessary and sufficient condition for machine thought. That is,

> S3: A machine deceiving the interrogator successfully is
>     equivalent to that machine thinking.

Notice, incidentally, that we assume that the notion 'passing a test' represents one completed action, rather than a process.

The logical interpretations, on the other hand, go like this:

L1: If machine X can pass the imitation game (C2) then it can think (E2). Machine X can pass the imitation game. Therefore, machine X can think.

That is, we have the argument form: If C2 then E2; C2, therefore E2.

Another logical interpretation goes like this:

L2: Only if machine X can pass the imitation game can it think. It cannot pass the imitation game. Therefore it cannot think.

That is, we have: If E2, then C2; not-C2; therefore not-E2. Notice that the introduction of the word 'only' before C2 in L2 changes the form of the argument.

Again, just as in the causal interpretations, both logical interpretations are possible, which then leads to a third logical interpretation:

L3: If and only if machine X can pass the imitation game can it think.

That is: If C2 then E2 and if E2 then C2, which is valid if C2 and E2 can be shown to be the case.

We shall have need to return to these relationships between C2 and E2 later, especially in the chapter on semantics (Chapter 4) where we shall present some more powerful tools, such as modal logic and temporal logic, for analysing the reformulations of the original question, 'Can machines think?' Our main concern here is to argue that Turing wishes to demonstrate, at the very least, the *possibility* of a machine passing the imitation-game, which would then, according to interpretation L1, demonstrate the possibility of machine thought and thereby solve the question, 'Can machines think?'

We shall now present some evidence to show that it is the logical interpretation that, for the most part, Turing wants to place on his imitation game, and later in this Chapter we shall cite his 'contrary views' which, we argue, add further constraints on the nature of the *conceptual* machine that is to play in the imitation game and the sorts of response it makes to questions. At the very least, we can be fairly sure that Turing does not want only a causal or scientific interpretation to be placed on his imitation game, although the following quote may lead one to believe so:

> . . . I believe that at the end of the century the use of words and general educated opinion will have altered so much that one will be able to speak of machines thinking without expecting to be contradicted. (Turing, 1950, p. 442)

However, a careful reading of this passage shows that Turing is not concerned with scientific advances which will lead to machine thought but 'the use of words and general educated opinion'. That is, it does not appear that Turing is concerned with his imitation game producing a scientific framework within which necessary and sufficient conditions could be identified and made to happen; indeed, we must take into account the need, on the causal interpretation, for past experience to guide us in the search for such necessary and sufficient conditions. But it is precisely this experience that was lacking in 1950 and would have continued to be lacking if Turing could not persuade philosophers and scientists that machine thought was a possibility and valid topic for research activity. Also, the reference to 'the use of words' does not necessarily imply that Turing believes that the question of machine thought would be solved empirically:

> If the meaning of the words 'machine' and 'think' are to be found by examining how they are commonly used it is difficult to escape the conclusion that the meaning and answer to the question. 'Can machines think?' is to be sought in a statistical survey such as a Gallup poll. But that is absurd. (Turing, 1950, p.433)

In any case, a causal interpretation based on the passage above is more than balanced by the following quotes:

> There are already a number of digital computers in working order, and it may be asked, 'Why not try the experiment straight away? It would be easy to satisfy the conditions of the game. A number of interrogators could be used, and statistics compiled to show how often the right identification was given.' The short answer is that we are not asking whether all digital computers would do well in the game nor whether the computers at present available would do well, but whether there are *imaginable* computers which would do well. (Turing, 1950, p. 436) (my italics)

> It was suggested tentatively that the question, 'Can machines think?' should be replaced by 'Are there *imaginable* digital computers which would do well in the imitation game. (Turing, 1950, p. 442) (my italics)

And in another reformulation, he writes:

> . . . 'Let us fix our attention on one particular digital computer C. Is it true that by modifying this computer to have an adequate storage, suitably increasing its speed of action, and providing it with an appropriate programme, C *can* be made to play satisfactorily the part of A in the imitation game, the part of B being taken by a man?' (Turing, 1950, p. 442) (my italics)

The reason why some commentators believe that Turing is asking for a scientific, or causal, question probably lies in the following passage:

> It will simplify matters for the reader if I explain first my own beliefs in the matter. Consider first the more accurate form of the question [i.e. the imitation game]. I believe that in about fifty years' time it will be possible to programme computers . . . to make them play the imitation game so well that an average interrogator will not have more than 70 per cent chance of making the right identification after five minutes of questioning. (Turing, 1950, p. 442)

It is clear that Turing is not proposing yet another interpretation of his imitation game but is instead stating his beliefs about what will actually happen, i.e. a certain sort of machine will be required to pass the game *in actuality*. But beliefs about the nature of such a machine actually to pass the test are different from the conceptual reformulation of the question which tests for the *possibility* of machine intelligence and thought.

So, for the remainder of this book, we shall adopt the view that it is the possibility of machine thought that interests Turing. That is, the point of the imitation game is this: given the original version, followed by the substitution of a computer for the man (the deceiver), is it possible for us to imagine that the interrogator will make as many mistakes concerning identification as the interrogator did in the original version?' If the answer is 'Yes, we can imagine such as situtation', then we are left with the problem of whether this is a premiss or a conclusion to an argument (L1 or L2 above), from a logical viewpoint. In other words, one interpretation is that if machines cannot pass the imitation game, they cannot think, which is different from saying that if they can pass the imitation game then they can think.

Returning to the two questions we said immediately sprang to mind, the second immediate question is whether the players of the new game are aware of the change in the rules. That is, when Turing says that the task of the interrogator is now to decide which is A (the computer) and which is B, is it important to the players that the new situation is spelled out to them? Does the interrogator now know that he or she is no longer dealing with a man and a woman but a machine and man or woman? Indeed, does it matter that B, the truth-teller, remains a woman? Does the truth-teller (B) know that he or she has a computer as a antagonist?

Fortunately, buried in his paper there is a phrase (already quoted) that answers these questions and makes clear what the new situation consists of. In the second reformulation of his imitation game, Turing writes:

> 'Let us fix our attention on one particular digital computer C. Is it true that by modifying this computer to have an adequate storage, suitably increasing its speed of action, and providing it with an appropriate programme, C can be made to play satisfactorily the part of A in the imitation game, the part of B being played by a *man*?' (Turing, 1950, p. 442) (my italics)

This quote should answer both the above questions. If a man takes the part of B, the truth-teller, then the man's role is not to claim to be a woman. Hence, the interrogator's task certainly appears to consist of deciding which of A and B is the man and which the computer. Also, if the man playing the role of B knows that his task is to help C make the right decision, it would appear that B knows that A, the deceiver and his antagonist in the game, is a computer. Furthermore, if C's task is to decide which is the human and which the computer, then he must know that a human and a computer are involved. Finally, we can assume that the intelligent computer is aware of the rules of the game and so will do its best to deceive C.

## 1.3  TURING'S IMITATION GAME: BACKGROUND

With these preliminaries out of the way, we can now move on to examine why Turing thinks that the original question, 'Can machines think?', is 'too meaningless to deserve discussion' and 'contained loaded terms', before looking at his reformulation of the original question in more detail. First, we need to introduce some basic concepts in the area of philosopy known as the philosophy of mind. The following exposition will necessarily be brief and so will not do justice to the fine detail of many of the concepts. Our focus, initially, will be on the philosophical doctrine known as naive dualism.

Naive dualism is an extremely simple form of philosophy which has its roots in the views of Descartes, who, in 1637. published *Discourse on the method* and, in 1642 *Meditations of first philosophy*. The references to his work will be taken from Anscombe and Geach's collected edition (Anscombe and Geach, 1970). We pay particular attention to the following passage by Descartes:

> . . . I have often noticed that highly intelligent persons to whom I have explained some of my views and who seemed to understand them distinctly at the time, have almost completely transformed them when reporting them, so that I could no longer acknowledge them as my own. Here I would beg posterity never to believe what is ascribed to me if I have not published it myself. (*Discourse on the method*, Part Six; Anscombe and Geach, 1970, p. 51)

Apart from noting that a philosophical version of the 'popular press' appeared to exist in the seventeenth century, we stress that naive dualism and Cartesian dualism — the form of dualism attributed to Descartes — share only the following theroetical 'axiom':

> Dualism is the view that a person consists of two entities — a mind and a body — and that these two entities interact in some way. The consciousness of a person resides in the mind. That there is such a conceptual division can be demonstrated by the fact that we can deny the existence of our body without being forced to deny the existence of our consciousness. Also, there is nothing in the notion of body that forces us to include within it the notion of mind, or consciousness.

On top of this axiom are built different conceptual edifices, of which Descartes' own is one. But we present a naive version of it, since the original version, i.e. Descartes', has a theological element which is important to his philosophy but which in the twentieth century would seem dated. Our naive view, although also dated, at least provides us with a foundation for developments that took place in the latter half of this century. This, then, is naive dualism.

> A person may introspect to monitor the workings of their own mind and can thus acquire indubitable knowledge of what is happening in their mind. A person has to infer the mental state of others by observing the bodily movements of others. But since these inferences are, in principle, not conclusively verifiable and since we cannot enter the minds of other persons to check if our inferences are correct, it follows that we can never be certain in our knowledge that another person is in a mental

state we say they are in. That person could be play-acting or pretending that they are in, say, pain, when in actual fact that person is not experiencing any pain. Moreover, since we can never know for sure the mental states of others, it is possible to believe that we can never know for sure that other minds do exist. That is, if we can never know for sure what mental state a particular person is in, then it is possible to believe that that 'person' does not have a mind at all, hence no mental states to speak of. We could have on our hands a machine that is programmed to behave in a certain way.

The last step above represents the view known as solipsism. What solipsism implies for the concept of a person is that I — as a person — have certain knowledge that I — and therefore my mind — exist but can never have certain knowledge that others have minds. Any such knowledge is both problematic and probabilistic. Therefore, others may not be persons in the same sense that I am a person.

This unhappy conclusion results from the premiss that when I report or describe my mental states ('I have a pain', 'I am depressed'), these reports or descriptions can be known to be true because I experience the mental states denoted by these words directly, and that when I describe or report another's mental states ('You are in pain', 'He is depressed'), these reports and descriptions can never be known conclusively to be true. Justifying interpretations we place upon the mental life of others is therefore problematic. No such problem is present when we decribe or report our own state of mind.

Next, for naive dualism, there is the question as to how mind and body are related. For Descartes, the answer is simple:

> It seems to me that the human mind is incapable of distinctly conceiving both the distinction between body and soul [the essence of which is to be conscious] and their union, at one and the same time; for that requires our conceiving them as a single thing and simultaneously conceiving them as two things, which is self-contradictory. (Letter to Princess Elizabeth, 28 June 1643; Anscombe and Geach, 1970, p. 279)

That is, for Descartes, the question of how the body and the soul are 'unified' cannot be answered. For naive dualists, however, the most sensible answer would be to say that the relationship is a two-way one. Not only does a physical event have a relationship with a mental event (e.g. my finger coming into contact with the sharp end of a needle is related to the sensation of pain), but also a mental event has a relationship with a physical (e.g. my wishing to have a cup of coffee is related to certain bodily movements such as filling the kettle with water).

But what exactly does this relationship consist of ? And how exactly are mental events different from physical ones? Let us look at the traditional answers to the second question first (Hospers, 1967).

Mental events do not appear to have any location, except the metaphorical location *in the head*. But if your head were cut open and we were to peer into it, would we see a lot of mental events, such as sensations, thoughts and desires? We may see a lot of neural activity, but neural activity is a physical activity, i.e. an ordered activity that takes place along certain connections (synapses). Hence, the first way to distinguished mental events from physical events is to say that physical events are spatial in that they have to occur somewhere, in some place. The physical event of a pin being stuck into you is at the tip of your little finger, but the pain you feel when the pin is stuck into you is not at the tip of your head, or at the bottom of your head, or anywhere else which can be described spatially.

Another way to distinguish between the two types of event is to say that physical events can be observed publicly, whereas mental events cannot. My pain is private, and you cannot observe it or inspect it. Only I can observe my pain. But anyone can observe a pin being stuck into a person's finger; I can observe a pin being stuck into my finger (perhaps even by myself) and can observe a pin being stuck into your finger. The sensations that occur when a pin is stuck into anyone's finger are, however, private.

Let us examine traditional answers to the first question, as to how the mental and the physical are related. The first and perhaps most obvious answer is to say that mental events *cause* physical events, and vice vesa. I wish to use a computer, and this wish causes certain bodily movements, such as sitting in front of a computer terminal, typing away on the keyboard, and so on. Likewise, physical events cause mental events. My hammering away on the keyboard may cause me to experience pain in my fingers as I type, but just like a budding guitarist who has bleeding fingers during a lengthy practice session, I may try to ignore the pain or even use it to elevate myself into a state of painful bliss.

The major problems with this answer concern the mechanisms which allow such causal interactions to take place. What if I wish to use the computer but remain in the same position, and do not make any movement towards the terminal? Is it possible for a mental state, such as the wish to do something active, not to cause a bodily movement? If so, then a mental event is not a sufficient condition of causing bodily movement but only one of perhaps many necessary ones. So what other necessary conditions exist, if any? If it is possible for a mental state, such as the wish to do something active, to exist without the appropriate behaviour being caused, then there must be something else in addition to the mental state that prevents the bodily movement. What is this something? And what caused that something? In any case, mental events are not supposed to occur anywhere at all, so how can a non-locatable, non-spatial event be an event at all?

Answers no doubt can be attempted for these questions, but as can be seen, the mechanism underlying causal explanation is not as obvious as it first appeared.

A second answer to the question concerning the relationship between the mental and the physical is to say that there is no interaction as such between the mental and the physical, and certainly no causal relationship between them. Instead, the mental and the physical *correspond* to each other, in that every mental event will have a physical correlate in the brain.

Causes can only be described in physical terms, hence, mental events cannot cause physical ones. All that can be said, according to this view — known as *psychophysical parallelism* — is that associated with, or corresponding to, mental events there will be physical ones, and vice versa. For instance, my alarm ringing at eight in the morning does not cause me to wake up; it just so happens that associated with the alarm going off is my awakening, but I can sleep (and frequently have slept) through the alarm. Even if I always wake up whenever the alarm goes off, that does not mean that tomorrow morning I shall wake up when the alarm goes off. The most that can be said is that if I wake up, then certain physical events have occurred, or are occurring, such as certain auditory nerves being jangled by the sound of the bell, but my auditory brain connections can be jangled without my waking up. Hence, proponents of this answer would argue that it is wrong to claim that I wake up *because* the alarm goes off, where the 'because' expresses a causal relationship. Rather, my waking up is directly correlated with the alarm going off. To claim anything more is, strictly speaking, not valid and is to use the notion of cause loosely. This is not to deny that mental events occur, only to deny that mental events cause physical ones, and vice versa.

As is apparent from the above account, one of the major problems with this answer is that it is difficult to see exactly what is being claimed. If a causal relationship between mental and physical is being denied, then the argument just seems to reduce to: 'There is the mental and there is the physical, and never the twain shall meet', which begs the question as to how the mental and physical are related, and also seems counter-intuitive. Surely there must be some relation between, say, a pin being stuck into your finger and the feeling of pain that is subsequently felt, and, say, the wish to make a cup of tea and moving my body in the direction of the kettle?

*Epiphenomenalism* is the view that physical events do cause mental events, but mental events, by their very nature, do not cause and cannot cause physical events. Hence, we have a one-way relationship. The word 'epiphenomenon', which signifies a secondary, or concomitant, symptom, is used to refer to the mind and its workings. That is, this view accepts that the physical can cause the mental, but not the other way around. In a sense, this view is a compromise between two-way interactionism and psychophysical parallelism, and therefore epiphenomenalism is susceptible, in its attempt to describe how the physical affects the mental, to the same problems as those that can be levelled against both the previous attempted explanations (psychophysical parallelism and two-way interactionism). That is, exactly how is the one-way causal chain between the physical and the mental achieved, given that mental events are not located anywhere, and what exactly is the status of mental events, given that they are merely concomitant with physical ones?

We may be starting to appreciate the complexity, and elusiveness, of the problems in this area, and in fact several of these views have re-appeared in modern guises during the last fifteen years, as we shall see. Turing's attempt to bypass debates such as these appears laudable, otherwise he would have to fit his theory into existing ones, or at the very least he would have to give a lot of background to the reader before being able to present his own view. Naive dualism certainly would not appeal to Turing, since the line of argument he would have to take looks like this:

(1)  Entities that have minds can think (axiom of dualism)
(2)  Humans have minds (asserted axiomatically or factually)
(3)  Therefore, humans can think

Some dualists may want to make the further claim that only humans have minds, not animals or other entities that inhabit our planet. Looking at the above approach that Turing would have to adopt if he wished to argue, along dualistic lines, that computers can think, he would have to introduce the assertion:

(2′)  Computers have minds

This would then lead to:

(3′)  Therefore, computers can think.

We may now see why Turing does not adopt a dualistic approach when tackling the question, 'Can machines think?'. To assert that computers have minds, axiomatically, would be very contentious even now, never mind 1950. It is very difficult to take seriously a definition of 'computer' as, say, 'mechanical entity with a mind', given that we want the computer to have a mind in the same way that we have a mind. If we allow any difference in the meaning of 'mind', depending on whether the term is used to refer to a human or computer mind, then the whole debate concerning whether machines can think reduces to one of simple definition, and the problem disappears, from a philosophical point of view. But such a terminological solution is not relevant or desirable here. We want to discuss whether it is *possible* to use the word 'mind' with the same meaning when it is applied to both human and computer minds. According to dualism, such a discussion would have to account for the fact that, if by 'computer' we mean just a mechanical entity, i.e. a body, in which everything is observable, in principle: its calculations, its symbolic manipulations from the top level of human-interpretable computer languages to the bottom level of ones and zeroes in the electronic circuits, then at every level the computer's behaviour can be located precisely. A computer, just like a body, is the object of cognition, but nothing in what we have said implies that the computer is a *subject* of cognition: when a computer completes a task, that is all there is to it. Computers feel no sense of achievement at having completed a task, or disappointment at not returning the expected result. It is neither happy to serve nor unhappy at being a slave. In fact, it is also possible to argue that, if anyone wants to claim, axiomatically, that computers have minds, that could be like claiming that a bachelor is a married man, i.e. it is a contradiction, and from a contradiction we can conclude any nonsense we like: if computers have minds, so do typewriters and rocks.

Turing therefore would not have been happy with a dualistic approach to the question, 'Can machines think?', because, as we have seen, he would have been sucked into a quicksand of problems. In any case, there is a deeper reason as to why dualism would not have been of much use to Turing, and this is because of the alternative to asserting, axiomatically, that computers can think. The alternative it to make this assertion empirically. That is, we observe that behaviour of other persons and listen to their reports of their own mental states, and when we observe that another individual says 'I have a pain in my stomach', we use analogy to conclude that that individual is in a state of pain. Observation stops at the level of behaviour since, as we have seen in our description of naive dualism, we cannot in principle observe the mental states of others.

At first, we may be tempted to adopt this approach with regard to machine thought. We can imagine that we observe a computer's behaviour and listen to its reports of itself. By anology, by using our own experience of the mental circumstances under which we make such reports and behave in such as way, we may or may not conclude that the computer is in the mental state that it asserts or reports of itself. Unfortunately, this empirical approach must contend with solipsism.

It is generally considered that solipsism represents the logical conclusion of any dualistic theory. The solipsistic arguments goes like this:

(1)  I do not know for certain that a person is in the mental state that I assert of that person, since I cannot verify the statement (I cannot enter the mind of that person).
(2)  This applies to all mental states I assert of a person.
(3)  Therefore, I do not know for certain that that person has any mental states or a mind at all.
(4)  That 'person' could be a robot or machine programmed to act in a certain way to fool me into believing it has a mind and is not a machine.

If these steps reflect the general tenor of dualism and, in particular, solipsism, then it makes no sense for Turing to apply a dualistic approach when attempting to answer the question, 'Can machines think?', because, by replacing the word 'person' by 'machine':

(1′)  I do not know for certain that a machine is in the mental state that I assert of that machine, since I cannot verify the statement (I cannot enter the mind of that machine).
(2′)  This applies to all mental states that I assert of a machine.
(3′)  Therefore, I do not know for certain that a machine has any mental states or a mind at all.
(4′)  That 'machine' could be a robot or machine programmed to act in a certain way to fool me into believing it has a mind and is not a machine.

Such an argument would only make sense if it were used to distinguish thinking machines from non-thinking ones, that is, if the notion of thinking machines is already off the ground. But as a way of answering the more fundamental question of whether machines can think, the last step (4′) contains an inconsistency which does not appear in (4). We know for certain that we are dealing with a machine in steps (1′)–(3′), and therefore there is no need to put quotation-marks around 'machine' in (4′). That is, if we know that the 'machine' could be a robot or machine, how can we then believe that it could be programmed to fool us into believing that it is not a machine?

Hence, dualism would appear to contain some axioms which, if it were to provide a theoretical framework for answering the question, 'Can machines think?', would lead to contradictory theorems.

Before leaving dualism, let us present two interesting quotes by Descartes:

> I went on to describe animals and in particular men . . . I confined myself to imagining that God should form a human body just like our own both in the outward shape of its limbs and in the interior arrangement of its organs, without using any matter but what I had described, and without placing in it, to begin with, any rational soul, or anything to serve as a vegitative or sensitive soul . . . Examining the functions that might result in such a body, what I found were precisely those that may occur in us unconsciously, without any co-operation of the soul, that is to say of the element distinct from the body of which I said above that its nature is merely to be conscious; the very operations in which irrational animals resemble us; but I could find none of the operations that depend on consciousness and are alone proper to us men . . . (*Discourse on the method*, Part Five; Anscombe and Geach, 1970, p. 41)

We shall see later, especially in the second volume, that this sort of 'mind game' concerning the construction of a perfect android has modern counterparts.

The second, and more relevant, quote as far as this chapter is concerned is the following:

> I specially dwelt on showing that if there were machines with organs and appearance of a monkey, or some other irrational animal, we should have no means of telling that they were not altogether of the same nature as those animals; whereas if there were machines resembling our bodies, and imitating our actions as far as is morally possible, we should still have two means of telling that, all the same, they were not real men. First, they would never use words or other constructed signs, as we do to declare our thoughts to others. It is quite conceivable that a machine should be so made as to utter words, and even utter them in connection with physical events that cause a change in one of its organs . . . but not that it should be so made as to arrange words variously in response to the meaning of what is said in its presence, as even the dullest men can do. Secondly, while they might well do many things as well as many of us or better, they would infallibly fail in others, revealing that they acted not from knowledge but only from a disposition of their organs. (*Discourse on the method*, Part Five; Anscombe and Geach, 1970, p. 42).

It could be argued that this is precisely the objection that Turing is hoping to overcome, or at least by-pass, in his paper. We shall return to this objection in Volume 2.

We now present a second philosophical doctrine that at first looks much more appealing as a provider of a framework that might allow Turing to answer his self-posed question. Again, the exposition of this doctrine — that of naive logical behaviourism or naive philosophical behaviourism — is going to miss out on a wealth of detail, but it is the general approach that is of interest here.

Perhaps it should be mentioned at this stage that since philosophical behaviourism is essentially a reaction to the dualistic conception of a person, and since Turing quite obviously is rejecting a dualistic framework within which to answer his question, Turing might be favourably disposed towards philosophical behaviourism, or at least philosophical behaviourists would be favourably disposed towards Turing adopting a non-dualistic approach. Indeed when we present naive philosophical behaviourism, it may look as if Turing comes very close to being a philosophical behaviourist. As an aside, it is interesting to note that one of the founding fathers of philosophical behaviourism, Ryle, was the editor of the philosophy journal *Mind* at the time Turing's paper appeared in it in 1950. Also, in his biography of Turing, Hodges (Hodges, 1983, p. 136) states that Turing and Wittgenstein had discussions many times whilst they were at Cambridge, first in 1937 and then later in 1939 when Turing sat in on Wittgenstein's lectures on the foundations of mathematics (Hodges, 1983, p. 152). Although Wittgenstein cannot be truly called a logical behaviourist, his views were interpreted by some of this followers as philosophically behaviourist in nature. Let us take a little time to develop the relationship between the philosophies of Ryle (but not Wittgenstein) and Turing a bit further.

In 1949, Ryle published his *Concept of mind.* Ryle's book is essentially a major attack on dualism. (Interestingly, although Ryle was concerned with a complete attack on Descarte's philosophy, not one actual reference to a paper or piece of work by Descartes occurs in the text of *Concept of mind*.) Imagine that the naive dualistic view we presented earlier is the more sophisticated 'official doctrine' that Ryle is concerned with. He calls it the 'dogma of the Ghost in the Machine', by which he means to describe in abusive terms the dualist's conception of a physical entity within which a spectre, an intangible, viz. a soul or mind, resides. Ryle introduces the phrase 'category mistake' to describe what had gone wrong with the dualistic approach.

Essentially, a category mistake consists of a misapplication of a category or concept. For example, if after watching 26 players come out onto the field for a First Division soccer match (i.e. 11 starting players and two substitutes for each side) you ask 'When do the teams appear?', you have made a category mistake: the appearance of people on the pitch was not of the 26 players *followed* by the teams but of the 26 players *of* the two teams. The category mistake committed here is of not knowing how to wield the concept 'team' and of an

. . . inability to use certain items in the English vocabulary. (Ryle, 1963, p. 19)

The example above is very similar to the second of Ryle's illustrations of a category mistake (p. 18). He goes on to write:

My destructive purpose is to show that a family of radical category mistakes is the source of the double-life theory [i.e. the mental and the physical]. The representation of a person as a ghost mysteriously ensconced in a machine derives from this argument. Because, as it is true, a person's thinking, feeling and purposive doing cannot be described solely in the idioms of physics, chemistry and physiology, therefore they must [when committing a category mistake] be described in counterpart idioms. As the human body is a complex organised unit, so the human must [according to the category mistake] be another complex organised unit, though one made of a different sort of stuff and a different sort of structure. Or, again, as the human body, like any other parcel of matter, is a field of causes and effects, so the mind must be another field of causes and effects, thought not . . . mechanical causes and effects. (Ryle, 1963, p. 20)

Ryle then presents a variety of arguments to back his case for the rejection of this 'dual-life theory', including some mentioned earlier which deal with the interaction between the mental and the physical, or perhaps better put, the lack of interaction. Large portions of his book are concerned with a reinterpretation, and solution, of problems originally couched in dualistic terms. Of particular interest to us is his treatment of intelligence and thought. In particular he rejects the 'intellectualist legend', which runs roughly like this.

. . . [An] action exhibits intelligence if, and only if, the agent is thinking what he is is doing whilst he is doing it, and thinking he is doing in such a manner that he would not do the action so well as if he were not thinking what he is doing (Ryle, 1963, p. 29)

For Ryle, the crucial objection to this view, which separates thought from intelligence, is that it leads to an infinite regress.

The consideration of propositions is itself an operation the execution of which can be more or less intelligent, less or more stupid. But if, for any operation to be intelligently executed, a prior theoretical operation had first to be performed and performed intelligently, it would be a logical impossibility for anyone ever to break into the circle. (Ryle, 1963, p. 31)

Ryle goes on to reject the idea that when we say that someone is intelligent we are describing someone's mental state or ascribing a quality of some sort to that person. Instead, he equates intelligence with a 'dispositional property':

When we describe glass as brittle, or sugar as soluble, we are using dispositional concepts, the logical force of which is this. The brittleness of glass does not consist in the fact that it is at a given moment actually being shivered. It may be brittle without ever being shivered. To say that it is brittle is to say that if it ever is, or ever had been, struck or strained, it would fly, or have flown, into fragments. To say that sugar is soluble is to say that it would dissolve, or would have dissolved, if immersed in water. (Ryle, 1963, p. 43).

Likewise, so say of someone that they are intelligent is to say that, *if* that person were, for instance, asked to solve a simple puzzle, *then* that person would solve it . Note particularly the 'if . . . then . . .' structure of the expression of a dispositional property or concept.

To possess a dispositional property is not to be in a particular state . . . , it is to be bound or liable to be in a particular state . . . when a particular condition is realized (Ryle, 1963, p. 43).

It is an easy matter to understand how the form of these rules, i.e. 'if . . . then . . .', natually gives rise to the expression *logical behaviourism*, just as it is easy to see how some commentator are tempted to regard Turing's reformulation as one that is sympathetic to the philosophy outlined above.

Turing takes a behaviouristic posture relative to the question ['Can a machine think?']. (Feigenbaum and Feldman, 1963, p. 9)

However, as we shall shortly see, there are ground for believing that Turing does not adopt a behaviourist posture, never mind a logical behaviourist one. But more on this later. Let us present a naive view of logical behaviourism.

The so-called philosophical or logical behaviourist does not regard the connection between so-called mental events and manifestations of mental events in behaviour as contingent — as the dualists may be forced to do because of the logical distinction dualists make between the mind and body, which then makes it difficult for them to find the logical connection between the two — but as logical. The connection is logical because the existence of a logical rule or criterion *justifies* us in ascribing so-called sensation words such as 'pain' to others. For the dualist, we make inferences from other person's behaviour and through past experience know that when we behave in that way we are experiencing a certain sensation. We describe the other person as experiencing a certain sensation on the basis of analogy. This inference, of course, cannot be conclusively verified. For the so-called philosophical or logical behaviourist, however, it is not a question of inferring correctly or incorrectly. Rather, our ascribing a sensation such as pain to another person is justified in part by the behaviour of that person. In other words, the philosophical or logical behaviourist is concerned not so much with the truth or falsity of the ascription as with the appropriateness, or soundness, of the ascription, where appropriateness and soundness are judged on the basis of logical rules and criteria.

Let us now examine the implications of this view for ascribing mental qualities to computers. If we ascribe cleverness or pain to others on the basis of their behaviour, and if the behaviour of others justifies us in our ascription, then it follows that we ascribe cleverness or pain to a computer on the basis of its behaviour, and its behaviour justifies us in our ascription. So, if we believe that the fundamental distinction between humans and non-humans lies in the speech-producing capability of humans, and it is on the basis of this speech-producing capability that we categorise living entities into humans and non-humans, then it follows that if a computer were to communicate with humans as capably as a human, we would be justified in ascribing to that computer the same range of mental predicates on the basis of its conversational behaviour as we would do on the basis of human conversational behaviour. And here we appear to have the essence of Turing's test for deciding whether machines can think, whether a computer system is artificially intelligent. This is a perfectly logical argument given the premiss that humans ascribe so-called mental qualities to others on the basis of their behaviour and that a computer may satisfy various human behavioural conditions. However, as we shall see next, it would be wrong to believe that Turing's approach is the same as naive logical behaviourism.

The standard reply to naive behaviourism is to say that logical behaviourism, with its emphasis on behavioural criteria and conditions, may allow us to ascribe qualities of a certain kind to living beings to which we would not normally ascribe such qualities. For instance, if a parrot behaves in a way that we would call intelligent when we see humans behave in that way (e.g. answering a question with a correct answer), the argument states that if the logical behaviourist is to be consistent in their use of behaviour criteria, the logical behaviourist would have to apply the predicate 'intelligent' to the parrot, with all the assumptions that the word 'intelligent' carries (e.g. symbol manipulation, decision-making, problem-solving . . .). The argument here is that since logical behaviourism does not appear to require reference to mental states, logical behaviourism cannot distinguish between ascription of mental qualities to humans and ascription of mental qualities to non-humans which behave 'in a human way'.

The logical behaviourist can counter-reply that the difference between human and non-human (i.e. animal) behaviour is one of degree and not one of kind. That is, human behaviour and animal behaviour are not essentially different. So it is possible for the same range of qualities to be ascribed to both humans and animals. However, the meaning of the predicates will be given in part by the way in which such ascription is made. That is, the phrases 'intelligent human' and 'intelligent parrot' do not necessarily use the word 'intelligent' in the same way and so we do not need to assume the same set of assumptions underlying the word 'intelligent'. The meaning of the word 'intelligent' may well be determined by the context in which it is used, by the 'form of life' in which the creature which is being attributed with intelligence is embedded, by convention, and so on. From our point of view, the implication of this counter-reply by the logical behaviourist is that the ascription of mental predicates to a non-human does not necessarily express the same information about the non-human that it expresses about a human.

If this is the case, then there is no problem about answering the question. 'Can machines think?', since the answer could be 'Yes, but computer thought is not the same as human thought; in fact they're completely different in that, in the case of a human, "thinking" means a mental activity, whilst in the case of a computer, "thinking" only means some electrical impulses being carried along wires and circuits.' Turing would not have been very happy about such a distinction in the meaning of 'thinking', since:

> . . . I believe that at the end of the century the use of words and general educated opinion will have altered so much that one will be able to speak of machines thinking without expecting to be contradicted.

That is, the force of the above quote appears to be that machines will, by the end of the century, be said to think in the same way as humans are said to think, and that we shall be able to say this without committing a logical, or semantic, error. Turing has to come up with some suitable level of description at which both human and computer behaviour could be adequately described, without fear of contradiction. We shall see in the next chapter how Turing, with help of his proposed 'universal Turing machine', believes that he provided a suitable level of description, and so a framework, to satisfy his purposes, but all we need to note here is that allowing the ascription of mental qualities to humans to have a different meaning from ascription of 'mental' qualities to intelligent computers would not have solved any philosophical problems. Hence, the adoption of naive logical behaviourism, with the implication inherent in the approach, would not have led Turing far. For this reason, we reject the view that Turing is proposing an essentially behaviourist reformulation of the original question, although no doubt his reformulation can be interpreted as behaviouristic. Our claim here is that such an interpretation does not then do justice to the other conceptual developments that Turing introduces — universal machines, functionalism, quintuples and informality of behaviour — which all form the conceptual framework within which Turing wants to reformulate, and answer, the original question.

In summary, it appears that if Turing adopts either naive dualism or naive logical behaviourism he would not get very far before coming up against the difficulties mentioned above. Instead, he chooses to bypass these problems, or so he believes, by adopting a different approach — an approach which, when fleshed out with some of his other views on machine theory — laid the foundations for the development of not only artificial intelligence but also computer science.

## 1.4   THE 'OBJECTIONS'

We now present, briefly, various objections that Turing envisages to his proposed approach for answering the question 'Can machines think?'.

(1) The Theological Objection, writes Turing, consists of claiming that God has given the capability of thought (a soul) to every human being, but not to machines. Hence, machines cannot think.

Turing replies that this argument is restrictive on God's omnipotence: if God wanted to, he could, in certain circumstances, give machines a soul and so allow them the capability of thought. 'The circumstances in question are discussed in the rest of this paper,' writes Turing, thereby giving more weight to our view that Turing is concerned about logical possibility of machine thought and intelligence. We shall not refer again to this objection.

(2)  The 'Heads in the Sand' objection is stated baldly as:

> The consequences of machines-thinking would be too dreadful. Let us hope and believe that they cannot do so.

Although Turing admits that the argument seldom is expressed in such an open way, he dismisses this objection by replying that is it based on the idea that human beings are superior in some way to other forms of life and that 'intellectual people', by placing a high value on the capability of thought, are inclinded to this view. He suggests that such objectors should console themselves in the idea of transmigration of souls and believes that the objection is not substantial enought to require refutation.

There is a modern counterpart to this objection which is very substantial indeed and cannot be dismissed so lightly. The modern counterpart is the view that AI is dehumanizing because of its adoption of a certain view concerning what it is to be human, viz. that a human being and his or her behaviour can be described or explained using the terminology and concepts of computational theory. Modern objectors argue that AI is yet one more attack from scientific and philosophical quarters on the notion of humanity. We shall not follow this up in these two volumes: we only point out there is a significant portion of AI literature devoted to this subject (see for instance, Boden (1981), Weizenbaum (1976), Rogers (1984)), and if Turing were to make a similar claim now, he probably would not be allowed to escape so easily.

(3)  The Mathematical Objection is more complex. It is based on Gödel's theorems of incompleteness and inconsistency. Essentially, the objection states that in a formal system of a sufficiently powerful kind, there will be formulae obtainable which cannot be both true and derived. That is, there will be at least one formula in the domain under consideration which is true but cannot be reached by the formal system, or can be reached by the system but cannot be true. If thinking machines are formal systems, then it follows that thinking machines are restricted in that, for instance, when asked a question in the imitation game, they will give wrong answers (i.e. formulae which are false) or not answer at all (i.e. cannot reach certain formulae). The sort of question Turing has in mind is: 'Here is the full description of another computer. Will this computer always return a truthful answer to every question put to it?' Given this limitation, objectors then state, says Turing, that we humans have no such limitations on our intellectual ability. Indeed, if we did, Gödel could not have derived these theorems (a theorem being both true and derivable) concerning the limits of formal systems. That is, we humans have no difficulty with such formulae: we accept them for what

they are, i.e. true but not derivable, or derived but not true, because we can escape from the formal system and use meta-formal system reasoning. No such escape route is possible with entities such as machines, which are only, or merely, formal systems, say the objectors. Hence, we humans will always be able to do something that 'thinking machines' cannot and so thinking machines can never fully replicate human thought.

Turing's reply is that objectors have not proved that human thought processes escape Gödel's findings, and that in any case we humans should not derive any satisfaction or smugness from such machine limitations. Humans often give wrong answers, and just because we triumph over one thinking machine which falls to this limitation, that does not mean that we can triumph over all machines, some of which may be more clever than we are.

We shall examine the basis of this Objection in some detail in Chapter 3.

(4) The Argument from Consciousness is the objection which claims that no machine can have emotions, experiences or thoughts, i.e. no machine can have consciousness. Without consciousness, emotions, experiences and thoughts are impossible. 'According to the most extreme form of this view,' writes Turing, 'the only way by which one could be sure that a machine thinks is to *be* the machine and to feel oneself thinking' (his italics).

Turing calls this the solipsist point of view and replies that anyone who holds such a view would have difficulty in justifying the ascription of consciousness to other human beings, never mind machines. Turing believes that the imitation game would provide a better test for ascribing consciousness, given that proponents of this objection may not wish to be forced into solipsism.

Interestingly, Turing goes on to write:

> I do not wish to give the impression that I think there is no mystery about consciousness . . . I do not think these mysteries necessarily need to be solved before we can answer the question with which we are concerned in this paper. (Turing, 1950, p. 447)

This again counts as evidence that he was not adopting a naive logical behaviourist view, but was perhaps leaning towards a view of consciousness that is similar to the one expressed by Wittgenstein in the *Philosophical investigations*. We shall return to this point in Part III, which includes developments in reductionism, materialism, dualism, and theories of consciousness.

(5) Arguments from Various Disabilities have the form: 'You will never be able to make a machine do X', where 'do X' may be 'enjoy strawberries and cream', 'fall in love', 'make moral judgements', 'be aware of what it's doing', and so on. That is, this objection claims that machines cannot think because of these disabilities, which human beings do not have.

Turing replies that the objection is based on induction: we see many computers which have these disabilities, from which we induce that all computers have these disabilities. However, this does not necessarily mean that computers will always have these disabilities. Secondly, Turing replies that may of these disabilities are common to human beings: not all of us enjoy strawberries and cream or fall in love, for instance. Making machines do these things '. . . would be idiotic'. A disability contributes to people not being friendly towards each other, for instance, because there is nothing in common, but that does not mean that people with disabilities are not intelligent or do not think.

As far as self-awareness is concerned — or the lack of it in the case of a machine, according to this objection — Turing replies that there is no reason why a machine cannot make up its own programs or modify existing ones to be more effective.

Essentially, Turing believes that this objection is a disguised form of the argument from consciousness.

(6) Lady Lovelace's Objection quite simply claims that machines can do only what they are told or programmed to do, and so they can never do anything new. Machines cannot think because the results they produce are not original.

Turing replies that this may be the case with human beings. After all, who or what is to determine originality? A so-called original idea may be the natural growth of an idea picked up whilst listening to a lecture or of following well-known general principles, such as those of logic. Turing argues that if this objection is rephrased as 'Machines can never take us by surprise', he himself has been regularly taken by surprise by the result of a computer calculation, usually because he has not bothered to work out beforehand what the result should be or because he made a mistake in his prediction of the result. He claims that philosphers and mathematicians in particular are prone to the fallacy that when a piece of information is presented to a human being all its consequences '. . . spring into the mind simultaneously with it', and this is plainly false since there would then be no need to formulate the rules of logic.

In the final section of his paper, Turing returns to Lady Lovelace's Objection (that machines cannot originate anything because they can only do what they are instructed to do) and tries to give support to his original reply. He uses the stages of learning that a child goes through as a model:

(1) the initial state of the mind, say at birth;
(2) the education to which it is subjected;
(3) other experience, not to be described as education, to which it has been subjected.

The first task of the programmers of the intelligent computer is to simulate (1) above. Then the education process can begin. Turing uses some behavioural concepts from psychology (i.e. the concepts of reward and punishment) to describe what such an approach could partly consist of and which presuppose no feelings on the part of the machine. But, crucially, another part of the process is the provision of commands to the computer which '. . . regulate the order in which rules of [a] logical system . . . are to be applied' and an example of such a command might be 'If one method has been proved to be quicker than another, do not use the slower method.' But not all such commands need have been explicitly give to the computer by its programmers. The computer may have used induction — a general principle fed to it by its programmers — to generate such as command. We now have a 'learning machine':

> An important feature of a learning machine is that its teacher will often be very largely ignorant of quite what is going on inside, although he may be able to some extent to predict his pupil's behaviour . . . Most of the programmes which we can put into this machine will result in its doing something that we cannot make sense of at all, or which we regard as completely random behaviour. Intelligent behaviour presumably consists in a departure from completely disciplined behaviour . . . (Turing, 1950, p. 458–459)

Hence, Turing's more elaborate reply is that we shall not be able to predict with certainty the behaviour of a truly intelligent machine which has gone through the stages outlined above, just as we cannot predict with certainty the behaviour of an adult even if we have personally educated that adult from birth ourselves. But no one then claims that an adult can do only what that adult is told to do, so why should we believe the same is true of the intelligent computer?

We examine a modern counterpart of this objection in Part II.

(7) The Argument from Continuity in the Nervous System is the objection that machines are discrete devices having states, whereas the nervous system is continuous. Since we cannot '. . . mimic the behaviour of the nervous system with a discrete-state system', and since thought and intelligence are based on a continuous system, machines cannot think or be intelligent.

Turing replies that this objection will make no difference to his imitation game and the way it is played. In Part III, we shall examine modern counterparts to this objection which may not be so easy to dismiss. We shall examine developments in neuron theory, cognitive science, and connectionism and the claim that machine intelligence, and therefore thought, are not possible unless the underlying architecture of the machine is similar to a human brain.

(8) The Argument from Informality of Behaviour is the objection that machines have no choice but to follow the instructions of a program. If they are confronted by new situations which they have not been programmed for, they make a decision which then gives rise to further difficulties.

In reply, Turing writes:

> From this it is argued that we cannot be machines . . . [The argument]

seems to run something like this. 'If each man had a definite set of rules of conduct by which he regulated his life he would be not better than a machine. But there are no such rules, so men cannot be machines.' The undistributed middle is glaring. I do not think the argument is ever put quite like this, but I believe this is the argument used nevertheless. (Turing, 1950, p. 452)

Turing replies in a curious way. He first distinguishes between 'laws of behaviour' and 'rules of conduct', meaning, by the former 'laws of nature' (e.g. 'If you pinch him he will squeak') and, by the latter, '. . . precepts such as "stop if you see red lights", on which one can act, and of which one can be conscious'. Next, he tries to bridge the 'undistributed middle' in the objection by substituting 'laws of behaviour which regulate his life' for 'laws of conduct by which he regulates his life', resulting in the modified objection

If each man had a definite set of rules/laws of behaviour which regulate his life he would be no better than a machine. But there are no such rules, so men cannot be machines.

(Let us ignore the inconsistency of the proposed substitution, which over-looks the difference between 'rules' and 'laws'.)

Turing now states that the undistributed middle is no longer insuperable, since machines are indeed regulated by laws of behaviour, but replies that it is not so easy to convince ourselves of the absence of complete laws of behaviour as of complete rules of conduct. That is, Turing claims that it is not possible to determine the circumstances under which we should stop looking for laws of behaviour regulating a person (e.g. 'If you pinch him, he will squeak', presumably). Finally, Turing gives an example of how it is impossible to determine the circumstances under which one would stop looking for more laws of behaviour:

. . . [S]uppose we could be sure of finding such laws if they existed. Then given a discrete-state machine it should certainly be possible to discover by observation sufficient about it to predict its future behaviour, and this within a reasonable time, say a thousand years. But this does not seem to be the case. I have set up on the Manchester computer a small programme using only 1,000 units of storage, whereby the machine supplied with one sixteen-figure number replies with another within two seconds. I would defy anyone to learn from these replies sufficient about the programme to be able to predict any replies to untried values. (Turing, 1950, p. 452–453)

This part of Turing's paper is very curious indeed. This formulation of the objection does not do justice to the objection that human *thought* is not rule-governed, whereas machine thought, by its very nature, is. Also the way he formulates the central argument in the objection:

If each man had a definite set of rules of conduct by which he regulated his life he would be no better than a machine. But there are no such rules, so men cannot be machines (Turing, 1950, p. 452)

clearly is not valid. It has the form 'If P then Q; not P; therefore not Q'. A better formulation of the objection would be, for example:

> If man is no better than a machine, then there is a definite set of rules of conduct by which he regulates his life. There is no such definite set. Hence man is better than a machine.

This, it may be argued, still does not get to the heart of the Objection, but at least the 'argument' is given an argument form.

Further, his description of 'rules of conduct' and 'laws of behaviour' does not seem immediately relevant, nor is his proposed substitution of one phrase for the other, strictly speaking, possible because of word differences. His example at the end seems to be a non sequitur. In Part IV, we shall re-examine this Objection and restate it in modern terms, given the developments in rule notation and rule theory since the appearance of his paper. Worthy of note here is Turing's adoption of 'rules of behaviour', which seems to suggest that he was familiar with naive logical behaviourism, where rules of behaviour are logical rules. Turing's example of such a rule, though, 'If you pinch him, he will squeak', could have been better.

(9) The Argument from Extra-sensory Perception is an odd one and runs like this. Some humans have extra-sensory perception. Let us use two such humans in the imitation game, and the task of the telepathic interrogator is to identify which of A (the computer) and B (a human who is good at telepathic reception) is the human or computer. C holds up cards invisible to both A and B, and asks A and B to identify them. B will get more answers correct than the computer with a random-card generator. Hence, the imitation game does not work, since the telepathic interrogator can easily distinguish between B and C.

Turing's reply to this is even more curious. He suggests that the random-card generator of the computer may also be susceptible to the telepathic powers of the interrogator and so the identification may not be easy after all. 'With ESP anything may happen,' writes Turing. We shall not return to this objection.

Finally, we stress that we have concentrated on the philosophical sections of Turing's paper and have not examined a significant section of it which deals with digital computers, universal digital computers, and other computational concepts. We shall rectify this oversight in Chapter 2.

This concludes our lengthy, by necessary, examination of Turing's paper. Parts of the paper are good, other parts puzzling. However, the approach is exciting and refreshing. One of our tasks is to see how well Turing's suggested approach has fared since the paper's publication.

## 1.5  CONCLUSION

The aim of the rest of the book is to re-examine some of these Objections in the light of modern developments in formal theory and philosophy of mind. In order to be able to do this, we need to present and describe in some detail these developments, and the book is split into two parts: Part II, in the volume, will concentrate on formal developments, especially in function theory, computation theory, logic theory, and logical semantics. At the end of the chapter on function theory and computational theory, we shall be in a better position to re-assess Lady Lovelace's Objection. At the end of the chapter on logic theory, we shall re-assess the Mathematical Objection. And at the end of the chapter on logical semantics, the Argument from Informality of Behaviour will be re-assessed. The Argument from Consciousness, the Arguments from Various Disabilities, and the Argument from Continuity in the Nervous System will be re-assessed in the second volume after the relevant developments in the philosophy of mind have been examined. Let us first prepare the ground for Part II.

Gödel's theorems of incompleteness, and the unsolvability of the halting problem, both to be introduced and explored in Chapters 2 and 3 have prompted much discussion on the existence of necesary differences between human and machine. If there are such differences, it follows that machines will never be able to do anything that humans can do, and so AI is necessarily constrained in its goals, objectives and theoretical power. The aim of these chapters is to examine these arguments in greater detail. Perhaps the most famous exponent of the view that Gödel's theorems of incompleteness have provided necessary logical and conceptual constaints of AI has been Lucas, who in his 1961 paper *Minds, machines and Gödel* argued that Gödel's theorems had proved that mechanism was false. Briefly, Lucas wrote that Gödel has showed how, in any formal system of a sufficiently powerful kind — say, a system of arithmetic — there will be formulae which cannot be proved within the system, but which we can see to be true. We humans can see that such systems will contain such formulae and that such systems will therefore be incomplete: we can do this because we can 'stand outside' the system. Also, by standing outside the system, we see that such formulae are not only meaningful but also true. Now, according to Lucus, Gödel's theorem must apply to computers, because

> it is of the essence of being a machine . . . that it should be a concrete instantiation of a formal system.

If the computer is consistent and is of a sufficiently powerful kind, it will not be able to produce the formula which cannot be proved in the system but which nevertheless we can see to be true. Since we humans can see this, but the computer cannot from within the system itself, it follows that the computer cannot be a complete or adequate model of the mind. Lucas concludes: '. . . minds are essentially different from machines.' The material in Chapters 2 and 3 will allow us to examine the above claim in some detail.

Tied in with these concepts is Lady Lovelace's Objection, that computers can do only what they are told to do. An evaluation of this Objection rests on a proper understanding of the underlying theory of computation, and this is explored in the next chapter. We shall see that Searle's Chinese Room Argument can be interpreted as a modern version of this Objection.

The Argument from Informality of Behaviour is re-assessed once developments in logical semantics are examined, since the core of this Objection rests on the idea that computers only follow rules and have no understanding of the rules they follow. If we accept that computers are programmed with rules that can be called 'logical', an examination of of logical semantics will be necessary before we can re-assess the force of this Objection.

In Part II, some degree of formality of presentation is required. Reading formal notations is like listening to jazz music — the more one does it, the easier and more enjoyable it becomes! Little previous knowledge of the material is assumed, but nevertheless beginners to formal aspects may find Part II difficult at first. The main point to remember is that the underlying ideas are quite simple: expressing these ideas precisely and concisely, and making inferences from these ideas rather than speculative guesses, require the use of formal notations. As far as possible, we have tried to keep the formalisms simple and to explain the notations and concepts as we go along. An Appendix describing the Greek alphabet is included to aid exposition.

## REFERENCES

Anscombe, E. and Geach P. T. (eds) (1970) *Descartes: philosophical writings*, revised edition. Nelson.

Boden, M. (1981) *Minds and mechanisms: philosophy, psychology and computational models*. Harvester Press.

Feigenbaum, E. A. and Feldman, J. (eds) (1963) *Computers and thought*. McGraw-Hill,

Halpern, M. (1987) Turing's test and the ideology of artificial intelligence, *Artificial Intelligence Review*, **1** (2), 79–93.

Haugeland, J. (1986) *Artificial intelligence: the very idea*, MIT Press.

Hodges, A. (1983) *Alan Turing: The Enigma of Intelligence*, Counterpoint.

Hofstadter, D. R. (1979) *Gödel, Escher, Bach: an eternal golden braid*. Harvester Press.

Hofstadter, D. R. (1982) The Turing test: a coffeehouse conversation, in Hofstadter, D. R. and Dennett, D. C. (eds), *The mind's I*, pp. 69–92. Penguin.

Hospers, J. (1967) *An introduction to philosophical analysis*, second edition, Routledge and Kegan Paul.

Hutchins, W. J. (1986) *Machine translation: past, present, future*. Ellis Horwood.

Lucas, J. R. (1961) Minds, machines and Gödel, *Philosophy*, **36**. Reprinted in Anderson, A. R. (ed.) (1964) *Minds and machines*. Prentice-Hall.

Michie, D. (1982) *Machine intelligence and related topics, Gordon and Breach*. (The quote in Chapter 1 is taken from a paper in this book which originally appeared in the *New Scientist*, 22.2.1980.)

Mill, J. S. (1843) The real cause of a phenomenon, in *A system of logic*, Book III, Chapter 5.

Rogers, P. C. (1984) AI as a dehumanizing force, in Yazdarni, M. and Narayanan, A. (eds), *Artificial intelligence: human effects.* Ellis Horwood.

Ryle, G. (1963) *The concept of mind*, Penguin. The book was originally published by Hutchinson in 1949.

Searle, J. R. (ed.) (1971) *The philosophy of language.* Oxford University Press.

Shaffer, J. A. (1968) *The philosophy of mind*, Prentice-Hall.

Turing, A. M. (1950) Computing machinery and intelligence, *Mind*, **LIX** 433–460.

Weizenbaum, J. (1976) *Computer power and human reason: from judgement to calculation.* Freeman.

**PART II**

# THEORETICAL FOUNDATIONS AND CONCEPTS

# 2

# Computation

## 2.1 COMPUTABILITY AND COMPUTATION

Let us first introduce the notions of compatability and computation. We start with some statements that use quite a few technical words, and then we shall go on to explain the words.

Computational theory is all about defining a 'computing device' that will be general enough to compute every 'computable function'. In 1936, Turing suggested the use of a machine, now called a Turing machine (TM), which is considered to be the most general computing device. Church's thesis of 1936 may be interpreted as stating that any computable function can be computed by a TM. Since it is not possible to give a mathematically precise definition of our notion of 'computable function', we can never hope to prove Church's thesis formally. However, from the definition of a TM it is apparent that any computation that can be described by means of a TM can be mechanically carried out; and conversely, any computation that can be performed on a modern-day digital computer can be described by means of a TM. Moreover, all other general computing devices that have been proposed, e.g. by Church, Kleene (1936) and Post (1936), have been shown to have the same computing capability as TMs, which strengthens our belief in Church's thesis.

Although this chapter will re-assess Lady Lovelace's Objection once we have presented various developments in automata theory and function theory, much of the material here will also be useful for re-assessing the Mathematical Objection and the Argument from Informality of Behaviour, and this is because of the following relationship between the concepts of TM and computability:

(1)  if TMs are indeed the most powerful type of computing device imaginable, in that every computation that can be carried out mechanically can be carried out on a TM, or

(1′) if, conversely, any computation that can be described by means of a TM can be mechanically carried out, and

(2)  if it can be shown that there is some process that we humans can perform but a TM cannot perform computationally,

then it follows that we humans can do something that even the most powerful computing device imaginable cannot.

The conclusion is important not only for the Mathematical Objection, but also in some respects for Lady Lovelace's Objection and the Argument from Informality of Behaviour. The premisses of the above are based on computation theory.

One of the problems we face when trying to explain the concept of a TM is that the subject can be approached in one of three ways. A TM can be considered as an 'acceptor', or as a 'generator', or as an 'algorithm' (Manna, 1974). An acceptor is a device that has the task of deciding whether some input to it satisfies some condition or another. For instance, in the context of language theory, an acceptor for the English language may have the task of distinguishing 'The dog the cat hates is chased by the tiger' as a grammatical sentence of English, whereas 'The dog the cat hates likes is chased by the tiger' is not. An acceptor must not, of course, make mistakes. If it cannot distinguish grammatical English sentences from ungrammatical ones correctly in all cases, it is not very useful, since its decisions cannot be relied upon.

A generator, again in the example of the English language, would have the task of producing (i.e. generating) only grammatically correct sentences of English. Hence, it does not take an input as such; its task is to produce, as output, sentences of English.

Whereas the notions of acceptor and generator are usually bound up with language theory, an algorithm is a finite sequence of steps that performs some task. An algorithm must always stop at some stage with the right answer. It may have inputs as well as outputs, and algorithms perform a wide variety of functions, not necessarily linguistic.

Our first priority in this section will be to examine the notions of TM, but in our early remarks we have introduced many terms which may not be familiar. So, let us try to describe some of these terms.


## 2.2 FUNCTIONS

We shall approach the concept of function from the viewpoint of set theory. By adopting the approach, we shall provide what is known as an *extensional* account of functions; as opposed to providing an *intensional* account. In Chapter 4 we provide a more detailed account of the differences between 'extension' and 'intension'. But first, here is an extensional account, which explains functions as **sets of ordered pairs**.

Given two sets **S** and **T**, a relation **R** from **S** to **T** is called a *function* if every element **s** which is a member of the set **S** appears once and only once as the left-hand entry of an ordered pair **(s,t)** which is a member of the set **R**. A relation **R** from a set **S** to a set **T** is simply a subset of the *product* of **S** and **T**. We say that **s** is related to **t** by the relation **R** if **(s,t)** is a member of the set **R**.

We now describe some fundamental concepts of set theory.

Given any sets **A** and **B**, the *product* of **A** and **B**, signified by the notation **A×B**, is defined to be the collection of all *ordered pairs* **(a,b)** such that **a** is a member of the set **A** and **b** is a member of the set **B**.

By an *ordered pair*, we mean that **(a,b)** and **(a',b')** are regarded as equal only when **a** is the same as **a'** and **b** is the same as **b'**. Thus, **(a,b)** is the same as **(b,a)** if, and only if, **a** is identical to (is the same as) **b**.

For instance, if we had the following sets **X** and **Y**:

$$\mathbf{X} = \{\mathbf{Alan, Bob, Charles}\} \quad \mathbf{Y} = \{\mathbf{Deb, Erica, Freya}\}$$

that is, **X** is a set of three individuals, and **Y** is a set of three individuals, the *product* **X** × **Y** would consist of the following nine *ordered pairs*:

| | | |
|---|---|---|
| **(Alan, Deb)** | **(Alan,Erica)** | **(Alan,Freya)** |
| **(Bob,Deb)** | **(Bob,Erica)** | **(Bob, Freya)** |
| **(Charles,Deb)** | **(Charles,Erica)** | **(Charles,Freya)** |

i.e. all distinct combinations of a member of the first set with a member of the second set, *in that order*. A relation, say, **has-as-girlfriend**, between **X** and **Y** is defined as another set, say:

$$\mathbf{has\text{-}as\text{-}girlfriend} = \{\mathbf{(Bob,Erica),(Charles,Deb)}\}$$

That is, of all possible combinations of a member of **X** with a member of **Y**, **has-as-girlfriend** picks out only two, namely, **(Bob,Erica)** and **(Charles, Deb)**. If in the real world **Alan, Bob, Charles, Deb, Erica**, and **Freya** are people, say, members of the Computer Science Department at the University of Exeter, and *if* the symbol **has-as-girlfriend** means what it usually means in the real world, then we have just succeeded in expressing in a mathematical way the information that of all the possible combinations of someone having a girlfriend given these six individuals, exactly two combinations are true. The *relation* **has-as-girlfriend** has the task of identifying those instances which are true. It doesn't matter to us *how* this identification is done (e.g. by asking tutors, or friends, etc.) as long as, if it is necessary to provide a 'how' explanation at any stage, in principle it is possible to come up with some strategy or rule for doing so. The symbol **has-as-girlfriend** can therefore be interpreted as a shortened way of describing the strategy, whatever it is, and at the level of *specification*, the person who introduces the relation need not declare the rule or strategy and may want simply to theorize about the relation. We assume, of course, that the strategy or rule, if supplied, will always be correct for those cases it does cover, i.e. it will not return a wrong answer. For instance, if the strategy for identifying who is a girlfriend of whom returns incorrect answers, then the strategy is not of much use, since it cannot be relied upon to describe the real world correctly. Proving that a strategy is correct can be quite complex, but for our purposes in this section proof is not important.

There are other ways of representing relations. Consider the *graphical* representation of a relation **R** in Fig. 2.1. There will be exactly one arrow emanating from each node **s** that belongs to **S** leading eventually to one element **t** of **T**. That is, '**t** is related to **s** by **R**'.

The notation **tRs** is used to denote that element **t** is related to element **s** by **R**. Notice that we have **t** on the left-hand side of **R** and **s** on the right-hand side of **R**. So, **has-as-girlfriend(Bob,Erica)** can be translated as '**Erica** is related to **Bob** by **has-as-girlfriend**.' If we now write

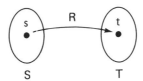

Figure 2.1

$$f(s) = t$$

in place of **tRs**, or

$$t = f(s)$$

or

$$f{:}S \rightarrow T$$

or

$$\mathbf{f}$$
$$\mathbf{S \rightarrow T}$$

we have rewritten the set relationship in function form. Here, **S** is called the *domain* and **T** the *co-domain* of the function

$$\mathbf{f{:} \, S \rightarrow T.}$$

For instance, consider the following relation:

$$\{(s1, t5), (s2,t3), (s3, t2), (s4, t3)\}$$

This particular relation (unnamed) consists of **t5** being related to **s1**, **t3** to **s2**, **t2** to **s3**, and **t3** to **s4**. This is shown in graphical form in Fig. 2.2.

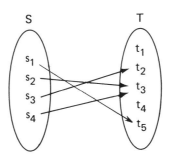

Figure 2.2

But for functions we use the notation:

$$f(s1) = t5 \qquad f(s2) = t3 \qquad f(s3) = t2 \qquad f(s4) = t3$$

We can now formalize the notion of function in terms of sets. A relation **f** from a set **X** to a set **Y** is called a function from **X** to **Y** if the following two conditions hold:

(1) the domain of **f** is **X**, and
(2) no two distinct ordered pairs in **f** have the same first value.

Hence, a function is a type of relation which is single-valued in that if **f(x)** is not equal to **f(y)**, the **x** is not equal to **y**. Moreover

> **f** is the set of ordered pairs (**x,y**) such that **x** ∈ (is a member or element of) **X** and **y** ∈**Y**, and **y**=**f(x)**;

> **f** is defined on the *domain* **X** where for each element **x** in **X** there is **y** such that **y**=**f(x)**; and

> the *range*, or *image*, of **f** is all those **y** of the co-domain **Y** such that there exists **x** where **y**=**f(x)**.

Now let us consider some properties of functions.

An *injective*, or *one-to-one*, function is one in which distinct domain elements are related to distinct co-domain elements. That is, the situation in Fig. 2.3 will never occur in the case of injective functions:

Figure 2.3

A function is called *surjective* if each co-domain element **t** can be written as **t**=**f(s)** for some domain element **s**.

The *inverse*, or *converse*, of a function can be defined as a reversal of ordered pairs. For instance, if **f** is as shown in Fig. 2.4. it can

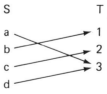

Figure 2.4

be described as follows:

$$f=\{(a,3),(b,1),(c,2),(d,3)\}$$

The inverse of **f**, symbolized by **f**$^{-1}$ can be described as follows for the above example:

$$\mathbf{f}^{-1} = \{(3,a),(1,b),(2,c),(3,d)\}$$

However, $\mathbf{f}^{-1}$ above is not a function at all, since **3** is mapped onto distinct elements **a** and **d**.

If **f: A→B** and **g: B→C**, we define the *composition* of **f** and **g**, symbolized as (**f°g**), from **A** to **C** as

$$(\mathbf{f°g})(\mathbf{x}) = \mathbf{g}(\mathbf{f}(\mathbf{x})).$$

For example, if **f** is **father** and **g** is **mother**, then asking for the **mother** of the **father** of someone, i.e. **mother(father(x))**, is equivalent notationally to **(father°mother)(x)**.

We informally introduce the idea of a *partial* function. A partial function **f(x)** is to be understood as one for which there may be no value defined for some, or even any, (domain) values of **x**. If **f(x)** happens to be defined for all values of **x**, then we call it a *total* function.

Let us now provide an example that uses the concepts outlined above. Informally, consider **Teacher** and **Student** to be the two sets shown in Fig. 2.5 related by **teaches**. Then, out of the total number of ordered pairs

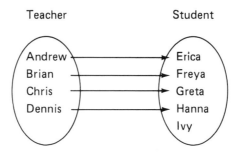

Figure 2.5

**Teacher x Student**, i.e.

**(Andrew, Erica)**
**(Andrew, Freya)**

.

.

**(Andrew, Ivy)**
**(Brian, Erica)**

.

.

**(Brian, Ivy)**
**(Chris, Erica)**

.

.

**(Chris, Ivy)**

**(Dennis, Erica)**

.

.

**(Dennis, Ivy)**

(twenty ordered pairs), the relation **teaches** picks out only four, i.e.

**teaches** = {**(Andrew, Erica), (Brian, Freya), (Chris, Greta),
(Dennis, Hanna)**}

We could write, in relational form,

**Andrew teaches Erica (Erica is related to Andrew by 'teaches')**
**Brian teaches Freya (Freya is related to Brian by 'teaches')**
**Chris teaches Greta (Greta is related to Chris by 'teaches')**
**Dennis teaches Hanna (Hanna is related to Dennis by 'teaches')**

or, in functional form,

**teaches (Andrew) = Erica**
**teaches (Brian) = Freya**
**teaches (Chris) = Greta**
**teaches (Dennis) =  Hanna**

Notice that in this example **teaches** happens to be a function, since it is not the case that a perticular teacher teaches more than one student. (In the real world, **teaches** will be a relation (and not a function) that maps one **Teacher** value onto many **Student** values.) Also, the domain of **teaches** is {**Andrew, Brian, Chris, Dennis**}, i.e. all four individuals; the co-domain of **teaches** is {**Erica, Freya, Greta, Hanna, Ivy**}, i.e. all five individuals; the range, or image, of **teaches** is {**Erica, Freya, Greta, Hanna**}, i.e. only four individuals, since **Ivy** is not related to any domain element.

We can make an important observation concerning the interpretation of functions at this point. The form **teaches (Andrew)=Erica** expresses the information that when **Andrew** is input to the function **teaches, Erica** is the value that results. Similarly, when **Brian** is input to the same function, **Freya** is the value returned, and so on. So when *interpreting* this notation, that is, when claiming that **teaches (Andrew)=Erica** *means*, or is saying, that in the real world Andrew teaches Erica, notice that we are not talking about symbolic relationship between symbols **'Andrew'** and **'Erica'**. Instead, what is being claimed is that two physical beings, Erica and Andrew are related in the world under examination, and that when Andrew the individual is 'fed' to some procedure or function labelled **teaches** Erica the individual results. In Chapter 4 we shall examine logical semantics, which uses this approach in an attempt to explain how a language is related to the real world.

Notice also that the function **teaches** is injective (i.e. one-to-one), since no two members in the domain of **teaches** are mapped onto the same individual in the co-domain (i.e. each **Teacher** value has exactly one **Student** value). However, **teaches** is not surjective, since there is one value in the co-domain, **Ivy**, which is not the value returned for any value in the domain. It is possible to define the inverse function **teaches**$^{-1}$ as follows:

> **teaches:** {(Andrew, Erica), (Brian, Freya), (Chris, Greta), (Dennis, Hanna)

> **teaches**$^{-1}$: {(Erica, Andrew), (Freya, Brian), (Greta, Chris), (Hanna, Dennis)

Note that injectivity is preserved with **teaches**$^{-1}$.

If we now have another function, say, **boyfriend**, which is:

> **boyfriend: Student → Postgraduate**

or

> **boyfriend (Erica) = John**
> **boyfriend (Freya) = Kevin**
> **boyfriend (Greta) = Lawrence**
> **boyfriend (Ivy) = John**

the *composition* of **teaches** and **boyfriend**, written **teaches°boyfriend**, from **Teacher** to **Postgraduate** is, for **Andrew**

> **(teaches°boyfriend)(Andrew)**

which is

> **boyfriend (teaches (Andrew))**

which *evaluates*, first, to

> **boyfriend (Erica)**

i.e. **teaches (Andrew)=Erica**, and, secondly, to

> **John**

i.e. **boyfriend (Erica)=John**. By means of composition, we can now start with a **Teacher** value and end with a **Postgraduate** value via a **Student** value.

The function **teaches** is *total*, i.e. every value in the domain is mapped into some value in the co-domain, whereas **boyfriend** is partial, since **Hanna** does not have a **boyfriend**. Notice that we have skipped over the crucial question of how it is that **Hanna**, which is part of our formal description, *is* the real Hanna, or how it is that **boyfriend**, also part of our functional notation, somehow refers to a real relationship of some sort between two real people. That is, we have ignored the question that concerns the relationship between a formal system and its associated world. So crucial is this question that many researchers dealing with formal systems ignore it altogether, being content to allow our intuition interpret the symbols in the first instance, and relying on well-established semantic models if a formal explanation is required. To help in this intuitive process, they use, just as we did, symbols such as **teaches, Student, boyfriend**, and so on, which are taken from the language of English. In the chapter on logical semantics we shall examine these 'semantic models' in more detail.

From such humble beginnings, a very powerful notation, together with rules for manipulating the notation, i.e. a *calculus*, can be built. For the moment, let us be content with this brief introduction to functions. Before we look at *computable* functions, let us introduce the notion of *machine*, specifically, a *Turing machine* (TM). We stress that we are introducing an *abstract* machine, i.e. a theoretical construct, and not an actual machine as such. Also, let us concentrate on the notion of a TM being an *acceptor*, rather than a *generator* or an *algorithm*. We shall tie up the relationship between these three notions later in this chapter. Just as with functions, we shall first describe a TM formally, using various technical terms, before explaining the terms in more detail.

## 2.3  TURING MACHINES

Let us consider a TM to be a machine **M** over an *alphabet* of individual letters, called $\Sigma$ with **M** consisting of three parts:

(1)  First, there is a *tape* divided into *cells*. The tape is infinite to the right and left, i.e. it can be extended indefinitely in either direction as the need arises. We are allowed to put markers on the tape to split it up into finite regions, if we wish. The tape symbols include the letters of $\Sigma$, subsets of which are used for input and output. Each cell contains one symbol.
(2)  Secondly, there is a tape *read/write head* which scan one cell of the tape at a time. In each move, the head prints a symbol on the cell scanned, replacing what was written there, and then *moves* one cell left or right depending on whether the tape-drive mechanism moves the tape one cell right or left. A *null-move*, i.e. no move of the head at all, is allowed.
(3)  Thirdly, there is a program, which we can represent by a *finite directed graph* (FDG).

Let us start our explanation with the last technical concept. An FDG consists of circles and arrows. The circles are called *vertices*, the arrows are called *arcs*. For instance, the basic structure of an FDG is shown in Fig. 2.6.

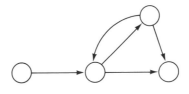

Figure 2.6

The vertices are identified, typically, by indices such as **i** and **j**. Let us insert some vertex identifiers, as in Fig. 2.7.

The indices represent the states of the machine, and traversing, or following, an arc means that the machine *switches* from one state to another. So, for example, traversing the arc between **i** and **j** as in Fig. 2.8 means that

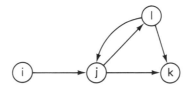

Figure 2.7

Figure 2.8

the machine switches from a state identified as **i** to a state identified by **j**. Arc traversal is not arbitrary but is determined by some conditions. These conditions are included in some information placed above an arc. Placing such information above an arrow is known as *labeling* the arc.

All FDGs have at least one *start* state (circle or vertex), which we shall signify with an arrow going into it from nowhere, and at least one *halt* state, which we shall signify with two rings. Our example now becomes as shown in Fig. 2.9.

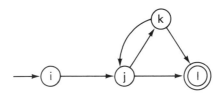

Figure 2.9

Let us examine the arc labels in more detail. Each arc label is of the form given in Fig. 2.10 where **α** and **β** are letters of ς, and **γ** is one of **L** (for

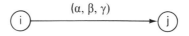

Figure 2.10

move left) or **R** (for move right) or **H** (for halt). This indicates that if during computation we are in a state **i** andd symbol $\alpha$ is scanned, we proceed to state **j** while the head prints symbol $\beta$ in the scanned cell and moves one cell right, or left, or halts depending on whether $\gamma$ is **R**, **L**, or **H**.

## 2.4   QUINTUPLES

Putting all this together, we can regard each combination of arc label and the two vertex indices which are connected by the arc as a *quintuple* having the following form:

$$(q_1, \alpha, \beta, q_j, \gamma)$$

The *interpretation* of this quintuple is as follows: if the machine is in state $q_i$ and letter $\alpha$ is read from the tape, then the machine prints letter $\beta$, moves into state $q_j$, and moves the head one cell $\gamma$ (either right, or left, or halts). Nothing forces us to include always an input, an output, and a move. For instance, quintuples of the form

$$(q_1, \phi, \phi, q_2, \phi)$$

can be used, meaning: 'If the machine is in state $q_1$ and no input occurs, no output is generated and the machine switches to state $q_2$, but the tape stays where it is,' The symbol $\phi$ is used to denote *null*.

For the moment, let us assume that if the computation eventually reaches a halt state, we say that the input string is *accepted by the TM*. If we reach a state **i** where the symbol scanned by the tape head is different from an expected $\alpha$, then there is no way to proceed with the computation and input string is *rejected* by the TM.

We now consider an example. The TM shown in Fig. 2.11, let us call it

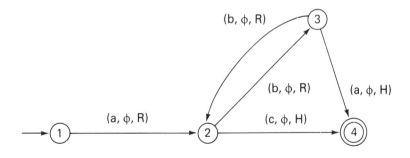

Figure 2.11

$TM_1$, with an alphabet $\varsigma$ consisting of only three symbols, **a**, **b**, and **c**, *accepts* strings of the form

**ac**
**abbc**

aba
abbba
etc.

One way to represent such strings is to say that the set of strings accepted by $TM_1$ must start with the symbol **a**, and if a string ends with an **a** there must be an odd number of **b**s between the two **a**s, whereas if a string ends with a **c**, there must be an even number (including zero) number of **b**s. No other strings are accepted by TM $TM_1$. A concise way to represent this information is as follows:

$\{ab^na\}$, such that $n = 1, 3, 5 \ldots$ or
$\{ab^mc\}$ such that $m = 0, 2, 4 \ldots$

These two descriptions allow us to represent concisely the sorts of strings accepted by $TM_1$. That is, $\{ab^na\}$ represents what is acceptable to $TM_1$ as a set of strings where there is an **a** followed by $n$ occurrences of **b** and terminated by an **a**, in that order.

The crucial step consists of representing the FDG and all the information contained in it as quintuples. The set of quintuples, in the above case, is not difficult to construct. We first code the information of how to get from $q_1$ to $q_2$:

$(q_1, a, \phi, q_2, R)$

That is, if the machine is in $q_1$ and **a** is encountered, output nothing, move into state $q_2$ and move the tape head one position to the right. This codes for the switch shown in Fig. 2.12. We shall have two quintuples to describe how

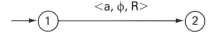

Figure 2.12

to leave $q_2$:

$(q_2, b, \phi, q_3, R)$

and

$(q_2, c, \phi, q_4, H)$

These code for the switches shown in Fig. 2.13.

Two quintuples represent the information about how to leave $q_3$:

$(q_3, b, \phi, q_2, R)$

and

$(q_3, a, \phi, q_4, H)$

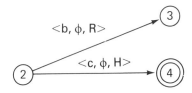

Figure 2.13

These code for the switches shown in Fig. 2.14.

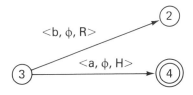

Figure 2.14

Hence, the five quintuples:

$(q_1, a, \phi, q_2, R)$
$(q_2, b, \phi, q_3, R)$
$(q_2, c, \phi, q_4, H)$
$(q_3, b, \phi, q_2, R)$
$(q_3, a, \phi, q_4, H)$

represent the instructions which are necessary to determine whether a string of symbols conforms to the structure demanded by $TM_1$.

For instance, if we wish to decide whether **abbbbc** is an acceptable string, we split the string into its individual symbols, viz., **a, b, b, b, b,** and **c,** put each of these symbols into consecutive cells on the tape (from left to right), place the tape head over the first **a,** and *run* $TM_1$, i.e. perform the computation according to the five quintuples. The sequence of the computation for **abbbbc** is as follows:

$(q_1, a, \phi, q_2, R)$
$(q_2, b, \phi, q_3, R)$
$(q_3, b, \phi, q_2, R)$
$(q_2, b, \phi, q_3, R)$
$(q_3, b, \phi, q_2, R)$
$(q_2, c, \phi, q_4, H)$

i.e. six steps.

Since $TM_1$ finishes in a halt state after the last symbol has been read the string **abbbbc** is accepted. If, however, we had started $TM_1$ off on the string **abbbc**, then, after the following computation sequence, no continuation is possible:

$$(q_1, a, \phi, q_2, R)$$
$$(q_2, b, \phi, q_3, R)$$
$$(q_3, b, \phi, q_2, R)$$
$$(q_2, b, \phi, q_3, R)$$

i.e. there is no quintuple (instruction) which describes what is to happen if the machine is in $q_3$ and a **c** is encountered. In such cases, $TM_1$ stops and is not in a halt state; the string is therefore rejected, i.e. the string does not conform to the required structure.

## 2.5 AN INTRODUCTION TO BASIC AUTOMATA THEORY

There are several points to note in the above account of a TM. First, notice that there are some gaps in our formal presentation, such as end-of-string markers which indicate to $TM_1$ that there are no more symbols in the string. For instance, according to our presentation, the string **abbbbca** is accepted by $TM_1$, since after processing **abbbbc** $TM_1$ is in a halt state, which means acceptance of the string, even though one more symbol remains to be processed (and indeed renders the string unacceptable). Hence, there is an inconsistency between what is acceptable to this TM, i.e. $\{ab^mc\}$ where $m=0,2,4\ldots$, and what is actually accepted by a TM if given the quintuples above. It is possible to overcome this, and other objections, by, for instance, changing quintuple

$$(q_2, c, \phi, q_4, H)$$

to be

$$(q_2, c, \phi, q_4, R)$$

and then adding the further quintuple:

$$(q_4, \phi, \phi, q_4, H)$$

i.e. if in $q_4$ and no more input is possible, then output nothing, remain in $q_4$ and halt. So, if any symbol occurs after a sequence of valid ones, rendering the whole string unacceptable, this can now be identified. The important point is that the gaps in our presentation can be filled by adding more quintuples to take care of them. However, our purpose is not to provide a full account of TMs, but only an account that is sufficient for the rest of the chapter.

We should, however, clarify one issue. In the above modification of our original quintuple to $(q_4,\phi,\phi,q_4,H)$ the machine *halts in a halt state*, a halt state being one identified by the corresponding FDG. It just so happens that $q_4$ is an *accept* halt state. We could have *reject* halt states as well. For instance, we could introduce $(q_4,a,\phi,q_5,H)$, where we use new halt state, $q_5$, which is entered if, and only if, an **a** is found after entering $q_4$. The two new quintuples for $q_4$ are not incompatible: they complement one another in that if there is no further input after $q_4$ is reached, the string is accepted, otherwise if an **a** is encountered, $q_5$ is entered, a reject halt state is reached, and no further processing of the string is required to reject it. (The string may terminate with one million **a**, for instance, which it would be inefficient and inelegant to process if the first terminating **a** could be used to reject the string.) Hence, halt states need not all be accept states.

A second point to note is that the notion of computation is crucially dependent on our being able to come up with a 'correct' FDG, as well as a correct set of quintuples for expressing the FDG in computational terms, or any other correct description of the steps involved in the acceptance of strings. If our FDG is wrong, i.e. does not provide a correct characterization of what is acceptable, or if the set of quintuples is wrong, i.e. does not accept what it should, then the TM will also be incorrectly programmed. It is for this reason that a notion such as computation is idealized, or abstracted away from the methods one may have used to arrive at it. In the real world, a program very rarely works the first time it is tried: debugging and rewriting are usually involved. But the notion of computation leaves all such low-level 'detail' behind and instead focuses on the specification of a program and its 'execution', i.e. its running on an abstract, idealized machine which is not affected by power cuts, faulty tapes and restricted memory.

A third point to note is that our example fails to use the full power of a TM. We have included null inputs, null outputs, null moves, moves only to the right, and so on. In fact, computation theory has identified four classes of machine, the most general and powerful of which is the TM, and for certain types of problem more restricted, hence 'simpler', abstract machines are all that are required. These simpler machines are called *finite automata* (FA), which are the weakest type, *pushdown automata* (PDA), which are stronger, and *linear bounded automata* (LBA), which are stronger still. The domain of computational problems is classified according to which type of machine is sufficient to provide a computational solution. Hence, there will be problems that require only the power of an FA, whereas other problems may require the full power of a TM. What is interesting for us to note is that some problems, even with the full power of a TM available, cannot be completely solved. This again leads us on to the Mathematical Objection, but more of this later. All that we need to do here is to identify the types of language, using **a**, **b**, and **c**, which each of these automata can handle.

An FA can handle languages of the form:

$$\{a^m b^n c^p\}, \; m \text{ greater than } 0, \; n \text{ greater than } 0, \; p \text{ greater than } 0$$

That is, any combination of **a, b** and **c**, in that order, is acceptable. The number of occurrences of each letter is arbitrary. Hence, the following strings are acceptable by an FA:

**abbbbcc** $\{a^1 b^4 c^2\}$

**aaaaaaabccc** $\{a^7 b^1 c^3\}$

An FA to handle these strings is shown in Fig. 2.15.

A PDA is required whenever the language requires there to be a

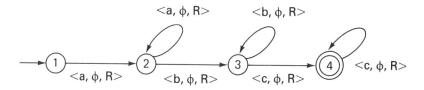

Figure 2.15

relationship of some sort between two of the three characters, e.g.

$$\{a^m b^m c^n\}$$

where it is stipulated that there must be an equal number of **as** and **bs**. The FDG of Fig. 2.15 must be rewritten in such a way that the number of **as** is somehow recorded so that each **a** can be checked against each **b**, once all the **as** have finished in the string. Our quintuples will have to do more work then those in Fig. 2.15, and the resulting automaton will only accept strings such as:

**aaabbbc** $\{a^3 b^3 c^1\}$

**aaaaaaaaaabbbbbbbbbbccc** $\{a^{10} b^{10} c^3\}$

Although the FA above will also accept such strings, it will in addition accept strings which do not conform to the $\{a^m b^m c^n\}$ requirement. The appropriately PDA however, will accept only strings that conform to this requirement and will reject all others. Hence, **abbbcc**, i.e. $\{a^1 b^3 c^2\}$, which is accepted by the previous FA will not be accepted by the appropriate PDA, since the *m* condition — that there be an equal number of **as** and **bs** — is not met.

The third type of automaton, an LBA, will accept strings where there is some sort of relationship between the occurrence of all three letters, such as

$(a^n b^n c^n\}$, **n greater and 1**

The automaton will have to count not only the number of **as**, but also the number of **bs** and **cs** to ensure that there are equal numbers of each. The quintuples will now have to do even more work than those of the PDA so that strings such as

**aaabbbccc** $\{a^3 b^3 c^3\}$

**aaaaaaabbbbbbbccccccc** $\{a^7 b^7 c^7\}$

are accepted. So, whereas $\{a^3 b^3 c^1\}$ is accepted by the PDA above, this string will be rejected by an LBA, since the *n* condition — that there be an equal number of **as**, **bs** and **cs** — is not met.

There has historically been much debate as to what sort of language requires the power of a TM, rather than an LBA, i.e. whether all languages can be handled by, at most, an LBA, but we won't go into this debate here. The basic finding of automata theory is that if there is a language that requires the full power of a TM, all that the TM can do is to accept those strings which are sentences (valid strings) of the language but the TM may loop forever, for some strings which are not sentences, in its attempt to demonstrate that such strings are not sentences of the language. We shall explore this possibility further below.

Notice that a string such as $\{a^7b^7c^7\}$ is accepted by all the automata. The notion of 'increasing power' is therefore tied up with the odd idea that there are *fewer* strings that the more powerful machines accept, since there are more conditions to be met. The further up the hierarchy one goes, the 'fussier' becomes the machine.†

Notice also that the quintuples which form a program that can be run on a TM can themselves be coded and put into a tape for another TM to operate on as data. For instance, we can bundle up the five quintuples of $TM_1$, put them on a tape and feed the tape to another TM, the task of which is to accept all TM programs that consist of seven quintuples exactly. Our five-quintuple input will therefore be rejected by the other TM. We shall describe the coding process shortly.

And finally, it may appear that our examples are trivial enough to be done by humans, so what is the need fo a machine? Although our examples are indeed trivial and deliberately so, it does not take long to find examples which would take a human a lot longer to work out but which can be more efficiently handled on a machine, e.g. 'Multiply 2 743 382 910 678 by 77 877 787 778 and then divide by 453 287'.

But the main point here is to describe a notation which allows us to specify clearly and unambiguously the exact steps that a machine, or human, must perform if they are to solve a particular task *correctly*.

We now mention some properties of TMs. If each $q_i$ and $a$ combination in the quintuple is unique, we have a *deterministic* TM. Another way of stating this is to say that in the associated FDG all arrows leaving a certain vertex must have distinct input conditions to the next vertex. If we examine the five original quintuples of $TM_1$, we notice that each $<q_i,a>$ pair is indeed unique; $TM_1$ is deterministic. If, however, we modify $TM_1$ slightly to represent the FDG in Fig. 2.16, i.e. we add the quintuple $(q_1,a,\phi,q_4,H)$, then we have a non-deterministic TM, since there are now two quintuples, i.e. $(q_1,a,\phi,q_2,R)$ and $(q_1,a,\phi,q_4,H)$ which have the same $q_i$ and $a$ conditions, namely, $<q_1,a>$. Notice that a deterministic TM may be described as a TM that 'has no choice', given a certain input and a certain current state, whereas a non-deterministic TM is one which 'has a choice of states' to switch to given a certain input and a certain current state.

It can be shown (although we shall not do so here) that a non-deterministic TM has exactly the same power as a deterministic TM. Thus, a non-deterministic TM is no more powerful than a deterministic TM, despite the notion of 'choice' just introduced.

In our discussion on TMs, we have mentioned that a string may be

---

† I am grateful to Antony Galton for reminding me of this important, but easily forgotten, aspect of computational theory.

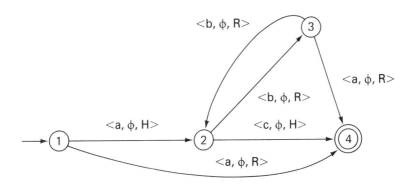

Figure 2.16

accepted or rejected. However, there is a crucially important third possibility: *the TM may loop forever in its attempt to decide whether a string is valid.* That is, the TM may not stop at all.

Consider the FDG in Fig. 2.17 and its associated quintuples:

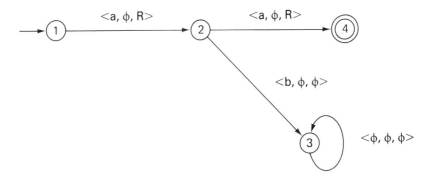

Figure 2.17

$$(q_1,a,\phi,q_2,R)$$
$$(q_2,b,\phi,q_3,\phi)$$
$$(q_2,a,\phi,q_4,R)$$
$$(q_3,\phi,\phi,q_3,\phi)$$
$$(q_4,\phi,\phi,q_4,H)$$

This TM, let us call it **TM$_2$**, will accept the string **aa**. All other strings, except **ab**, will cause **TM$_2$** to halt in a reject state. But **ab** will throw **TM$_2$** into a loop, whereby, in $q_2$, **b** will be input, **TM$_2$** will switch to $q_3$, where it will then loop forever in that state with no input, no switch of state and no tape-head movement. Hence, **TM$_2$** loops for the input **ab**.

In this example, we deliberately designed **TM₂** to loop. In fact, it is a very simple matter to write a correct FDG and its associated quintuples which will accept the strings **aa** and **ab** and reject all others. Moreover, with the examples we have used so far, the TMs will always halt, given a correct solution to the problem. But, and this is the crux of the matter, proofs demonstrating the limits of what machines can do rest on there being a class of problems which, even when correctly represented by means of FDGs and quintuples, cause the TM 'running' the program to go into an eternal loop. Since we humans do not go into an eternal loop when tackling the same problems, it follows that we are not TMs. But TMs are condsidered to be the most powerful type of computer imaginable. Hence, we humans cannot be machines, since we can do something more (i.e. not go into a loop) than even the most powerful machine imaginable.

But we are jumping ahead of ourselves!

From the above, we can see that a TM can be regarded as an idealized version of a real computer in which the individual steps are made as simple as possible (e.g. 'If in state $q_i$ and input **a** encountered . . .'). The idea of an *effective procedure* can be introduced informally as a procedure which can be broken down into very simple steps which are carried out in accordance with a set of rules. The idea is a formalization of that of an *algorithm*, or standard method of solving a problem. One could, for instance, write down (as we did) an algorithm for deciding whether a string of symbols is acceptable. This informal idea of an effective procedure evidently includes TMs, in that any procedure which can be carried out on a TM is an effective procedure. The converse argument, that any effective procedure can be carried out by a TM, is known as the *Church–Turing thesis*. One compelling but philosophically intriguing argument for accepting the thesis is that no one has thought of a process that could reasonably be called an effective procedure which cannot be carried out by a TM. The crucial word here is 'reasonably'!

## 2.6  COMPUTABLE FUNCTIONS

We have spent most of this chapter introducing some basic notions. We provided an extensional account of functions rather than an intensional one. We introduced the notion of quintuples, FDGs, and automata. Although much of the earlier material may not have been entirely necessary for what follows, it does no harm to introduce such material. At the very least, even experts may have been reminded of some simple, but easily forgotten, aspects of computational theory. For novices, the introduction may well have been of help in clarifying many technical words and concepts used in not only computational theory but also contemporary philosophy of mind and artificial intelligence. The later chapters build on this introduction. For instance, the notions of extension and intension, which appear regularly in philosophical logic and philosophy of language, will reappear in later sections of the book, where they should cause no conceptual difficulty.

But as far as this chapter is concerned, we are in a position to tie up a few loose strands.

A *function* is *computable* if it can be calculated on a TM that *halts for every input*. Calculations of such functions correspond to effective procedures. A *partial computable function* is defined only for some values of its arguments. The corresponding TM will halt only for some values of its arguments. Such functions correspond to problems which have a method of solution which may or may not terminate.

We can now explain these concepts in terms of computation theory. First, let us give a definition of function in terms of the behaviour of TMs. A function $f(x)$ will be said to be Turing-computable if its value can be computed by some TM whose tape is initially blank except for some *standard representation* of the argument $x$. When the machine stops the value returned by $f$ for its argument $x$ is left on the tape. In other words, we can define a function to be Turing-computable if all the information necessary for returning a value for the function, given a certain argument, is contained within the program of a TM and no extra information needs to be placed on the tape. Essentially, the tape is used for input and output, but the TM containing the program which represents the function does the rest. It therefore follows that a function must be describable as a sequence of steps that a TM can understand, i.e. in the form of quintuples.

By *standard representation* is meant, for example, an *unary representation* or a *binary representation*. In unary representation, numerals, for instance, are represented by ones. Thus, the numeral '3' is represented as '111'. So, $f(3)$ is represented as $f(111)$. If $f$ is a function which squares its argument, the answer, in unary form, would be '111111111' i.e. nine ones. In binary representation, binary form is used. Hence the numeral '3' would be represented in binary '11', and the answer for $f(11)$ would be '1001', i.e. nine represented in binary.

We now formalize the class of partial functions, called T-C (for Turing-computable) functions, as TMs which take arguments in the domain and map them, or convert them, into values in the co-domain. For some arguments, there will be no value in the co-domain, because, quite simply, the TM (function) may loop forever. That is, a partial function cannot provide a complete mapping for all its arguments. In the case of $f$ above, where $f$ stood for squaring its argument, it will be possible to provide a complete mapping, but there are some functions which may not return a value at all, since the TM which computes the function may loop forever. For example, consider the function that takes **pi** as its argument and returns **1** if ten consecutive 5s occur in the decimal expansion of **pi**. If **pi** does not contain ten consecutive 5s, the TM executing the quintuples may run forever!

So far, our functions have had one argument, as in $f(x)$. It is possible to have functions with more than one argument, such as **add(2,3)**, and the result of this function would be '5'. We now provide a more general definition of T-C functions which takes into account functions with more than one argument. A partial function $f(x_1,...,x_n)$, where $n$ is greater than or equal to one, which maps the argument values onto a single value in the co-domain, is said to be T-C if there is a TM **M** which behaves as follows:

(1) if $f(x_1,\ldots,x_n)$ is undefined, then **M** will loop forever;
(2) if $f(x_1,\ldots,x_n)$ is defined, then **M** will eventually halt (either rejecting or accepting the input) with a tape containing the one value of $f(x_1,\ldots,x_n)$ followed only by blanks.

Remember that the phrase 'partial function' indicates that $f(x_1,\ldots,x_n)$ may be undefined for some arguments $(x_1,\ldots,x_n)$, in contrast to a 'total function' for which $f(x_1,\ldots,x_n)$ is defined and yields a result for all possible *n* arguments. For instance, **add** is a total function, no matter how many arguments it takes.

That concludes our brief introduction to computable functions.


## 2.7   CODING QUINTUPLES

We now come to the crux of the matter. The quintuples we have introduced set out the structure of a TM **M** which will compute a function; the quintuples describe the relationships between states, inputs and outputs of **M**. We now demonstrate that it is possible for this list of quintuples to be coded in some standard representation, put onto a tape, and fed into another TM **M'**. For instance, if we represent quintuples in binary notation, we could have on the input tape (with 0s marking positions):

$$0\,0\,0\,0\,0\,0\,0*0\,0\,0\,0\,0\,0\,0*0\,0\,0\,0\,0\,0\,0*\ldots$$

where each sequence of seven 0s can be described as follows:

first two 0s, $q_i$, i.e. current state;
third 0, input symbol;
fourth 0, output symbol;
fifth and sixth 0, new state;
seventh 0, direction of tape-head;
*, punctuation mark between quintuples.

For instance, all five quintuples of $TM_1$ can be stored in this form on the tape. The quintuples are

$$(q_1, a, \phi, q_2, R)$$
$$(q_2, b, \phi. q_3, R)$$
$$(q_2, c, \phi, q_4, H)$$
$$(q_3, b, \phi, q_2, R)$$
$$(q_3, a, \phi, q_4, H)$$

We use two bits for coding the states (four states), two bits for the input and output letters **a**, **b**, **c**, and $\phi$ (for no input), and two bits for the directions **L**, **R,** and **H**. We may decide on the following codes:

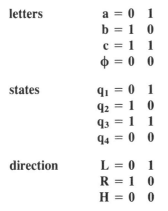

| letters | a = 0 | 1 |
|---|---|---|
| | b = 1 | 0 |
| | c = 1 | 1 |
| | φ = 0 | 0 |
| states | $q_1$ = 0 | 1 |
| | $q_2$ = 1 | 0 |
| | $q_3$ = 1 | 1 |
| | $q_4$ = 0 | 0 |
| direction | L = 0 | 1 |
| | R = 1 | 0 |
| | H = 0 | 0 |

Our tape with the five quintuples will look like this:

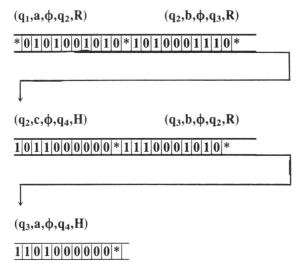

$(q_1,a,\phi,q_2,R)$                                    $(q_2,b,\phi,q_3,R)$

$(q_2,c,\phi,q_4,H)$                                    $(q_3,b,\phi,q_2,R)$

$(q_3,a,\phi,q_4,H)$

We also need to represent the string that **TM₁** is to accept or reject. Let us assume it is **abbbbc**. This is converted into binary notation and placed at the beginning of the tape:

**string to be tested          quintuples of TM₁ →**

| * | 0 | 1 | 1 | 0 | 1 | 0 | 1 | 0 | 1 | 0 | 1 | 1 | * | 0 | 1 | 0 | 1 | 0 | 0 | 1 | 0 | * | 1 | 0 | . . . . |

Let us call the TM that has all the information concerning TM₁ and its tape **TM₂**. That is, **TM₂** is a TM which has as its tape a description of the quintuples of **TM₁** and the string that **TM₁** is to accept or reject. The behaviour of **TM₂** will itself be describable by means of quintuples, of course, and this behaviour will be described below.

We may require some additional information to be stored, such as the start state of **TM₁**, which symbol in the string it starts with, how exactly to read in and write out the symbols, etc. All this information can also be coded and put onto the tape of **TM₂**.

The behaviour of $TM_2$ may be described in the following way. It starts with a particular state-symbol pair $<q_i,s_j>$, searches for the corresponding quintuple $<q_i,s_j,s_k,q_1,d_m>$ and carries out the instruction. $TM_2$ accesses the string and prints the required output, updates the location of the tape-head if necessary and replaces the old state description of $TM_1$ with a new one. $TM_2$ then prepares to read the next symbol of the string and continues as before. This behaviour can be described in terms of quintuples, if one wishes, but we shall not provide such a description here.

A TM which has all of another TM's quintuples and arguments represented on its tape is known as a Universal TM (UTM). A UTM simulates a TM's behaviour for all values of the function that the TM represents. We can, however, simulate a TM's behaviour on just one value by feeding in that value together with the TM's moves for that particular value only, as we did in the above example. Thus, we can construct several different TMs which simulate a TM's behaviour on different values. We are in effect saying that each value of $x$ in a function $f(x)$, where $f$ is a T-C function, can have its own TM representation, hence its own TM.

We have seen how for an even a simple task, such as deciding whether a string is acceptable, the construction of a finite number of instructions (by means of, for instance, a FDG), their conversion into quintuple form, and then the computation that results, are all fairly complex. Imagine what it would be like once we started to do something really difficult, such as multiplying two numbers, or dividing one number by another, or checking if one string appears within the other. Of course, in computer languages that we use every day, such functions (operations) are represented by certain symbols (e.g. $*$, $/$, and **member**, respectively), and the physical realization of these operations on computers may vary enormously. The approach we have outlined in this section, it must be stressed, is theoretical, or idealized. The theoretical fact that to express a particular function may require, say, six hundred quintuples, two hundred thousand cells, and perhaps ten thousand steps in the computation sequence is of no practical concern. It is the principle involved here that is important — the principle that a computation can be broken down into primitive steps, each of which conforms to a certain structure, which can be run on the one sort of abstract machine we have been dealing with, a TM.

So far, no one has provided a problem for which it has been shown that no breakdown into such primitives is possible. This does not mean that just breaking a problem down into primitive steps will necessarily mean that the TM will always halt at some stage with an answer. If a function is total, i.e. if it is defined for all values that lie in its domain, then we can guarantee that the associated TM will halt with an answer (value or result). If the function is partial, we have a problem. In such cases, it may not be possible to know before the computation starts whether the associated TM will halt with the right answer. All that can be said is that if the partial function is defined for the particular argument it is given, it will certainly halt with the correct answer. It may take some time (theoretically!) to do so, but it will eventually stop with an answer. But if the partial function is given an argument for which it is not defined, sometimes it will stop with a nice 'undefined' response, and at other times it may loop forever, trying to find a solution and not realizing that the value is undefined. We are now quite close to providing some examples of the behaviour of TMs given such partial functions, and therefore to understanding the impact of proofs demonstrating the limits of computability.

## 2.8 ALGORITHMS

During our introduction to automata concepts, a gradual shift has taken place. We started off by looking at automata as acceptors (of strings), but whilst discussing functions we moved onto the idea that automata were generators: given a blank tape with only the arguments provided, the TM 'generates' a result and replaces the arguments on the tape with the value that results, given the arguments. In order to present a proof of the limits of computability in a simple form, and also to bring the material up-to-date, let us present the third way of looking at TMs, namely, as algorithms.

When a TM with input tape is started in operation, it may be a very long time before it completes its computation and comes to a halt. For many 'machine-tape' pairs, as we have seen, this will never happen — the computation may go on forever. It would be very useful to have a decision procedure of some type which would help us determine whether, given a machine **M** and input tape **t**, the process will ever halt.

Given Turing's thesis that TM computations include all effective procedures, if there does exist such a decision procedure, there must exist a TM which can carry out the procedure. That is, if we humans can do it, then a TM can do it. The term 'decision procedure' here means a single set of instructions, given once and for all, that will enable us to solve the *halting problem* for every machine–tape pair. The decision will return a 'yes' if the machine will halt and 'no' if the machine will not halt.

Another way of looking at the decision procedure is to consider classes of yes/no problems, i.e. problems for which the answer is always either 'yes' or 'no', and seeing whether there is any algorithm (computing device) for solving the problems in that class. We say that a class of yes/no problems is solvable if there is some algorithm and an associated TM which for any problem in that class always halts with a correct 'yes' or 'no' answer. A 'yes' answer is returned when the TM reaches an 'accept' halt, and the 'no' answer is returned when it reaches a 'reject' halt. If no such algorithm (TM) exists, we say that the class of problems is unsolvable.

It is important to note what is *not* being claimed. The unsolvability of a class of problems does not mean that we cannot determine the answer to a specific problem in that class.

In effect, we are looking for a total function which, when fed with a partial function as its own argument, will be guaranteed to return a value to us. The value will tell us whether the partial function will return a value to us or not. In other words, we want a function, say, $f(g,n)$, which returns, for example, **1** if partial function **g** returns a value for argument **n**, and **0** if **g** does not return a value for **n**.

Unfortunately, many interesting classes of yes/no problems are unsolvable. A weaker notion of algorithms is introduced, which involves algorithms only partially solving problems in the class. That is, if the answer to the problem is 'yes', the 'algorithm' will eventually halt with a 'yes' answer, but if the answer is 'no', the 'algorithm' may supply no answer at all. The word 'procedure' is usually used to denote an algorithm in this sense. More precisely, a class of yes/no problems is said to be partially solvable if there is a procedure ('algorithm') (or TM) that will take any problem in the class as input and

(1) if the answer to the problem is 'yes', the procedure ('algorithm') will eventually reach an 'accept' halt, but
(2) if the answer to the problem is 'no', the procedure ('algorithm') either reaches a 'reject' halt or never halts.

This sense of solvability is clearly weaker than the original one in that if a class of yes/no problems is solvable, then it is also partially solvable.

## 2.9   AUTOMATA THEORY AND THE LIMITS OF COMPUTABILITY

We are now finally in a position to present a proof that demonstrates that even the most powerful machines imaginable are limited in what they can do. The proof that follows is adapted from Minsky (1967, pp. 148–150).

Minsky's proof demonstrates that it is not possible to construct an algorithm which takes an arbitrary TM **M** with input tape **t** (i.e. a machine--tape pair) and which always determines whether or not **M** will halt if given **t**. The proof therefore demonstrates the *unsolvability of the halting problem*. The form of argument is a *reductio ad absurdum*. That is, we assume the opposite of what we want to prove is true, and then show that the result is nonsense. From this we can conclude that the opposite of the opposite of what we want to prove, i.e. that we wanted to prove in the first place, is true.

Let us assume that there does exist a TM (algorithm) **A** which will decide whether or not any TM computation will ever halt, given the description $d_M$ of TM **M** and its tape **t**. Diagrammatically (from Minsky):

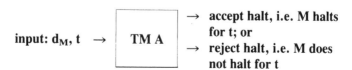

The box represents TM **A**, which we can consider to be a set of quintuples which express **A**. The quintuples operate on another set of quintuples which express **M** and the tape that **M** itself operates on. The task of **A** is to run **M** on any **t** to determine whether **M** will halt for **t**.

That is, if **A** does exist, only one of two outcomes is possible: either **A** accepts, or **A** does not accept. In both cases, **A** halts. Also, **A** must demonstrate that **M** will halt, in whatever state, for all arguments, i.e. for any **t**. Hence, **A** will halt no matter what **t A** runs with **M**. Also, **A** must halt for any **M**. This is the point of the exercise, namely, to construct a set of quintuples which will take any other set of quintuples (any other TM) with any input (**t**) and which will always correctly determine whether **M** will halt for **t**. We have assumed we can construct **A**.

If **A** can solve the halting problem for all description pairs $(d_M, t)$, then it can certainly stop for the special $(d_M, d_M)$, where the tape **t** which is fed to **M** is a description of **M**. The two items of information previously required by **A** — the description of **M** and of the tape **t** — are now the same. If **A** were to process this pair, we would get:

$$\text{input:} \quad d_M, d_M \quad \rightarrow \quad \boxed{\text{TM A}} \quad \begin{array}{l} \rightarrow \text{ \textbf{accept halt, i.e. M halts for}} \\ \phantom{\rightarrow} \text{ \textbf{t}=}d_M\text{\textbf{; or}} \\ \rightarrow \text{ \textbf{reject halt, i.e. M does not}} \\ \phantom{\rightarrow} \text{ \textbf{halt for t}=}d_M \end{array}$$

Whatever the internal structure of **A** may be, we know that its FDG must contain two halt exits, one printing 'yes' if $(d_M, d_M)$ ever halts, and one printing 'no' if $(d_M, d_M)$ never halts. For instance, let us assume that the FDG for **A** contains $q_a$ (for the **accept** halt) and $q_r$ (for the **reject** halt):

**TM A**

$$\boxed{\begin{array}{l} \ldots \rightarrow q_a \\ \ldots \rightarrow q_r \end{array}}$$

Let us now construct a TM **B**, which applies TM **A** on $(d_M, d_M)$ as input, with one modification. Whenever **A** is supposed to reach the 'yes' halt, instead **B** will loop forever:

**TM B**

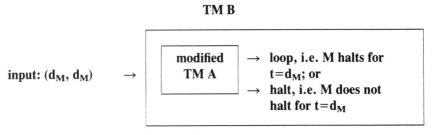

$$\text{input: } (d_M, d_M) \quad \rightarrow \quad \boxed{\begin{array}{l} \text{modified} \\ \text{TM A} \end{array}} \quad \begin{array}{l} \rightarrow \text{ \textbf{loop, i.e. M halts for}} \\ \phantom{\rightarrow} \text{ \textbf{t}=}d_M\text{\textbf{; or}} \\ \rightarrow \text{ \textbf{halt, i.e. M does not}} \\ \phantom{\rightarrow} \text{ \textbf{halt for t}=}d_M \end{array}$$

That is, we modify $q_a$ in TM **A** as follows, so that TM **B** results:

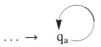

$$\ldots \rightarrow q_a \circlearrowright$$

Now, the above can be achieved for any arbitrary TM **M**. Since **B** (modified TM **A**) itself is a TM, we let **M** equal **B**. Replacing **M** by **B** wherever **M** occurs in the above figure, we get:

**TM B**

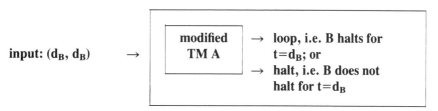

What this diagram shows is that **B** halts if **B** applied to $d_B$ does not halt, and **B** does not halt if **B** applied to $d_B$ halts! This contradiction leads us to conclude that **B** cannot be constructed, and hence nor can **A**, since **B** was constructed quite legitimately out of **A**. Hence, an algorithm (TM) for solving the halting problem of TMs does not exist. The halting problems of TMs is unsolvable.

Let us pause for a second. We assumed a TM **A** could be built, for which we constructed TM **B**. But TM **B** led us to a contradiction, and since **B** was constructed legitimately out of **A**, it follows that **A** cannot be built. Hence, the unsolvability of the halting problem has been demonstrated using the notion of TMs. Now, could a machine demonstrate the unsolvability of the halting problem in the same way? That is, above is a proof that has been constructed by a human (Minsky, in this case), read and understood by humans. Could there be a computational version of this proof that a machine could provide?

Let us work through the proof again, this time using a computer program. Let us assume that a machine $M^*$ constructs the following program and calls it **A**:

**program A;**

   · · ·
   · · ·
   **input (M,t);**

      · · ·
      · · ·
      **function accept (X,Y): . . . end {function accept};**
      · · ·
      · · ·
      **if accept (M,t) then writeln ('M halts for t');**
      **if not accept (M,t) then writeln ('M does not halt for t');**
      · · ·
      · · ·
   **end. {program}**

where **accept** is assumed to be constructable so that it returns 'true' or 'false' for all (X,Y) pairs, where X is $d_M$ and Y is t.

The next step for $M^*$ is to replace in **A** a description of $d_M$ being fed to itself:

**program A;**

```
input (dM,dM);
    ...
    ...
    function accept (X,Y); ... end; {accept}
    if accept (dM,dM) then writeln ('dM halts for dM');
    if not accept (dM,dM) then writeln ('dM does not halt for dM');
end.
```

The stage after this consists of editing program A to form program B, by modifying the first output statement:

**program B;**
```
    input (dM,dM);
        ...
        ...
        function accept (X,Y); ... end; {accept}
        if accept (dM,dM) then
            repeat z:=true until z=false;
        if not accept (dM,dM) then writeln ('dM does not halt for dM');
    end.
```

We assume **z** is declared as a Boolean variable earlier in the program.
The final stage consists of feeding **B** into itself, as $d_M$:

**program B;**
```
    input (dB,dB); {description of B and its tape, i.e. itself, fed into itself}
        ...
        ...
        function accept (X,Y); ... end; {accept}
        if accept (dB,dB) then
                repeat z:=true until z=false;
        if not accept (dB,dB) then writeln ('dB does not halt for dB');
    end.
```

Now *we* can see that program B states that B goes into a loop if $d_B$ is accepted by $d_B$, so how can **accept** ($d_B$,$d_B$) return **true** (signifying an accept halt condition) for this condition to be triggered? But there is nothing in the program that allows $M^*$ to reach this conclusion. Instead, what is required is a higher-level reasoning process that *interprets* **B** as leading to a contradiction. But a higher-level reasoning process, by its very definition, means higher-level to program **B**. The only process which is higher than program **B** is $M^*$. The task of $M^*$ was to construct programs **A** and **B**, not to reason about them. This means that $M^*$ cannot identify the contradiction, because it was not meant to!

If it is argued that $M^*$ could nevertheless be programmed to reason about programs such as **A** and **B** and to identify contradictions, we are back to where we started. That is, let us assume that $M^*$ is programmed as follows:

**program $M^*$;**

```
      . . .
      . . .
   input (A,t);
      . . .
      . . .
   function accept (X,Y): . . . end {function accept};
      . . .
      . . .
   if accept (A,t) then writeln ('A halts for t');
   if not accept (A,t) then writeln ('A does not halt for t');
      . . .
      . . .
   end. {program}.
```

But this is exactly where Minsky's proof started from, except that wherever M occurred in the program, A does! We humans can see immediately that by modifying the accept halt statement and allowing $M^*$ to take a description of itself, together with its input, as input, we shall end up with the following program:

**program $M^*$;**

```
   input ($d_M^*$,$d_M^*$); {description of B and its tape, i.e. itself, fed into itself}
      . . .
      . . .
   function accept (X,Y); . . . end; {accept}
   if accept ($d_M^*$,$d_M^*$) then
           repeat z: =  true until z = false;
   if not accept ($d_M^*$,$d_M^*$) then writeln ('$d_M^*$ does not halt for $d_M^*$);
   end.
```

We humans see that $M^*$ cannot be built. That is, we cannot build a program to identify and recognize inconsistencies without a further, higher-level program, say, $M^{**}$, being built to spot contradictions in $M^*$. But $M^{**}$ will be prone to the same problems that befell $M^*$ and may require $M^{***}$ to be built, which in turn requires $M^{****}$, etc. (Proponents of the Mathematical Objection would claim at this point that what Minsky's proof demonstrates is that we humans will always be one step ahead of the machine. That means that there will always be something that we humans can do that a machine cannot. Hence, mechanism — the view that the mind can be fully explained in mechanistic, or computational, terms — is false. This is good preparation for Gödel's findings in the next chapter, incidentally.)

One immediate, interesting implication of this proof is that no machine could ever discover the limits of its own power for itself. It requires human reasoning to be able to identify the limitations the most powerful machines imaginable possess. Even a TM cannot discover that it will go into a loop for some functions, since it would go into loop first before it could make this discovery, and by that time it would be too late!

Another implication of this proof is that we humans cannot be considered as UTMs since it is quite obvious that we do not go into a loop when confronted with problems for which we have no answer. That is, if the human reasoning process is modelled by a UTM, where the problem is considered to be on the tape and the reasoning process consists of the machine that operates on it, then the above proof demonstrates that for certain problems humans must go into an infinite loop. But we humans don't. However, the proof is obviously valid for UTMs. Hence, we cannot be UTMs. But a UTM is the most powerful computer or machine imaginable. Hence, we cannot be machines, even the most powerful imaginable. It therefore follows that mechanism is false.

There are various ways to answer these arguments, and in the next chapter we shall present some of them. All that we need do here is to remind ourselves that the proponent of the proof demonstrating the unsolvability of the halting problem, namely Marvin Minsky, himself did not see the proof as placing a limit on the applicability of AI. He, and many other AI researchers, accepted the validity of his proof (and of the Mathematical Objection), but their conclusion was very different. If formal computation theory demonstrated that computing machines were limited in power, then this showed that for AI purposes computing machines should not be driven by formal constraints. That is, the assumption of the above proof is, crucially, that a TM could be formally described in terms of automata theory, function theory, and as we shall see later, logic theory. If the halting problem lay across the formal path, then this showed that the formal path was not the one to be followed in AI and that other, less formal paths were to be explored. Minsky himself went on to propose an informal structure called *frames*, and other AI researchers also developed informal methods and techniques for AI research.

## 2.10  AI AND COMPUTATION

We are now in a position to re-assess Lady Lovelace's Objection. If we remember, this Objection, according to Turing, was that machines can only do what they are told, or programmed, to do, and so can never do anything new. Machines cannot think because the results they produce are not original.

Looking at the above exposition of automata theory, we can see that in some sense this is true. That is, no matter how an instruction or rule is presented to a computer (e.g. by FDGs, functions, 'if ... then ...' format, quintuples), it can, in theory, be 'broken down' into a sequence of primitive steps that a machine with a read/write head and indefinitely long tape can process. The behaviour of the machine can then be described as a sequence of state switches depending on the symbols read. The tape acts as memory for the machine, and the total system can be described as a mechanical process.

Turing himself proposed three responses to this Objection. First, he argued that just because machines in Lady Lovelace's time could not 'originate' anything, that did not mean that machines in the future could not think for themselves. That is, whilst it is certainly currently true that machines have to be programmed explicitly by a human to perform a series of computations, that does not mean that in future a machine could not originate programs for itself. Therefore, Turing's first response was to claim that the Objection rested on empirical fact and not logical fact.

His second response was to say that the Objection rested on what was meant by 'doing something new' and 'original work':

> Who can be certain that 'original work' that he has done was not simply the growth of the seed planted in him by teaching, or the effect of following well-known general principles? (Turing, 1950, p. 450).

Instead, Turing agued that if the Objection was rephrased as 'A machine never takes us by surprise', he himself was constantly surprised by the results of computers. Even if the surprise is the result of not being bothered to work long-hand through all the quintuples that express a program or instruction, that does not detract from the empirical fact that he has been surprised.

And his third response was to say that philosophers and mathematicians have been subject to the 'fallacy' that '. . . as soon as a fact is presented to a mind all consequences of that fact spring immediately into the mind simultaneously with it' (Turing, 1950, p. 451). This, argued Turing, was simply false.

We should now be able to see that Turing's responses do not really get to the heart of the Ojection, except perhaps for his third response. As far as his first response is concerned, he has claimed that the objection that machines can only do what they are told to do can be answered by the saying that this does not mean that in future a machine may not be able to do more than it is told to do. But this is to overlook the force of the claim, which is that *necessarily* machines can only do what they are told to do, and this is because, theoretically, any instruction or program on the computer can be represented by a sequence of, say, quintuples which make the machine behave the way it does. These quintuples may well be programmed by a human programmer, or they may well be generated by a computer itself: for instance, We can imagine a computer 'translating' a program in the computer language LISP into a set of quintuples which it then executes. Nevertheless, at all stages of the translation and execution process, the computer is not originating anything at all, since even the translation process will be governed by a set of instructions that the computer has to follow. That is, the computer can only do what it is told to do, and that is a necessary truth concerning computers. Turing's first response does little to rebut that charge.

His second response was to throw the question back at the proponents of Lady Lovelace's Objection by asking them for a clarification of what is meant by 'originating something'. Again, this is not a strong response, since there is quite clearly something essentially different about being an executor of instructions and *thinking* about executing instructions. Although Turing mentions briefly that this idea of thinking about executing instructions can be 'mimicked' by a UTM which takes another TM with its tape and executes the quintuples of that TM, he needs to show the processes of the UTM correspond to 'thinking'. This does not mean that such a correspondence cannot be found; only that Turing did not provide one.

His third response gets closer to the heart of the matter, where he explicitly questions the force of the Objection by asking for criteria for when something is judged to be new. Even then, Turing does not manage to refute the general force of the Objection. For instance, imagine we have a set of quintuples which, we are told, represent the process of multiplying two numbers. We try, manually, to work through the quintuples for two very large numbers. In principle, if we worked at it hard and long enough, no doubt we would come up with a result. We could then make a computer work through the same two numbers, using the quintuples and the tape, and the machine will come back, probably more quickly, with a response. Imagine that the two responses are different. Given the amount of effort and time that we took to work through the quintuples, there would no doubt be the temptation to say that the computer's response was correct, because there was room for error when we worked through the quintuples. But to say that a machine has less scope for error, or works more quickly, is a long way from saying that the machine has intelligence, or thinks, otherwise humans would have been tempted to attribute intelligence or thought to, say, sewing machines, which also have less scope for error and work more quickly. What is required by Turing is an argument that there is something about the rules, or quintuples, being followed, or executed, that leads to the possibility of intelligence, or thought. Again, this is not to claim that such an argument cannot be found; only that Turing himself did not provide it.

One contribution that AI can make to computation theory is precisely to concern itself with the question of how it is possible for the machine to come up with something new in virtue of, or some would say 'despite', being a quintuple-executor or rule-follower. That is, there is no doubt that we humans are creative. There is also no doubt that blind rule-following cannot lead to creative behaviour. But that does not mean that computers necessarily only follow rules blindly and therefore cannot be creative. Rather, AI can have as its objective the study of rule systems such that they are 'graded': some rule systems are more limited than others. For instance, let us look at one existing 'grading' in the area of linguistic theory.

According to Chomsky (1959), there are four types of grammar: Type 0, Type 1, Type 2, and Type 3. Rules of Type 3 grammars (regular grammars) are of the form:

$$A \rightarrow \sigma B$$

which is to be interpreted as 'The category symbol **A** can be rewritten as a string of terminal symbols $\sigma$ (symbols which cannot be further rewritten) followed by another category symbol B (a symbol which can be further rewritten in that it appears on the left-hand side of some rule in the grammar)'. Another form of rule in a Type 3 grammar is:

$$A \rightarrow \sigma$$

i.e. the category symbol **A** can be rewritten as a string of terminal symbols **σ**. Type 2 grammars (context-free grammars) have rules of the form

$$\mathbf{A} \rightarrow \boldsymbol{\beta}$$

which is to be interpreted as: 'The category symbol **A** can be rewritten as **β**, where **β** is any mixture of category symbols and terminal symbols.'

Rules of Type 1 grammars (context-sensitive grammars) have rules of the form:

$$\boldsymbol{\alpha} \rightarrow \boldsymbol{\beta}$$

which is to be interpreted as: 'Any mixture **α** of category and terminal symbols can be rewritten as any other mixture **β** of category and terminal symbols.' There is one restriction on such rules, which is that the length of string **α** must be less than or equal to the length of string **β**.

Finally, we have Type 0 grammars (unrestricted grammars) which also have rules of the form:

$$\boldsymbol{\alpha} \rightarrow \boldsymbol{\beta}$$

i.e. any mixture **α** of category and terminal symbols can be rewritten as any other mixture **β** of category and terminal symbols, but with no restrictions concerning the length of **α** and **β**.

For example, if non-terminal symbols are **X**, **Y** and **Z** and terminal symbols are **a, b** and **c**, the following rules exemplify those that can be found in the four types of grammar.

Type 3

$$\mathbf{X} \rightarrow \mathbf{a\,b}$$
$$\mathbf{X} \rightarrow \mathbf{a\,b\,Y}$$

Type 2

$$\mathbf{X} \rightarrow \mathbf{a\,b}$$
$$\mathbf{X} - \mathbf{Y\,Z\,a\,b\,Z}$$

Type 1

$$\mathbf{a\,X\,b} \rightarrow \mathbf{a\,b\,c\,b}$$
$$\mathbf{X\,Y} \rightarrow \mathbf{a\,X\,Y\,b}$$

Type 0

$$\mathbf{a\,X\,b\,c} \rightarrow \mathbf{a}$$
$$\mathbf{X\,Y\,a} \rightarrow \mathbf{X\,b\,c\,a\,Z\,c}$$
$$\mathbf{X\,Y\,Z\,a\,b\,c} \rightarrow \boldsymbol{\Phi}\ (\text{null})$$

However, although Type 0 grammars are called 'unrestricted' grammars, it is almost universally accepted by grammarians, linguists, and computer scientists that there is one restriction on such grammars, which is that there must be at least one symbol on the left hand side of a Type 0 rule. That is rules of the form

$$\Phi \rightarrow \beta$$

are not allowed.

Invoking certain assumptions, we can interpret such grammatical rules as 'if ... then ...' rules, where the part on the left-hand side of the arrow is considered to be the antecedent or condition, and the part on the right-hand side of the arrow the consequent or action. This means that we can now convert these language rules into quintuples or FDGs so that a grammar can be represented computationally. The important point is this: just as Chomsky ties up the type of grammar with 'power', in that Type 3 is the weakest form of grammar, whereas Type 0 is the strongest, in terms of language derivation and adequacy (Chomsky's view was that a grammar of at least Type 1, and for theoretical reasons a Type 0 grammar, was needed for adequately describing natural language), so AI could have as its focus the study of 'rules of natural intelligence', where rule systems are classified as to their descriptive or explanatory adequacy in the domain of intelligence. The search would then be for a classification of rule systems for natural intelligence similar to, but not identical with, the one proposed by Chomsky for natural language. One immediate effect of such a study would be the adoption of the working hypothesis that intelligence is not just an undivided, unstructured domain, but, just like natural language, can be subdivided into distinct subdomains which are classified according to the type of 'intelligence rule' required to describe adequately what goes on in that domain.

We shall return to this topic in the next volume. Our only motivation here is to point out that, whilst it is obviously true that human intelligence is creative, and whilst it is obviously true that a computer 'blindly' executing quintuples does not conform to our criteria of what counts as intelligent, these facts do not in themselves necessarily lead to the conclusion that intelligence is rule-free, or that computers cannot be intelligent. In addition to Lady Lovelace's Objection, which deals with *rule-following*, we have introduced another element into the debate, namely, that the *form* of the rules being followed may be important as well.

We have wandered close to the territory covered by the Argument from the Informality of Behaviour, so we shall leave the debate here, for the moment. Further discussion on some of these points will also be picked up in the later part of Chapter 4, where we shall discuss what it means to follow *semantic* rules. Let us now present a modern view of Lady Lovelace's Objection; one which makes absolutely explicit the force of the original Objection.

Searle has gained much publicity during the 1980s with his general attacks on what he calls 'strong AI' as well as with the now famous *Chinese Room Argument* (Searle 1980). (Incidentally, the format of Searle's paper is quite similar to Turing's original, except, of course, Searle is attacking the claims of certain AI researchers: there is a definition of AI, followed by a 'mind game', and then an evaluation of certain objections.) Let us summarize the main points of Searle's attack.

(1) There is a distinction between *strong* and *weak* AI. According to *weak* AI,

> ... the principal value of the computer in the study of the mind is that it gives us a very powerful tool. For example, it enables us to formulate and test hypotheses in a more rigorous and precise fahsion than before. (Searle, 1980, p. 282)

According to *strong* AI,

> ... the computer is not merely a tool in the study of the mind; rather the appropriately programmed computer really is a mind in the sense that computers given the right programs can be literally said to *understand* and have cognitive states. And, according to strong AI, because the programmed computer has cognitive states, the programs are not mere tools that enable us to test psychological explanations; rather, the programs are themselves the explanations. (Searle, 1980, pp. 282–283 his italics)

Searle makes clear that it is *strong* AI that he is concerned with in his article.

(2) After providing a brief description of the work of Schank and others at Yale University (Schank and Abelson, 1977), which deals with natural language processing and story 'understanding', Searle questions the claims of these workers that the machine can be literally said to *understand* the story. The questioning takes the form of the following thought experiment (slightly amended to convey the general point, whereas the original thought experiment was concerned with scripts, stories and questions, all aspects of the work of Schank and his fellow researchers). According to Searle, 'A way to test any theory of the mind is to ask oneself what it would be like if one's own mind actually worked on the principles that the theory says all minds work on' (Searle, 1981, p. 284). Hence, the thought experiment is meant to be a logical extension of what Searle takes strong AI to be, at least in the case of natural language 'understanding', so that the impossibility of the strong AI thesis can be demonstrated.

(3) Imagine that we are locked in a room. We know no Chinese. We are given two batches of Chinese writing (we may not even recognize the squiggles as Chinese), together with a set of rules in English for correlating the first batch with the second. We

> ... understand these rules as well as any other native speaker of English. They enable [us] to correlate one set of formal symbols with another set of formal symbols, and all that 'formal' means here is that [we] can identify the symbols entirely by their shapes. (Searle, 1980, p. 284)

The idea is that when, in the locked room, we receive some 'input' (Chinese, although we may not know this) on a card, say, through a flap in a wall, we check each symbol on the card against the symbols on the first batch of (Chinese) writing we were given, use the (English) rules for correlating that symbol with another symbol on the second batch of (Chinese) writing, and write that symbol down on an 'output' card. At the end of correlating all the symbols on the input card with symbols on the second batch of (Chinese) writing, and after writing down the (Chinese) symbols in the right order on the output card, we push the output card back through the flap into the outside world and consider our job done, for that particular input. If another input card enters the room, we go through the same process for that card, and the next, and so on.

(4) The point of the experiment is this:

> Suppose that after a while [we] got so good at following the instructions for manipulating the Chinese symbols . . . that from an external point of view — that is, from the point of view of somebody outside the room in which [we are] locked — [our] answers are indistinguishable from those of native Chinese speakers. (Searle, 1980, p. 285)

According to *strong* AI, we now *understand* Chinese, whereas in fact we understand no Chinese at all but are simply 'behaving like a computer', i.e. we are manipulating *uninterpreted* symbols. Also, following the rules, by itself, does not provide a sufficient condition for understanding Chinese, since no explanation of understanding has been given. If it is claimed that the above process gives us a necessary, as opposed to a sufficient condition, for understanding, Searle's answer is that there is no reason to suppose that this claim is true.

Searle then describes four responses to this thought-experiment, and calls these 'The Systems Reply', 'The Robot Reply', 'The Brain Simulator Reply', and 'The Combination Reply'. We shall return to these Replies in the second volume, since they are not relevant to our discussion of the Chinese Room Argument from the viewpoint of computational theory.

We should now be able to see that Searle's Chinese Room Argument (point (3) above) is a modern, and much expanded, version of Lady Lovelace's Objection, where Searle grants strong AI adherents their theory, but goes on to show that even if their theory is granted, we still cannot claim that the computer 'understands' anything, or even that we have supplied a necessary condition for understanding. Let us look again at some details of the thought-experiment.

The crucial part of the thought-experiment is the following supposition:

> Suppose that after a while [we] got so good at following the instructions for manipulating the Chinese symbols . . . that from an external point of view — that is, from the point of view of somebody outside the room in which [we are] locked — [our] answers are indistinguishable from those of native Chinese speakers.

With this supposition, Searle seems to grant to *strong* AI researchers that the rule set being followed by us in the room is at least sufficient, together with the original batches of Chinese script, for producing behaviour that is 'indistinguishable' from native speakers of Chinese. Hence, it follows, from a computational point of view, that the set of rules which allow the computer to correlate one symbol with another must be adequate for producing behaviour that is indistinguishable from a Chinese native speaker. Let us imagine that the rules are expressed in the form of quintuples. There may be several hundred of them or, as seems more likely, several hundred thousand, if not millions, if the computer is to produce behaviour which is indistinguishable from Chinese native speakers. For instance, there will need to be quintuples that store previous input cards so that the computer is not stumped by the simple command: 'Repeat the previous answer.'

From an efficiency point of view, we can immediately see that the amount of time required to process a simple Chinese sentence and produce an output that is indistinguishable from a native Chinese speaker is going to be very long indeed, especially since a simple symbol-by-symbol correlation is not going to work. Early machine translation attempts in the 1950s effectively knocked such a translation strategy on the head: the famous 'spoof' sentence, 'The spirit is willing but the flesh is weak', after it had been translated by the sort of strategy that Searle grants, first into Russian and then back into English, produced the sentence, 'The whisky is OK but the steak is rare'. Hutchins (1986), in his history of machine translation, has many examples of word-to-word translations based on mechanical dictionaries that required considerable pre- and post-editing in order for the translated sentence to resemble something that was 'indistinguishable' from what a native speaker would expect. Yet, the Chinese Room Argument is based on a strategy that strong AI researchers would reject. Instead, a more plausible language strategy is required.

This questioning of the soundness of the Chinese Room Argument may appear trivial, but in fact it is not, because the computational implications of adopting another strategy which will allow us, locked in the room, to produce linguistic behaviour which is indistinguishable from a native Chinese speaker, are considerable. We stated earlier that the weakest sort of machine, the FA, is not powerful enough to cope with certain linguistic structures, such as $a^n b^n$, where $n$ is arbitrarily large. Now, if a natural language, such as Chinese, is shown to possess such linguistic structures from a grammatical point of view, i.e. the grammar for Chinese can derive such structures, and if it is important for the Chinese Room Argument that the weakest type of automaton should be assumed to reside in the room, namely, an FA rather than a PDA, the syntax of Chinese sentences must be restricted to the derivation of structures of the form $a^m b^n$, where $m$ and $n$ are some upper constant limits to the number of as and bs. But then the problem might surface of whether Chinese has structures of the form $a^n b^n c^n$, where $n$ is some arbitrary number. That is, if Chinese has dependencies between three structures, no matter how many in number, an automaton of at least the power of an LBA is required. By keeping to the FAs, PDAs, and LBAs, proponents of the Chinese Room Argument can at least ensure that we, in the room, will not loop forever in our attempt to extract the grammatical structure of a Chinese sentence, since the class of grammars that are associated with these automata, if not *tractable*, i.e., 'always solvable in a reasonable amount of time and/or space on an ordinary computer' (Barton *et al.*, 1987, p. 2), are at least guaranteed to be computable, i.e. it halts for every input. If a proponent of the Chinese Room Argument is forced to adopt the power of a TM in order for us to produce behaviour which is indistinguishable from a native Chinese speaker, we in the room, if we follow the rules 'blindly', may well not halt for a certain input Chinese string which is not a sentence of Chinese: we would guess that a native Chinese speaker could then distinguish our behaviour from one of his native colleagues'!

Now, none of this may matter for Searle, since he could argue that he doesn't care in the slightest what sort of automaton resides in the room. He can give way on all the assumptions of *strong* AI researchers, except one: at the end of the day, no matter what the strategy adopted for translating, and no matter what the power of the machine, the computer still does not understand anything, since it is only following rules which do not depend on the symbols being interpreted. In other words, it cannot be the case that solely by virtue of following rules a computer understands in the way that we understand, and this is because the computer is manipulating uninterpreted symbols. However, in granting so much, he may well also have demonstrated the *possibility* of strong AI. If we list the concessions that Searle is willing to make, each is very impressive, from an AI point of view. That is,

(1) if the rules that the computer follows are not simple correlation rules between symbols but highly complex rules (requiring the power of TMs, or at least LBAs) that are required to extract the syntactic structure of input sentences;
(2) if the rules that the computer follows are assumed to have been constructed out of some prior semantic theory which has extracted the semantics of sentences well enough to be able to map input sentences onto output sentences with no further semantic analysis being required;
(3) if the computer is to be prevented from looping so that its behaviour is indistinguishable from a native speaker's;
(4) if the computer is to return responses in real time so that its behaviour is indistinguishable from a native speaker's; and
(5) if the computer '... get[s] so good at following instructions' that its answers are indeed indistinguishable from a native speaker's

that is quite a significant number of important concessions. The most important of these may well be (2).

A strong AI researcher may now want to claim that, as long as Searle is in a granting mood, he may as well grant that the computer can interpret the symbols as well. That is, why stop at syntax? What is so special about language that allows syntax to be rule-governed and programmable, but not semantics? After all, if the rules that we use in the room work on uninterpreted symbols, and if our linguistic behaviour is nevertheless indistinguishable from a native speaker's, that must be because some prior semantic theory has allowed the (human) compiler of the rules to associate, *in a rule-governed way*, symbols of one sentence with symbols of another sentence. If this association is not rule-governed, the implication is that there may well be a sentence that we could not associate with another, simply because the rules we follow do not specify what is to happen to a sentence with just that combination of symbols. This may then lead to behaviour which *is* distinguishable from a native speaker's. If there is a rule-governed way of associating symbols of one sentence with symbols of another sentence, then since the compilation of the formal rules we follow in the room must be based on the semantic rules that the human compiler has used in order to construct the formal rules presented to us, it follows, according to the Church–Turing thesis, that this process of rule compilation must also be expressed in computational form. In other words, the Chinese Room Argument satisfies Searle's objective only because Searle has begged the question in the first place of the nature of the rules we are given in the room. He states, in his original version of the argument, that they are English rules. But we, in the room, must be able to *understand* these rules first in order to associate Chinese symbols. Even if these English rules were simply of the form: 'Look for symbol 1 in the dictionary; if found, replace with symbol 2 associated with symbol 1 in the dictionary', a lot of prior interpretation has occurred, including the association between symbols in the dictionary in the first place. Who compiled the dictionary? How was it done? If there is a rule-governed process behind this compilation, then the process can be expressed in computational terms so that instead of looking up dictionary entries, we in the room now *compute* the meaning of symbols when they are presented to us and return appropriate answers. In principle, what is the difference, and why should Searle prefer one method to another?

In fact, as we shall see in Chapter 4 logical semantics is precisely that area of philosophy that attempts to lay down, in rule-governed form, the meaning of sentences. If Searle disagrees that logical semantics says all there is to say about the meaning of sentences, then his quarrel is not just with strong AI researchers but also some colleagues in his own profession who are working in the area of formal semantics.

Another aspect of the Chinese Room argument is this. Searle is asking us to consider the strong AI position to be equivalent to, first, granting the various concessions (1)–(5) above, and *then* considering the question of whether the computer can understand anything by just following rules manipulating uninterpreted symbols. It may be quite in order for an AI researcher who wants to demonstrate at least the *possiblity* of strong AI that *in the process of conceding these five points*, an intelligent computer results. That is, it might make no sense to grant these concessions and then question whether the computer understands English, or Chinese; rather, understanding cannot be divorced from the process by which understanding takes place. That is, understanding is not the sort of thing which is left over after the formal manipulations have been conceded. Instead, there may well be some sort of formal manipulation involving the use of semantic concepts and rules which give rise to the possibility that some degree of 'formal understanding' can be achieved. Although this may appear to be using the notion of understanding in two different ways — one if we are dealing with computer understanding, and the other if we are dealing with human understanding — this does not make the notion of computer understanding *impossible*. If Searle then argues that human understanding is different from computer understanding, proponents of strong AI can ask Searle exactly what it is about human understanding that is left out of their (formal) account. The danger is that the argument between Searle and strong AI researchers may then 'loop', in that whatever Searle claims is left out can, according to strong AI researchers, be programmed into a computer, and the result, according to Searle, still does not fully describe, or explain, understanding. (We have left out of our discussion the notion of 'causal power' which Searle also appeals to in his argument, but shall return to this topic at the end of the next Chapter.)

We may be reaching the point where the argument is concerned more with who 'owns' the notion of understanding (philosophers, or strong AI researchers?), or whose methodology is better for tackling the notion of understanding (the philosophers', or the AI researchers'?) than with a discussion on the conceptual nature of understanding, although, of course, the methodological question cannot be divorced entirely from the conceptual. Nevertheless, we can summarize the main point of what has come out of our discussion on the relationship between AI and computation so that we can carry it over into the next volume. It is this: the question, 'Can machines think?', and Lady Lovelace's Objection to this question, may well be interpreted, from a computational point of view, as: 'Are there appropriate rule systems and rule formats, and can intelligence, understanding and creativity be subcategorized appropriately, such that the following of one sort of rule as opposed to another gives rise to, or is equivalent to, intelligence, understanding or creativity in the one case but not in the other?'

## REFERENCES

Barton, G. E., Berwick, R. C. and Ristad, E. S. (1987) *Computational complexity and natural language*. MIT Press.

Chomsky, N. (1959) On certain formal properties of grammars, *Information and control*, **2**(2), 137–167.

Church, A. (1936) An unsolvable problem of elementary number theory, *American Journal of mathematics*, **58**, 345–363.

Hutchins, W. J. (1986) *Machine translation: past, present, future*. Ellis Horwood.

Kleene, S. C. (1936) General recursive functions of natural numbers, *Mathematisch Annalen.*, **112**, 727–742.

Manna, Z. (1974) *Mathematical theory of computation*. McGraw-Hill Kogakusha.

Minsky, M. L. (1967) *Computation: finite and infinite machines.* Prentice-Hall.

Post, E. L. (1936) Finite combinatory processes — formulation 1, *Symbolic Logic*, **1**, 103–105.

Schank, R. C. and Abelson, R. P. (1977) *Scripts, plans, goals and understanding*, Lawrence Erlbaum Associates.

Searle, J. R. (1980) 'Minds, brains, and programs', *The Behavioral and Brain Sciences*, **3**, 417–424. Reprinted in Haugeland J. (ed.) (1981) *Mind design*, MIT press, from which the page references in this chapter are taken, and in Hofstadter, D. R. and Dennett, D. C. (eds) (1981) *The mind's I: fantasies and reflections on self and soul.* Penguin.

Turing, A. M. (1936) On computable numbers, with an application to the entscheidungsproblem. *Proceedings of the London Mathematical Society, Series 2*, **42**, 230–265; correction, **43**, 544–546 (1937).

Turing, A. M. (1950) 'Computing Machinery and Intelligence', *Mind LIX*, pp. 433–460.

# 3

# Logic

## 3.1 INTRODUCTION

The best way to explain logic is by throwing ourselves into it. Logicians usually teach the logic they were taught, i.e. they adopt the formalisms and notations learned during their first exposure to logic. Our exposition of logic is heavily influenced by Copi's approach (Copi, 1967). Logicians, of course, claim that it does not matter which logic is taught or described, since notational differences (i.e. differences in the use of symbols and rules) are not important to the study of logic.

Just as we did in the previous chapter, we shall provide a summary of logic before going on to explain the technical concepts in more detail.

The syntax of a logical language may be defined in terms of its *terminal* symbols:

(1) a set of predicate symbols $\mathbf{P} = \{\mathbf{Q,R}. . .\}$ (capital letters)
(2) a set of individual constants $\mathbf{C} = \{\mathbf{a,b}. . .\}$ (lower-case letters taken from the beginning of the alphabet)
(3) a set of variable symbols $\mathbf{V} = \{\mathbf{x,y}. . .\}$ (lower-case letters taken from the end of the alphabet)
(4) a set of function symbols $\mathbf{F} = \{\mathbf{f,g,h} . . .\}$ (lower-case letters)
(5) a set of logical connectives $\mathbf{L} = \{\sim, \wedge, \rightarrow, \vee, \leftrightarrow\}$ standing for *negation, conjunction, implication, disjunction*, and *if and only if*, respectively
(6) two quantifier symbols $\forall$, and $\exists$, standing for *for all* and *there exists*, respectively
(7) punctuation symbols ( ), , (comma), {}

Using the above symbols, the objective is to specify the syntactically correct strings, called *well-formed formulas*, or *wffs* ('wuffers'), that constitute the legal statements in the language. The rules for building wffs in the language require that *terms* and *atomic formulae* be defined first.

The *terms* are defined recursively as follows:

(1) a constant is a term;
(2) a variable is a term;
(3) if $\mathbf{f}$ is a function symbol or predicate symbol of $n$ arguments and if $\mathbf{t_1}, . . . ,\mathbf{t_n}$ are terms, then $\mathbf{f(t_1}, . . . ,\mathbf{t_n})$ is a term;
(4) There are no other terms.

Terms form the arguments of *atomic formulae*. The atomic formulae are defined as follows:

> If **P** is a predicate letter of **n** arguments (**n** greater than 0) and if $\mathbf{t_1}, \ldots, \mathbf{t_n}$ are terms, then $\mathbf{P(t_1, \ldots, t_n)}$ is an atomic formula.

When *n* is zero, the atomic formula is called a *proposition*. Hence, *propositional logic* can be defined as a restricted subset of the language described above, i.e. predicate and function symbols without arguments, and no ∀ or ∃. An atomic formula, or the *negation* of the atomic formula, will be referred to as a *literal*.

*Wffs* are defined using atomic formulae, parentheses, the logical connectives and the quantifiers as follows:

atomic formulae are wffs;
if A is a wff and **x** is an individual variable, then (∀**x**)A is a wff and so is (∃**x**)A;
if **A** is a wff, so is (**A**) and {**A**};
if **A** and **B** are wffs, then ~ **A**, **A**→**B**, **A**∧**B**, **A**∨**B**, **A**↔**B** are wffs;
the only wffs are those obtained from finitely many applications of the above.

A wff in which all variables are quantified, i.e. no variable is free, is called a *closed* wff, otherwise it is *open*. Most of the work in logic deals only with closed wffs. For instance, in the following formula, (∃**x**) **P(x,y)**∧**Q(x)**, the first two occurrences of **x** are *bound* (i.e. not free), and the third occurrence is not bound (i.e. is free), wheras in (∃**x**){**P(x,y)**∧**q(x)**}, as the bracketing signifies, all three occurrences of **x** are bound. With each formula is associated a formula called the *universal closure*, which is obtained by adding a universal quantifier for each variable having a free occurrence in the original formula.

Using these syntax rules, we can determine the syntax structures of wffs and distinguish them from non-wffs. For example,

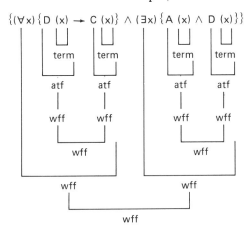

atf = atomic formula

Let us now provide an informal account of the formal description above. The main task of logic is usually agreed to be that of distinguishing between correct and incorrect *arguments*. An argument consists of two or more propositions, or statements, such that one, the *conclusion*, follows from the others, called the *premisses*. The passage from premiss (or premisses) to conclusion is known as *inference*, and formal logic is therefore sometimes defined as *the theory of logical inference*.

In *propositional logic*, i.e. the language with no quantifiers, variables or constants, the proposition, or statement, signified in capital letters, is taken to be the primitive logical unit. In *predicate logic*, the statement is broken down into further logical primitives by means of subject, predicate, and, where necessary, quantifiers. We shall concentrate first on propositional logic.

## 3.2  PROPOSITIONAL LOGIC

Consider this example:

**If the cat is hungry, it miaows. The cat is hungry. Therefore it miaows.**

Although the argument appears obvious, the task of propositional is to demonstrate the *validity* of such arguments. There are two ways to do this: either by *truth tables*, or by *rules of inference*.

In either case, there are certain steps we must go through. First, we pick capital letters of the alphabet to represent propositions in the argument. For instance, we could represent **The cat is hungry** by **H**, and **The cat (or it) miaows** by **M**. We would then have the *form*:

**If H then M. H. Therefore M.**

It is usual in propositional logic to use the lower case letter (**p, q, r** . . . ) to represent any proposition which occurs in an argument. Also, English 'connectives', such as *if* and *then* are also dropped and either replaced by their corresponding *logical connectives* or not replaced at all. For instance, the logical connective $\wedge$ replaces the English words *and*, *but*, *moreover*, and *also*, and is known as *conjunction*.

Let us adopt the *truth table* method, first of all. The extension, or meaning, of $\wedge$ is given by the following *truth table*, which signifies the result of two propositions being conjoined:

| p | q | p$\wedge$q |
|---|---|---|
| t | t | t |
| t | f | f |
| f | t | f |
| f | f | f |

For instance, reading across the first row, if **p** is true, i.e. **t**, and **q** is true, i.e.

**t**, then the conjunction of **p** and **q** is true, i.e. **t**. But if one or other, or both, of **p** and **q** is false, i.e. **f**, the result is false, i.e. **f**.

The logical connective ∨, for disjunction, replaces the English word *or*, and its meaning can be given extensionally as follows:

| p | q | p∨q |
|---|---|-----|
| t | t | t |
| t | f | t |
| f | t | t |
| f | f | f |

The *implication* connective, which replaces the English words *If . . . then . . . , therefore, it is implied from this that, consequently, is a sufficient condition for, it follows that,* and *only if,* has the following extension:

| p | q | p→q |
|---|---|-----|
| t | t | t |
| t | f | f |
| f | t | t |
| f | f | t |

*Material equivalence,* or ↔, is used for *if and only if,* and is unpacked using *implication*:

| p | q | (p→q) | ∧ | (q→p) |
|---|---|-------|---|-------|
| t | t | t | t | t |
| t | f | f | f | t |
| f | t | t | f | f |
| f | f | t | t | t |

That is,

| p | q | p↔q |
|---|---|-----|
| t | t | t |
| t | f | f |
| f | t | f |
| f | f | t |

The final connective, ∼ , which stands for *not*, or negation, is described as follows:

| p | ∼p |
|---|-----|
| t | f |
| f | t |

That is, negation has the effect of reversing the truth value of a proposition: if **p** is **true**, then **p̄** is **false**.

When individual propositions combine with each other to form a complex proposition, the result of such a combination is known as a *truth-functionally compound statement*, or *complex* statement, or *molecular* statement, i.e. a statement composed out of smaller 'atoms' or atfs. For instance, if we had:

$$(A \wedge B) \rightarrow C$$

we would construct the following table, or truth table, taking into account all possible values of **A, B** and **C**.

| A | B | C | (A∧B) | →C |
|---|---|---|-------|-----|
| t | t | t | t | t |
| t | t | f | t | f |
| t | f | t | f | t |
| t | f | f | f | t |
| f | t | t | f | t |
| f | t | f | f | t |
| f | f | t | f | t |
| f | f | f | f | t |

For instance, let us look at the second row, where **A** is **true, B** is **true**, and **C** is **false.** First, the combination of **A∧B** results in *true*, and **true**→ **C**, where **C** is **false,** results in *false.* The term *truth-functionally compound statement* arises because we can express this information in function terms:

**implies (and (A B) C)**

First, **and (A B)** is evaluated, to give, for the second row of the above table, **and (t t)**, which returns **t**, and this value then replaces **and (A B)** in the above function to leave us with **implies (t C)**. **C** evaluates to **f** (again, in the second row), and this replaces **C** to give us **implies (t f)**, which evaluates to **f**.

For a compound proposition of three different arguments, as above, eight combinations of the *truth values* of the arguments will occur, each combination corresponding to one row of the table. The general rule for working out how many rows of a truth table are required is given by raising 2 to the power of the number of distinct arguments. For instance, if there are three different arguments in a compound statement, there are $2^3$ different rows, i.e. eight. For six different arguments in a compound statement, such as

$$(A \rightarrow (B \vee (C \wedge D))) \wedge (A \rightarrow (E \vee F))$$

there will be $2^6$, i.e. 64 different rows.

Here is another example:

$$\{(p \wedge q) \vee (p \vee r)\} \rightarrow (r \leftrightarrow q)$$

Let us work out the value of the *main*, or *outermost* connective, i.e. the connective which separates the left hand part of an expression from the right hand part, which in this case is → . First we fill in all possible combinations of truth values:

$$\{(p \wedge q) \quad \vee \quad (p \vee r)\} \rightarrow \quad (r \leftrightarrow q)$$

| | | |
|---|---|---|
| t t | t t | t t |
| t t | t f | f t |
| t f | t t | t f |
| t f | t f | f f |
| f t | f t | t t |
| f t | f f | f t |
| f f | f t | t f |
| f f | f f | f f |

We start with the innermost connectives of the formula, which are $(p \wedge q)$ and $(p \vee r)$.

$$\{(p \wedge q) \quad \vee \quad (p \vee r)\} \rightarrow \quad (r \leftrightarrow q)$$

| | | |
|---|---|---|
| t t t | t t t | t t |
| t t t | t t f | f t |
| t f f | t t t | t f |
| t f f | t t f | f f |
| f f t | f t t | t t |
| f f t | f f f | f t |
| f f f | f t t | t f |
| f f f | f f f | f f |

Next, we evaluate the connective, $\vee$.

$$\{(p \wedge q) \quad \vee \quad (p \vee r)\} \rightarrow \quad (r \leftrightarrow q)$$

| | | | |
|---|---|---|---|
| t t t | t | t t t | . |
| t t t | t | t t f | . |
| t f f | t | t t t | . |
| t f f | t | t t f | |
| f f t | t | f t t | |
| f f t | f | f f f | |
| f f f | t | f t t | |
| f f f | f | f f f | |

Next we evaluate $\leftrightarrow$.

$$\{(p \wedge q) \quad \vee \quad (p \vee r)\} \rightarrow \quad (r \leftrightarrow q)$$

| | | | |
|---|---|---|---|
| . | . | . | t t t |
| . | . | . | f f t |
| . | . | . | t f f |
| | | | f t f |
| | | | t t t |
| | | | f f t |
| | | | t f f |
| | | | f t t |

Finally, we evaluate $\rightarrow$.

$$\{(p \wedge q) \quad \vee \quad (p \vee r)\} \rightarrow \quad (r \leftrightarrow q)$$

| | | | | | |
|---|---|---|---|---|---|
| t t t | t | t t t | t | t t t |
| t t t | t | t t f | f | f f t |
| t f f | t | t t t | f | t f f |
| t f f | t | t t f | t | f t f |
| f f t | t | f t t | t | t t t |
| f f t | f | f f f | t | f f t |
| f f f | t | f t t | f | t f f |
| f f f | f | f f f | t | f t f |

We now come to the central point of propositional calculus. Truth-functional expressions such as the one above are categorized according to the pattern of **t** and **f** *that falls under the main connective*. Where the main column of the truth table contains only the value **t**, the expression is said to be *logically true* or a *tautology*. If only **f** values occur in the main column, we have a *logically false* or *self-contradictory* expression. In those cases where a mixture of **t** and **f** values occurs beneath the main connective, as in the case above, we have a *contingent* expression.

If we recall that an argument consists of two or more propositions, such that one, the conclusion, supposedly follows from the others, the premises, it follows that every argument can be expressed as a *material implication* of which the premiss or premisses constitute the antecedent and the conclusion the consequent. Hence, every argument can be expressed as an *implication* and the general form of the argument can be tested by means of a truth table.

This can be made clear by means of an example.

> **If Simba is hungry, she miaows. She doesn't miaow. Therefore Simba isn't hungry.**

If **H** represents **Simba is hungry,** and **M** represents **She miaows,** we have the following logical argument:

$$\{(H \rightarrow M) \wedge \sim M\} \rightarrow \sim H$$

We then assign all possible truth values to the propositions:

$$\{(H \rightarrow M) \quad \wedge \sim M\} \quad \rightarrow \sim H$$

| | | | |
|---|---|---|---|
| t  t | t | t |
| t  f | f | t |
| f  t | t | f |
| f  f | f | f |

We then work out the results of the inner connectives $\rightarrow$ and $\sim$.

$$\{(H \rightarrow M) \quad \wedge \sim M\{ \quad \rightarrow \sim H$$

| | | |
|---|---|---|
| t t t | f t | f t |
| t f f | t f | f t |
| f t t | f t | t f |
| f t f | t f | t f |

We evaluate the inner ∧.

$$\{(H{\to}M) \ \wedge \ {\sim}M\} \quad \to \ {\sim}H$$

|         |   |     |        |
|---------|---|-----|--------|
| t t t   | f | f t | f t    |
| t f f   | f | t f | f t    |
| f t t   | f | f t | t f    |
| f t f   | t | t f | t f    |

**Finally, we calculate the result of the outer →.**

$$\{(H{\to}M) \ \wedge \ {\sim}M\} \qquad \to \ {\sim}H$$

|     |   |     |
|-----|---|-----|
| .   | f | t f |
| .   | f | t f |
| .   | f | t t |
| .   | t | t t |

Since only **t** appears under the main connective, this argument is logically valid. In fact, all arguments of the form

$$\{(p{\to}q) \wedge \ {\sim}q\}{\to} \ {\sim}p$$

are tautologous.

Now consider:

**If Simba miaows, then Freya is hungry or Simba is hungry. Freya is hungry. Therefore, if Simba miaows then she isn't hungry.**

If **M** stands for **Simba miaows, F** for **Freya is hungry,** and **H** for **Simba is hungry,** we have the argument

$$\{\{M{\to}(F{\vee}H)\} \ \wedge \ F\}{\to}(M{\to} \ {\sim}H)$$

which has the general form

$$\{\{p{\to}(q{\vee}r)\} \ \wedge q\}{\to}(p{\to} \ {\sim}r)$$

The truth table is

| {{ p→ | (q∨r)} | ∧q} | →(p→ | ∼r) |
|-------|--------|-----|------|-----|
| t t   | t t t  | t t | f    | t f  f t |
| f t   | t t f  | t t | t    | t t  t f |
| t t   | f t t  | f f | t    | t f  f t |
| t f   | f f f  | f f | t    | t t  t f |
| f t   | t t t  | t t | t    | f t  f t |
| f t   | t t f  | t t | t    | f t  t f |
| f t   | f t t  | f f | t    | f t  f t |
| f t   | f f f  | f f | t    | f t  t f |

Note that one false value occurs under the main connective, namely, in the row where all the asserted (i.e. unnegated) propositions are true! Hence, the argument is invalid. Thus, an argument is valid if and only if it is a tautology.

This concludes our introduction to the propositional calculus (PC). From this brief introduction, we would not like to give the impression that there are no problems with PC when it is used to analyse natural language expressions. (McCawley 1981, pp. 49–82) provides an extended discussion of the difficulties facing logicians and linguists when they attempt to translate natural language sentences into PC formulae. McCawley's concern is especially with the overlap between the connectives of PC ('and', material implication, 'or') and their English language equivalents. (Baker and Hacker 1984, pp. 168–205) go one step further and provide a critical analysis of the belief that there is a 'rough correspondence' between logical constants and corresponding expressions in natural language. We shall not enter into this debate here but shall return to it in the next volume, especially in the chapter dealing with methodology.

## 3.3  THE PREDICATE CALCULUS

The best way to introduce the predicate calculus, over and above the PC, is through Russell and his 1905 paper, 'On denoting', where he proposed a solution to a difficulty facing logicians. The phrase 'The present King of France' *denotes*, yet it does not denote! Superficially, it appears to be similar to 'The present Prime Minister of France,' yet there are deep differences. If, as we have seen in our account of the PC, every proposition has to be true or false, we can certainly say that the statement 'The present Prime Minister of France has four children' is true or false. If such a proposition appears in an argument, where validity of the argument depends on the truth value under the main connective being true irrespective of the values of the various propositions that make up the argument, then the negation of the statement 'The present Prime Minister of France has four children' is to be interpreted as claiming that the present Prime Minister of France has either fewer than, or more than, four children. But if 'The present King of France has four children' has to be either true or false, we have a problem: the statement is certainly not true, since there is no present King of France. That means that it has to be false, but the negation of this statement, i.e. 'The present King of France does not have four children', implies that the present King of France has either fewer than, or more than, four children. There appears to be no way, in the propositional calculus, of signifying the important fact that there is no present King of France. Thus, although in some sense we know the meaning of 'The present King of France', in another sense we do not know the meaning at all, since there is no King of France for the phrase to latch on to.

Frege (1982) had tried to overcome this problem by distinguishing, in a denoting phrase such as 'The present Prime Minister of France', two elements called the *sense* and the *denotation*. The *sense* of 'The present Prime Minister of France' is a complex of simpler parts, such as **present, Prime Minister, of, France,** and **the,** whereas the *denotation* of this phrase is a certain person who, in March 1982, *is* the present Prime Minister of France. Frege had then outlined a solution to the problem by saying that whereas the phrase 'The present King of France' has sense, it has no denotation. For Russell, whilst this was logically respectable, it did not give an exact analysis of why the problem arose in the first place. After all, the phrases 'The present Prime Minister of France' and 'The present King of France' were, superficially, of exactly the same form: what determined lack of denotation in the one case, but not in the other? Frege's answer was that denotation was to be unpacked in terms of class membership: 'The present Prime Minister of France' denotes a class, or set, of entities called 'present Prime Ministers of France' which contains exactly one member, namely, the present Prime Minister of France, whereas 'The present King of France' denotes a class, or set, of entities called 'present Kings of France' with no members. Russell's view was that this was an artificial procedure, since a Fregean analysis assumes not only that there is a denotation (a class) but also that there is none (no members of that class)!

Russell's own solution was to propose that denotation, or *reference*, was not to be separated from a phrase but was an essential *part* of a phrase. Phrases such as 'The present Prime Minister of France' were to be *analysed* into terms of the predicate calculus as follows:

**There exists some entity such that that entity is now Prime Minister of France**

Actually, some more logical apparatus is required to translate the meaning of **'the'**, which assumes that there is not just **some** individual who possess this property but also that there is *only one* such individual. We shall provide the appropriate formulation below, but the property of uniqueness, although important for Russell's Theory of Descriptions, will not be discussed here.

When a property is assigned to such phrases so that statements result, the predicate calculus would then make clear exactly what was being assigned the property. For instance, the sentence 'The present Prime Minister of France has four children' becomes

**There is some entity such that that entity is now Prime Minister and that entity has four children.**

Expressed in logic, this becomes a *conjunction* embedded within a quantified statement:

**There is some x such that x is now Prime Minister of France and x has four children**

This then becomes:

$$(\exists x)\{P(x) \wedge F(x)\}$$

where $P(x)$ stands for 'x is Prime Minister of France', and $F(x)$ stands for 'x has four children'. Since the sentence is expressed as a conjunction, it is true if both parts are true, and false if either part, or both parts, are false, i.e. if there is no present Prime Minister of France, or if the present Prime Minister of France does not have four children. Similarly, 'The present King of France has four children' will be analyzed into

$$(\exists x)\{K(x) \wedge F(x)\}$$

where **K(x)** stands for 'x is King of France', and **F(x)** stands for 'x has four children'. This statement likewise can be true if both parts of the conjunction are true, or false if at least one part is false. This statement is false since there is no individual that the **x** can be instantiated to, i.e. no present King of France exists. Thus, the introduction of the *existential quantifier* has helped us solve a puzzle. Notice also, by the way, that whereas in the English language phrases 'The present King of France' and 'The present Prime Minister of France' there appears to be reference to an individual, in the logical translation such references have disappeared: instead, we have a neutral *variable* being *predicated* of a certain property. 'The Prime Minister of France' becomes 'Some x such that x has the property of being Prime Minister of France'. That is, 'Prime Minister of France' becomes a *predicate* to be *ascribed* to individuals such as **x**, where **x** is an *individual variable*. We shall return to ascription, and its relation to sense and reference, in Chapter 4. For the sake of completeness, let us provide a first-order predicate calculus (FOPC) formulation of 'The present King of France has four children' in such a way that the meaning of 'the' is preserved:

$$(\exists x)\{K(x) \wedge F(x) \wedge (\forall y) [K(y) \rightarrow (y = x)]\}$$

i.e. 'There is some **x** such that **x** is King of France and **x** has four children and for all **y**, if **y** is King of France then **y** and **x** are the same individual.' Notice that conjunctive form is preserved, and that there is now another reason why 'The present King of France has four children' can be false, namely, if there is more than one King of France!

## 3.4  FORMAL SYSTEMS

We can now proceed to an examination of **formal systems.** Although the term *formal systems* is used extensively in computer science, mathematics, and artificial intelligence, as well as logic, it does us no harm to spell out in some detail what such systems consist of. A formal system (or axiomatic system) consists of

(1) a formal language (the syntax of one, namely, the predicate calculus, has just been described)
(2) a set of *axioms*
(3) a set of *rules of inference*

An *axiom* is a wff which is accepted as, or defined to be, universally true, i.e. valid. A *rule of inference* allows new wffs to be derived from existing ones.

Providing the syntax of a formal language, by itself, does not lead us very far. The syntax rules allow us to generate an infinite number of wffs, but all we have so far is a 'toy' notation and language, strings of well-formed symbols that do nothing and say nothing. The provision of axioms is the first step in elevating a formal language from its just being a system on paper to its saying something meaningful and true about the world.

Axioms are of two sorts. First, they can be universally valid formulae, called *logical axioms*, such as, for example,

$\mathbf{p} \lor \mathbf{q} \leftrightarrow \mathbf{q} \lor \mathbf{p}$ (commutation)

$\sim (\forall \mathbf{x})\ \mathbf{P(x)} \leftrightarrow (\exists \mathbf{x})\ \sim \mathbf{P(x)}$ (quantifier negation)

In the first case, *commutation* means that any compound statement of the form $\mathbf{p} \lor \mathbf{q} \leftrightarrow \mathbf{q} \lor \mathbf{p}$ is valid, or tautologous, in that the compound statement is always true irrespective of the truth values of the individual statements $\mathbf{p}$ and $\mathbf{q}$. For instance, '(Simba miaows or Freya is hungry) if and only if (Freya is hungry or Simba miaows)' is valid: if $\mathbf{S}$ stands for 'Simba miaows' and $\mathbf{F}$ stands for 'Freya is hungry', the logical statement $\mathbf{S} \lor \mathbf{F} \leftrightarrow \mathbf{F} \lor \mathbf{S}$ is true no matter what the truth values of $\mathbf{S}$ and $\mathbf{F}$. In the second case above, i.e. $\sim (\forall \mathbf{x})$ $\mathbf{P(x)} \leftrightarrow (\exists \mathbf{x}) \sim \mathbf{P(x)}$ where $\mathbf{x}$ is a variable symbol, and $\mathbf{P}$ a predicate symbol, what is being claimed is that the statement

(It is not the case that for all x, x is P) if and only if (There is some x such that it is not the case that x is P)

is valid. For instance, '(It is not the case that all cats are pretty) if and only if (There is some cat which is not pretty)' is valid.

The two logical equivalences above are called *logical axioms* since they would appear in any formal system of logic. Other logical axioms include:

$\sim (\mathbf{p} \lor \mathbf{q}) \leftrightarrow (\sim \mathbf{p} \land \sim \mathbf{q})$ (De Morgan's)

$\sim (\mathbf{p} \land \mathbf{q}) \leftrightarrow (\sim \mathbf{p} \lor \sim \mathbf{q})$ (De Morgan's)

$(\mathbf{p} \rightarrow \mathbf{q}) \leftrightarrow (\sim \mathbf{p} \lor \mathbf{q})$ (disjunctive syllogism)

The second form of axiom is the *non-logical* sort, and this is where the formal system impinges upon the real world, at which point we can say that we have a *formal theory* rather than just a formal system. Non-logical axioms are statements which are defined to be true of a world, or a subworld, or a domain. For example,

$(\forall \mathbf{x})\,(\forall \mathbf{y})\,(\forall \mathbf{z})\ \{\{\mathbf{Father\ (x,y)} \land \mathbf{Mother\ (y,z)}\} \rightarrow \mathbf{Grandfather\ (x,z)}\}$

(i.e. 'For all x, y and z, if x is the father of y and y is the mother of z, then x is a grandfather of z') is a non-logical axiom in that, in the domain or world under consideration, this relationship between $\mathbf{x}, \mathbf{y}$, and $\mathbf{z}$ is universally true.

Notice that in the above case the axiom is expressed in the form of an implication. It is possible to express statements of fact, in addition to rules, as axioms, e.g.,

**Father (alan, mary)     Mother (mary, sue)**

These non-logical axioms are asserted to be true of the domain, or world, of which the formal system to which they are added is a description, and therefore cannot be questioned from within the system itself. Obviously, the non-logical axioms must not contain any inconsistencies or contradictions, otherwise the formal system, together with the non-logical axioms, will be flawed from the start.

The rules of inference provide the mechanism whereby new formulae can be generated from existing formulae. For instance,

**If $\mathbf{p} \rightarrow \mathbf{q}$ and $\mathbf{q} \rightarrow \mathbf{r}$ then infer $\mathbf{p} \rightarrow \mathbf{r}$**

is the rule of *hypothetical syllogism*. If we had the following statements of the PC:

$$A \to B$$
$$B \to C$$
$$C \to D$$

we could infer, first $A \to C$ (a new statement), and then $A \to D$ (another new statement). Typically, these *inferences* would be set out as follows:

1. $A \to B$ (non-logical axiom)
2. $B \to C$ (non-logical axiom)
3. $C \to D$ (non-logical axiom)
4. $A \to C$ 1,2 Hypothetical Syllogism (HS)
5. $A \to D$ 4,3 HS

where, at lines 4 and 5 a justification is provided for the inference in terms of previous lines. Both $A \to C$ and $A \to D$ are *theorems* of the formal system which contains, in the above case, the PC, logical axioms (not explicitly described, since they will occur in every formal system), and the three non-logical axioms $A \to B$, $B \to C$, and $C \to D$.

Here is a simple *proof* in the FOPC for the argument:

1. Helen loves David.
2. Anyone who loves David loves Tom.
3. Anyone loved by Helen is intelligent.
4. Therefore, Tom is intelligent.

First, we translate the argument into FOPC, using the symbols **L** (for 'loves'), **I** (for 'is intelligent'), **h, d, t** (for 'Helen', 'David', and 'Tom'). We write out the non-logical axioms one at a time, on separate lines:

1. **L(h,d)**
2. **(∀x) {L(x,d) → L(x,t)}**
3. **(∀x) {L(h,x) → I(x)}**

We regard the conclusion as a purported theorem of the system, and add it as follows:

1. **L(h,d)**
2. **(∀x) {L(x,d) → L(x,t)}**
3. **(∀x) {L(h,x) → I(x)}**

where /?I(t) is to be interpreted as 'Does it therefore follow that Tom is intelligent?'

The **proof** looks like this:

1. **L(h,d)**
2. **(∀x) {L(x,d) → L(x,t)}**
3. **(∀x) {L(h,x) → I(x)}**
                        /?I(t)
4. **L(h,d) → L(h,t)** 2 Universal Instantiation (UI))

5. **L(h,t)** 4,1 Modus Ponens (MP)
6. **L(h,t)→ I(t)** 3 UI
7. **I(t)** 6,5 MP Quod erat demonstrandum (QED)

That is, at line 4 we universally instantiate line 2 by dropping the universal quantifier and replacing all occurrences of the universally quantified variable **x** with a constant **h** (for 'Helen'). Notice that *all* occurrences of a quantified variable that lie within the scope of a quantifier that quantifies over that variable must be replaced by the same constant letter. At line 5, from 4 and 1, i.e. from **L(h,d)→ L(h,t)** and **L(h,d),** we infer **L(h,t)** by the rule of Modus Ponens, which states that if we have the statements **p→ q** and **p** on two separate lines of a proof, we can derive **q**. At line 6, we universally instantiate **x** with respect to the constant **t**, and this allows us to derive, by Modus Ponens, **I(t)**, which was the purported theorem. We attach the signal QED (which literally stands for 'which is the thing which had to be proved') in order to make clear that we have succeeded in showing that **I(t),** i.e. 'Tom is intelligent', is indeed a theorem of the system.

Notice that the formal system is assumed. That is, we are assuming that underlying the non-logical axioms is a formal system consisting of a formal language, in this case the FOPC, a set of logical axioms that provide the universally true relationships between statements, and a set of rules of inference. The principles and tools of the underlying formal system can be used to provide a proof. Hence, by means of the base set of axioms and rules of inference, new formulae — theorems — can be derived.

Formal systems are differentiated according to the choice of different axioms and inference rules. Generally speaking, an axiom should not be included if it can be generated from a base set of axioms and the inference rules. The stress is on economy of assumption (or defininitions). If two differently axiomatised formal systems are claimed to provide two different ways of describing exactly the same domain, the formal system with fewer axioms is generally preferred. The overriding objective, though, is that all valid formulae of the language can be generated by means of the axioms and inference rules alone.

## 3.5  FORMAL THEORY

A formal theory can now be described as a formal system (formal language, logical axioms and inference rules) plus, crucially, some non-logical axioms about the domain under examination. Hence, the example given above was one of a formal theory, rather than simply a formal system. Here is another formal theory. The formal system here again consists of the FOPC as the formal language and the logical axioms and inference rules we would find in any, standard logical system. We add the following non-logical axioms:

1. **Farther(alan,mary)**
2. **Father(ken,june)**
3. **Mother(mary,albert)**
4. **Mother(mary,joan)**

**5.** $(\forall x)\,(\forall y)\,(\forall z)\,\{\{\textbf{Father(x,y)} \land \textbf{Mother(y,z)}\}\} \to \textbf{Grandfather (x,z)}\}$

where all the individual constants, variable symbols and predicate symbols are part of the language. Using these non-logical axioms and the underlying formal system, which we shall refer to as $\textbf{T}_1$, we can derive as a theorem **Grandfather(alan,albert)** as follows.

1.  **Father(alan,mary)**
2.  **Father(ken,june)**
3.  **Mother(mary,albert)**
4.  **Mother(mary,joan)**
5.  $(\forall x)\,(\forall y)\,(\forall z)\,\{\{\textbf{Father(x,y)} \land \textbf{Mother(y,z)}\} \to \textbf{Grandfather(x,z)}\}$
    /?**Grandfather(alan,albert)**
6.  $(\forall y)\,(\forall z)\,\{\{\textbf{Father(alan,y)} \land \textbf{Mother(y,z)}\} \to$
    **Granfather(alan,z)**}      5 UI
7.  $(\forall z)\,\{\{\textbf{Father(alan,mary)} \land \textbf{Mother(mary,z)}\} \to$
    **Grandfather(alan,z)**}      6 UI
8.  $\{\textbf{Father(alan,mary)} \land \textbf{Mother(mary,albert)}\} \to$
    **Grandfather(alan,albert)**      7 UI
9.  **Father(alan,mary)** $\land$ **Mother(mary,albert)**      1,3 Conj
10. **Grandfather(alan,albert)**      8,9 MP (QED)

First, we have three UIs, dropping **x, y,** and **z,** and replacing them with **alan, mary,** and **albert,** respectively. At line 9, we *conjoin* lines 1 and 3. The inference rule *conjunction* sates that if at any stage of the proof we have expressions (no matter how complex) **p** and **q** on separate lines, we can conjoin them on a new line of the proof by means of the $\land$ connective. *Conj* is used to signal this inference rule. At line 10, we use MP to drive the desired theorem.

An almost identical proof can be derived to show that **Granfather(alan, joan)** is also a theorem of $\textbf{T}_1$. At step 8, we instantiate with respect to **joan** and at step 9 we conjoin lines 1 and 4.

Both proofs depend crucially on UI. In the proof described above, replacing **x** with **alan, y** with **mary,** and **z** with **albert** leads us to the correct derivation. But there are other instantiations possible, such as replacing **x** with **ken,** which would not have led us to the desired theorem. The proof above represents the 'ideal' proof, in that all the false trails and instantiations are not described. That is, given the domain of individuals **alan, mary, ken, june, albert,** and **joan,** we chose just those constants when invoking UI that led us to a solution. Also, of the many rules of inference possible in a formal system, we chose just three in the above example, namely, UI, Conj, and MP. Proofs such as the one provided above are called **goal-driven,** in that the choice of instantiations and inference rules are dependent on the form and content of the purported theorem. But just because a certain choice of instantiations and inference rules does not lead us to the theorem, we cannot conclude that no proof exists for a purported theorem. As we shall see soon, there is a mechanical approach that we, and a machine, can adopt to satisfy ourselves that a purported theorem is indeed a theorem without necessarily being able to provide a *proof* of the theorem, if by *proof* we mean a formal sequence of steps leading from the axioms to the theorem. Before we can do this, though, we need to look at some properties of formal systems.

## 3.6   PROPERTIES OF FORMAL THEORIES AND SYSTEMS

We can show that, in the example above, the two statements are in fact theorems, and have been demonstrated to be so by proof, by using the following notation;

$$T \vdash F$$

which is to interpreted as

**Formula F is derivable, by means of a proof, from a theory T.**

That is, **F** is a theorem of the formal theory **T**, and can be formally derived by means of a proof. Hence, we can claim:

$$T_1 \vdash \textbf{Grandfather (alan, albert)}$$
$$T_1 \vdash \textbf{Grandfather (alan, joan)}$$

where $T_1$ is as we described above (i.e. a formal system, and the set of non-logical axioms). The $\vdash$ symbol, called 'turnstile', is a meta-language construct. Whereas $T \rightarrow V$ is to be interpreted as 'If **T** then **V**' $T \vdash V$ is to be interpreted as 'From premiss, **T**, **V** can be inferred' and as such is saying something *about* the formal system. What is being claimed with $T \vdash V$ is that **V** is a theorem of the formal system, i.e. that **V** can be derived by one or more rules of inference. Typically, axioms of a formal system are expressed using $\rightarrow$, whereas rules of inference are expressed using $\vdash$. For instance,

$$\{(P \rightarrow Q) \wedge P\} \rightarrow Q$$

is usually interpreted as an axiom within the formal system concerning a certain relationship between **P** and **Q**, whereas

$$p \rightarrow q, p \vdash q$$

is a rule of inference which state that whenever premises $p \rightarrow q$ and **p** occur in a formal system, then **q** can be derived (inferred). **p** and **q**, being propositional variables, can stand for a variety of different propositional forms. $\vdash$ therefore provides us with a way of characterizing theorems *relative* to a particular formal system, since different formal systems may well have different inference rules. The symbol $\dashv\vdash$ is also sometimes used as a meta-language construct, this time to indicate *deductive equivalence*. For instance, in Section 3.4, we provided two logical 'axioms': De Morgan's and Disjunctive Syllogism. It is probably more accurate to represent these not as axioms but as rules of inference, as follows:

$$\sim(p \vee q) \dashv\vdash \sim p \wedge \sim q$$
$$\sim(p \wedge q) \dashv\vdash \sim p \vee \sim q$$

$$(p \rightarrow q) \ \dashv \vdash \ (\sim p \vee q)$$

There is another, related notion for us to consider, though. The theorem **Grandfather(alan,albert)** is obviously true in all cases where the premises are true, i.e. the theorem is valid. Just as $\vdash$ is used to signify derivability or provability, given certain premises, the symbol $\models$ is used to signify validity, or truth in all states of affairs in which the premises are true. The phrase 'semantic entailment' is sometimes used to describe this relationship. So,

$$\textbf{T}_1 \models \textbf{Grandfather (alan, albert)}$$
$$\textbf{T}_1 \models \textbf{Grandfather (alan, joan)}$$

That is, $\textbf{T} \models \textbf{F}$ means: 'In all states of affairs in which $\textbf{T}$ is true, $\textbf{F}$ is true also'. Hence, **Grandfather(alan, albert)** is true is all states of affairs in which $\textbf{T}_1$ is true.

The distinction between $\vdash$ and $\models$ may seem an odd one to make. After all, if $\textbf{T}$ contains universal truths and the rules of inference generate new formulae, then must not the new formulae also be universally true?

The answer, unfortunately, is 'No', since, in addition to the logical axioms of a formal system, there is the set of non-logical axioms and these may be true only with respect to the particular domain they are meant to describe, not all domains. For instance, it may be possible to derive, by means of inference rules, the formula $\textbf{F}$:

$$(\exists x) \, (\forall y) \, (x = y)$$

where $=$ is the sign of *identity*. The claim is: **There is some x such that for all y, x is y**. If it is derivable from some system $\textbf{S}$ we could represent this as $\textbf{S} \vdash \textbf{F}$ but $\textbf{F}$ is only true in a domain that contains one individual, since it states 'Some entity x is identical with every entity y.' Since $\textbf{F}$ is not true when describing a domain with two or more individuals,

$$\textbf{S} \not\models \textbf{F}$$

Hence, a formula is valid if and only if it is true in all states of affairs, or under all interpretations.

We can now declare some properties of formal theories and systems. Although we shall present the properties as if they are properties of formal theories, these properties also belong to formal systems in general.

(1) a formula is invalid if there exists at least one state of affairs, called an *interpretation*, for which the formula is false;
(2) a formula is *unsatisfiable* if and only if it is false for every state of affairs (for every interpretation);
(3) a formula is *satisfiable* if and only if there exists at least one interpretation — called a *model* — for which the formula is true.

(We shall discuss models and interpretations in more detail in the next chapter.) Crucially, the interdependence between the notions of validity, derivability and satisfiability is as follows:

A formula $\textbf{F}$ is derivable if and only if $\sim \textbf{F}$ is unsatisfiable.

In formal terms,

$$\mathbf{T} \vdash \mathbf{F} \text{ if and only if } \mathbf{T} \not\models \sim\mathbf{F}$$

In other words, one way to demonstrate that **F** can be derived from **T** is to try and show that there does not exist any interpretation of the negation of **F** which is true.

Perhaps an easier way to understand the relationship between derivability and satisfiability is to say that a formula which is not derivable, or provable, is not valid, and if a formula is not derivable then there is at least one state of affairs in which it is false. The term 'valid' is used here in a slightly different sense from the one introduced earlier, when *argument* forms were characterized as valid, contradictory, or contingent. A *formula* is valid if it is true in all states of affairs, and a formula which is true in at least one state of affairs is said to be 'satisfiable'. The symbol $\models$ is used to signify that what appears on the right-hand side of this symbol is always true, given the truth of whatever appears on the left-hand side of the symbol. Hence, the symbol $\not\models$ signifies 'always false', or 'not satisfiable'.

A theory is **sound** if all the wffs that can be derived in the theory are *semantically entailed*, i.e. are valid and true. That is, if for any theory **T** all the derived formulae are valid, **T** is sound. A sound theory, therefore, is any theory in which all theorems are valid, i.e. true in all states of affairs. Another way to put this is:

If '**If T** $\vdash$ **F** then **T** $\models$ **F**' is true, the formal theory **T** is sound.

Another interesting property is *completeness*. A formal theory is *complete* (semantically) if every valid wff of the therory can be derived by means of the axioms and inference rules. That is, if for any theory **T** all the true (valid) formulae can be derived from **T** using the inference rules of the formal system, then **T** is complete. Another way to put this is as follows:

If '**If T** $\models$ **F** then **T** $\vdash$ **F**' is true, the formal theory **T** is complete.

As McCawley (1981, p. 74) puts it:

A logical system is said to be SEMANTICALLY COMPLETE if its rules of inference allow you to prove all the [formulae] that could stand a chance of being proved, that is, all [formulae] that are true in all states of affairs.

McCawley uses the term 'semantic completeness' to distinguish if from 'deductive completeness' (McCawley, 1981, p. 76):

A system is 'deductively complete' if for every [formula] A of the system, either A or $\sim$A is a theorem of the system.

We shall return to the topic of deductive completeness in Section 3.10.

A theory **T** is *inconsistent* if and only if both **T** $\vdash$ **F** and **T** $\vdash$ $\sim$**F** for some formula **F**. That is, if a theory derives both the asserted form and the negated form of a wff **F**, the theory is inconsistent. A theory is consistent, therefore, if and only if it is not inconsistent. This is known as a *syntatctic* *definition of consistency*, since consistency is unpacked in terms of a formal, i.e. rule-governed, relationship between theory and formula, i.e. between symbols. The general, *semantic*, notion of consistency, that a system of statements is consistent if it is possible for it to be true (as in 'That's consistent with the facts') — semantic, because the word *true* is mentioned — is an important one for logic, since it is through consistency that a series of marks on paper — the axioms, notations, and inference rules — can be judged as to its relevance to the real world. The obvious route of trying to demonstrate the consistency of a theory by actually showing it to be true will, unfortunately, not work once we deal with theoretical domains, as opposed to the domain of real entities. For instance, it is possible to theorize about phenomena and check these theories for consistency long before equipment can be built to measure and observe these phenomena ('oxygen', 'black hole', and 'quark', for example).

The final property that we shall mention can be described as follows. A formal theory **T** is *decidable* if it is always possible to determine whether it is or is not consistent. That is, a theory is decidable if it is always possible to determine wheither its formulae (couched in terms of a formal system) are theorems (true) or not. A formal theory is *undecidable* if it is *not* possible to determine whether it is or is not consistent.

We have briefly stated some of the more interesting properties of formal systems and theories. One of the important points to note here is that some formal systems are sound *and* complete, whereas others are not. 'Simple' formal systems based on the PC are sound, complete, and decidable. That is, the exclusive use of the PC will ensure that all true statements of the domain, given the axioms of the formal system, are derivable, i.e. can be reached by a proof (completeness), and that all statements derived by means of the inference rules are true (soundness). Moreover, this means that the PC is decidable, since it is always possible to determine whether a theory couched in terms of the PC is or is not consistent, i.e. whether the theory allows the derivation of a formula, **F**, and its negation $\sim$ **F**. Some elementary geometry systems which can be expressed in terms of the PC only are therefore decidable, in that there will be a *decision procedure* which will take any formula expressed in terms of the theory and will determine whether the formula is valid or not. Moreover, for all valid formulae, there will be a derivation from the axioms, via rules of inference, to that formula (theorem). For instance, one way to determine whether a formula is a theorem is simply to calculate, mechanically, all possible truth values of the individual propositions in the formula and see what the truth values are under the main connective. If there occurs one **F** value, the formula does not constitute a theorem. If only Ts occur under the main connective, we can, if we wish, try to derive a formal proof via the rules of inference which then provides a step-by-step demonstration of how the theorem can be derived from the axioms. We know that such a proof exists, since the formal system under consideration possesses the properties of completeness, consistency and decidability.

However, no such decision procedures exist for formal systems which deal with more complex domains, such as the domain of natural numbers. These domains require the 'power' of the FOPC in order to be expressed and represented adequately, but formal theories based on FOPC are undecidable. That is, no decision procedure exists which will take an arbitrary formula of the formal theory and always decide whether the formula is true (part of the theory) or not. That does not mean that there will not be *some* formula for which decidability will hold: rather, what is being claimed is that not all formulae can be neatly characterized by the decision procedure as theorem or non-theorem. For some formulae, the decision procedure will not be able to decide. Instead, the most that can be done is provide a 'semi-decision procedure' which can take an arbitrary formula and, if the formula is indeed a theorem (part of the theory), the semi-decision procedure will certainly say so. If, however, the formula is not a theorem, the semi-decision procedure may not be able to say so: sometimes it will, and at other times it won't. But just because the semi-decision procedure may not be able to say so does not mean that the formula is not a theorem: the semi-decision porocedure may just be taking a long time to determine that the formula is indeed a theorem. That is, just because the semi-decision procedure seems to be taking a long time to return an answer, that does not mean that the formula it is working on is not a theorem. In this situation, we are caught in the awkward position of not being able to conclude, from the fact that the semi-decision procedure is taking a long time, that the formula it is working on is not a theorem. If we did, and 'switched off' the procedure, it might have been the case that the semi-decision procedure was just about to show that the formula was indeed a theorem, but we switched it off too early. Hence, we will have made a mistake. The property of being *semi-decidable* belongs to a formal theory or system which will always allow us to determine whether it is consistent but only sometimes allow us to determine whether it is inconsistent. That is, a semi-decidable system is one in which valid formulae will certainly be identified and recognized, but invalid formulae may not. These formal properties are used extensively in the next subject we shall examine, namely, automated theorem proving.

## 3.7  THEOREM PROVING

Given a wff we can ask whether it is a theorem of a given theory, i.e. $\mathbf{T} \vdash \mathbf{F}$. If we are dealing with a theory couched in terms of the FOPC, this is an unsolvable problem as no procedure is guaranteed to terminate in a finite amount of time if the wff is not a theorem. The process is guaranteed to terminate in a finite amount of time only if there is a finite number of possible deductions or the given formula is indeed a theorem.

One way to prove a theorem mechanically is to apply inference rules blindly to axioms so as to derive all possible theorems. This is not a sensible approach to adopt, since there might be at every stage a choice of, say, ten inference rules, which will generate ten new wffs, each of which can be manipulated by one of ten rules, which will generate one hundred wffs, each of which can be manipulated by one of ten rules, etc. Even for a short proof, where the theorem may be 'only' six steps away from the premiss, many thousands of wffs will have to be generated, stored and manipulated. And we have been assuming only one premiss. Imagine if our theory had, say, twenty premisses: the interaction amongst the premisses also will have to be taken into account.

Instead of using a variety of inference rules and working forwards from the premisses to the theorem, we can — given the soundness and completeness properties — concern ourselves with the notions of satifiability and unsatisfiability. That is, instead of trying to derive, or deduce, **F** from the axioms, we can try to show that ∼ **F**, together with the given set of axioms, is unsatisfiable, i.e. we try to demonstrate **T** $\not\models$ ∼**F**. (Remember that a formula is derivable if and only if the negation of the formula is unsatisfiable.) Consequently, if from ∼ **F** and the given formal theory, we derive an unsatisfiable formula, this shows that ∼**F** together with the theory is unsatisfiable, i.e. **T** $\not\models$ ∼**F**. From this it follows that **T** $\vdash$ **F**, i.e. that **F** is derivable, even though we have not formally derived **F** by means of a staged proof. The question then arises as to how we identify an obviously unsatifiable formula, given this method. The answer lies in the three fundamental axioms of any logical system, namely,

> **p**∨ ∼ **p** (Law of Excluded Middle)
> ∼ (**p**∧ ∼ **p**) (Law of Contradiction)
> **p**→ **p** (Law of Identify)

The negation of any one of these laws would provide us with an unsatisfiable formula. Let us look at the Law of Excluded Middle:

> **p**∨ ∼ **p**

Obviously, the negation of this law is unsatisfiable, i.e. ∼ (**p**∨ ∼ **p**). With some simple manipulation, this becomes:

> ∼ (**p**∨ ∼ **p**)
> ∼ **p**∧ ∼ ∼ **p** using De Morgan's Rule
> ∼ **p**∧**p** using the Rule of Double Negation
> **p**∧ ∼ **p** using the Rule of Commutation

That is, any formula with the form **p**∧ ∼ **p** is unsatisfiable.

If we look at the second Law, namely, the Law of Contradiction, we see that another unsatisfiable formula would result by negating this Law:

> ∼ ∼ (**p**∧ ∼ **p**)

But, through the Rule of Double Negation, this becomes

> **p**∧ ∼ **p**

also.

The negation of the third Law gives us:

> ∼ (**p**→ **p**)

which also give us:

$\sim (\mathbf{p} \to \mathbf{p})$
$\sim (\sim \mathbf{p} \vee \mathbf{p})$ By the Rule of Disjunctive Syllogism
$\sim \sim \mathbf{p} \wedge \sim \mathbf{p}$ By the Rule of De Morgan
$\mathbf{p} \wedge \sim \mathbf{p}$ By the Rule of Double Negation

Hence, the negation of each of the three Laws leads to the same, unsatisfiable formula, namely, $\mathbf{p} \wedge \sim \mathbf{p}$. Consequently, if from $\sim \mathbf{F}$ and the given set of axioms we derive at any stage a formula that has the form $\mathbf{p} \wedge \sim \mathbf{p}$, then we can conclude that $\sim \mathbf{F}$ together with the axioms of the theory is unsatisfiable. Since the axioms must be true, it follows that it is the inclusion of the negated form of the theorem that leads to unsatisfiability. Hence, the unnegated form of the theorem, $\mathbf{F}$, is derivable.

Such procedures in which a contradiction, known as *the empty*, or *null formula*, is derived from the negation of the theorem to be tested and the set of axioms are called *refutation procedures*, as opposed to *affirmation procedures*, which work with the given axioms and theorem. Refutation procedures do not yield a formal proof (i.e. $\mathbf{T} \vdash \mathbf{F}$) but a result, namely that the formula $\mathbf{F}$ is valid. The best known refutation procedure is based on the *resolution principle* of Robinson (1965). It can be applied to wffs after they are put into a *standard normal form* called *clauses*, in which all variables are implicitly universally quantified. A clause is a disjunction of literals, and every set of wffs can be transformed to caluse form. The transformation is satisfiability preserving.

Before we examine the resolution principle, let us first look at the transformation process. The format to which we convert the wff in preparation for the resolution procedure is called *Skolem conjunctive form*, or just *conjunctive normal form*. The conversion (or transformation) process consists of a number of steps. To illustrate the transformation process, we use the following wff as an example:

$$(\forall x)\,(\forall y)\,(\forall z)\,\{\{\mathbf{Mother(x,y)} \wedge \mathbf{Mother(y,z)}\} \to \mathbf{Grandmother(x,z)}\}$$

**Step 1**
Eliminate $\to$ and $\leftrightarrow$. Apply the following conversion rules to any formula or subpart within a formula:

$$\mathbf{A} \to \mathbf{B} \text{ becomes } \sim \mathbf{A} \vee \mathbf{B}$$
$$\mathbf{A} \leftrightarrow \mathbf{B} \text{ becomes } (\sim \mathbf{A} \vee \mathbf{B}) \wedge (\mathbf{A} \vee \sim \mathbf{B})$$

where $\mathbf{A}$ and $\mathbf{B}$ stand for wffs, or subparts of wffs. So, in our example, we would now have: $(\forall x)\ (\forall y)\ (\forall z)\{\sim \{\mathbf{Mother(x,y)} \wedge \mathbf{Mother(y,z)}\} \vee \mathbf{Grandmother(x,z)}\}$

**Step 2**
Move $\sim$ inwards. Apply the following conversion rules to any formula:

| | | |
|---|---|---|
| $\sim (A \wedge B)$ | becomes | $\sim A \vee \sim B$ |
| $\sim (A \vee B)$ | becomes | $\sim A \wedge \sim B$ |
| $\sim \sim A$ | becomes | $A$ |
| $\sim (\forall x)A$ | becomes | $(\exists x) \sim A$ |
| $\sim (\exists x)A$ | becomes | $(\forall x) \sim A$ |

The rules are applied until all negations are immediately to the left of a propositional or predicate letter. So, in our example, we would now have:

$(\forall x)\ (\forall y)\ (\forall z)\ \{\{ \sim \textbf{Mother(x,y)} \vee \sim \textbf{Mother(y,z)}\} \vee$
$\textbf{Grandmother(x,z)}\}$

**Step 3**

Exchange $\exists$ for *Skolem functions*, if $\exists$ lies within the scope of a universal quantifier, otherwise replace with a designated constant. Let us look at Skolem functions in more detail.

Examine the following two statements:

There is some number **x** such that it is greater than all other numbers.

For any number **x**, there is some number that is greater than it.

In terms of the FOPC, we can state these as follows:

$(\exists x)\ (\forall y)\ G(x,y)$
$(\forall x)\ (\exists y)\ G(y,x)$

where $G(\textbf{w,v})$ stands for **w is greater than v.** Let us assume that each of these two statements is the non-logical axiom of two different theories, $\textbf{T}_1$ and $\textbf{T}_2$, respectively, both of which deal with the domain of the set of positive integers only (that is, with numbers greater than 0). In $\textbf{T}_1$, we have the axiom $(\exists x)\ (\forall y)\ G(x,y).$ Instantiating the quantified variables always takes place from the outermost quantifier inwards. Hence, when we instantiate the existential quantifier to, say, **20**, we shall have $(\forall y)\ G(20,y).$ When it comes to instantiating the universal quantifier, we are limited to all those numbers for which the relation **20 is greater** is true, i.e. to all those numbers between 1 and 19, inclusive. Hence, the first, existential instantiation effectively limits the domain of positive integers, after instantiation, to a finite set of numbers that the universally quantified variable can then be instantiated to. $\textbf{T}_1$ can therefore be interpreted as a theory which expresses true statements about a limited domain of positive integers, the limit being set by the first, existential instantiation. Hence $(\exists x)\ (\forall y)\ G(x,y)$ can be *interpreted* as generating a finite set of values, for 1 up to a value that corresponds to $\textbf{x} - 1$ any one of which will preserve the truth of the relation.

If we look at $\textbf{T}_2$, however, it contains a different axiom which states that for any number that is instantiated, there exists a number that is greater than it. Remembering that we must instantiate the outermost quantifiers first, let us universally instantiate **x** to **20**, i.e. $(\exists y)\ G(y,20).$ If we now want to instantiate the existentially quantified variable, how can we do so and still preserve the truth of this axiom? Again, if we *interpret* the first instantiation as generating a set of values, the generation will go on forever, since the set is infinite! We can see that **21** will satisfy the relationship, as will **22, 23,** and so on, but according to our interpretation we shall never be able to reach the stage of seeing this, since we shall forever be busy generating an infinite set.

Common-sense dictates that the proper interpretation of $(\forall x)$ $(\exists y)$ **G(y,x)** is this: Given an **x** value, we should be able to generate one **y** value by some simple method which uses the **x** value in order to come up with a **y** value that preserves the truth of the relation. For instance, the method might simply be: **Add 1 to the x value.** Hence, $(\forall x)$ $(\exists y)$ **G(y,x)** can be 'translated' into the following statement,

$$(\forall x) \; \mathbf{G(add1(x), x)}$$

where **add1(x)** stands for **add 1 to the x value, when x is instantiated.** If we now instantiate **x** to **20,** we have **G(add1(20),20)** (we replace all occurrences of **x**, wherever they occur in the axiom), which evaluates to **G(21,20).** This preserves the truth of the relation, without the necessity of trying to generate infinite sets. But, notice that in the 'translation' of the second axiom, we have introduced a function, **add1,** which is required to take the **x** value and return a result. This method of translation, called *Skolemization*, will work for all those wffs that have an existential quantifier within the scope of a universal quantifier, provided that we replace all occurrences of the existentially quantified variable with a function that takes as an argument the universally quantified variable.

Returning to our conversion example, we should now see that after Skolemization has taken place, we can adopt the rule that if any variables remain in the wff, they are universally quantified.

For instance, if we had

$$(\exists w) \; (\forall x) \; (\exists y) \; \mathbf{P(w,x,y)}$$

this transforms first to

$$(\exists w) \; (\forall x) \; \mathbf{P(w,x,f(x))}$$

where **f(x)** replaces the existentially quantified variable **y** which falls within scope of the universal quantifier, $(\forall x)$, and the $(\exists y)$ is dropped. It does not matter to us what **f** is, since at this stage it is just a marker for a function that we know we can provide once the interpretation of the wff becomes clear. Next, we replace the other, existentially quantified variable, **w**, with a designated constant, say, **a**. That is, since $(\exists w)$ does not fall within the scope of a universal quantifier, no Skolemization is required. $(\exists w)$ is now dropped also, leaving us with

$$(\forall x) \; \mathbf{P(a,x,f(x))}$$

Finally, $(\forall x)$ can be dropped on the understanding that any variables left in the formula at this stage are universally quantified, giving us:

$$\mathbf{P(a,x,f(x))}$$

Our conversion example contains no existential quantifiers, which means that we can drop all the universal quantifiers, leaving us with:

$$\{\{\sim Mother(x,y) \lor \sim Mother(y,z)\} \lor Grandmother(x,z)\}$$

## Step 4

Obtain the *conjunctive normal form*. A *clause* is a disjunction of *literals*, and a formula is in conjunctive normal form if and only if it expresses a series of clauses conjoined together. To obtain conjunctive normal form, we apply the following conversion rules until conjunctive normal form is realized (where **A, B,** and **C** stand for literals):

**A ∨ (B ∧ C) becomes (A ∨ B) ∧ (A ∨ C)**
**(B ∧ C) ∨ A becomes (B ∨ A) ∧ (C ∨ A)**

Since our example contains no conjunctions, it is already in clause form, i.e. it contains disjuncts only:

$$\{\{\sim Mother(x,y) \lor \sim Mother(y,z)\} \lor Grandmother(x,z)\}$$

But if, instead, the formulas had been:

$$\{\{\sim Mother(x,y) \land \sim Mother(y,z)\} \lor Grandmother(x,z)\}$$

this would have been converted into

$$\{\{\sim Mother(x,y) \lor Grandmother(x,z)\} \land \{\sim Mother(y,z) \lor Grandmother(x,z)\}$$

## Step 5

Rewrite in *standard normal form notation*. All parentheses except those around the function and predicate arguments are deleted. Commas are used between function arguments. Also, commas are used to separate clause, i.e. commas replace ∧. So, our example finally becomes:

$$\sim Mother(x,y) \lor \sim Mother(y,z) \lor Grandmother(x,z)$$

This clause of three *literals* is now ready to be input to a *resolution procedure*, to be described soon.

The sequence of steps described above is a simplified version of the actual conversion process. In truth, there are a couple of extra steps involved, and the conversion process is more complex, but our shortened exposition should be enough for our purposes. A fuller, and more formal, account is provided in Nilsson (1971).

Let us briefly provide another example. Consider the wff

$$(\forall x)\{P(x) \to \{(\forall y)\{P(y) \to P(f(x,y))\} \land \sim (\forall z)\{Q(x,z) \to P(z)\}\}\}$$

This wff contains a function **f**. Here is the conversion.

(1) Eliminate implication signs

$$(\forall x)\{\sim P(x) \lor \{(\forall y)\{\sim P(y) \lor P(f(x,y))\} \land \sim (\forall z)\{\sim Q(x,z) \lor P(z)\}\}\}$$

(2)  Reduce scope of negation signs:

$$(\forall x)\{\sim P(x) \vee \{(\forall y)\{\sim P(y) \vee P(f(x,y))\} \wedge (\exists z)\sim\{\sim Q(x,z) \vee P(z)\}\}\}$$

$$(\forall x)\{\sim P(x) \vee \{(\forall y)\{\sim P(y) \vee P(f(x,y))\} \wedge (\exists z)\{Q(x,z) \wedge \sim P(z)\}\}\}$$

(3)  Eliminate existential quantifiers:

$$(\forall x)\{\sim P(x) \vee \{(\forall y)\{\sim P(y) \vee P(f(x,y))\} \wedge \{Q(x,g(x)) \wedge \sim P(g(x))\}\}\}$$

That is, $g(x)$ replaces all occurrences of $z$, since $\exists z$ falls within the scope of $\forall x$.

$$\{\sim P(x) \vee \{\{\sim P(y) \vee P(f(x,y))\} \wedge \{Q(x,g(x)) \wedge \sim P(g(x))\}\}\}$$

(4)  Obtain the conjunctive form:

$$\{\{\sim P(x) \vee \sim P(y) \vee P(f(x,y))\} \wedge \{\sim P(x) \vee Q(x,g(x))\} \wedge \{\sim P(x) \vee \sim P(g(x))\}\}$$

That is, the underlying form of the wff at the end of step (3) is

$$\{\sim A \vee \{(\sim B \vee C) \wedge (D \wedge \sim E)\}\}$$

which is converted as follows:

$$\{\{\sim A \vee (\sim B \vee C)\} \wedge \{\sim A \vee (D \wedge \sim E)\}\}$$
$$\{\{\sim A \vee (\sim B \vee C)\} \wedge \{(\sim A \vee \sim E)\}\}$$
$$\{\{\sim A \vee (\sim B \vee C)\} \wedge (\sim A \vee D) \wedge (\sim A \vee \sim E)\}$$

(5)  Rewrite in standard normal form notation:

$$\sim P(x) \vee \sim P(y) \vee P(f(x,y)), \quad \sim P(x) \vee Q(x,g(x)), \quad \sim P(x) \vee \sim P(g(x))$$

*Resolution* as developed by Robinson (1965) can be defined simply for the PC — that is, the language without quantifiers and terms — as follows:

If the set of clauses $\{p \vee q, \sim p \vee r\}$ is satisfiable, then so is the set $\{p \vee q, \sim p \vee r, q \vee r\}$. The clause $q \vee r$ is derived from the clauses $p \vee q$ and $\sim p \vee r$ by using the *resolution principle*, which deletes the complementary propositions $p$ and $\sim p$ from the two clauses and forms a disjunction of the remaining parts. A resolvent of the form $p \vee p$ is simplified to $p$ only.

For example, if we had

$$\{\sim A \vee B \vee C, A \vee D\}$$

we could form the new clause set

$$\{\sim A \vee B \vee C, A \vee D, B \vee C \vee D\}$$

by cancelling out $A$ and $\sim A$ in the first two clauses and forming a new clause by taking the remnants of the two clauses in which $A$ and $\sim A$ appear. The remnants are connected together by disjunction.

At the propositional level, the resolution principle acts as a cancellation law which, given two clauses with complementary literals, forms a new derived clause. The literals in the two clauses on which the cancellation law is applied are referred to as the *resolved literals*, while the newly formed clause is called the *resolvent*.

Consider the set of clauses $\{\mathbf{p} \lor \mathbf{q}, \sim \mathbf{q} \lor \mathbf{r})$, which may be thought of as the axioms of the system. If we want to determine whether $\sim \mathbf{r} \rightarrow \mathbf{p}$ is a theorem, we can proceed in one of two ways. First, we can negate $\sim \mathbf{r} \rightarrow \mathbf{p}$, convert the negated wff into clause form, insert the clause into the axiom set, and try to derive the null clause, i.e. a contradiction. If we do, that tells us that the negated wff cannot be satisfied, hence the non-negated wff, i.e. $\sim \mathbf{r} \rightarrow \mathbf{p}$, must be a theorem. This is to use resolution with a refutation strategy. Or, secondly, we can try to derive $\sim \mathbf{r} \rightarrow \mathbf{p}$, or, rather, its clausal form $\mathbf{r} \lor \mathbf{p}$ (after double negation) from the axiom set as it stands. This is to adopt an affirmation strategy.

If we adopt the refutation strategy, we negate $\sim \mathbf{r} \rightarrow \mathbf{p}$, i.e. $\sim (\sim \mathbf{r} \rightarrow \mathbf{p})$, convert it into $\sim (\sim \sim \mathbf{r} \lor \mathbf{p})$ and then into $\sim \mathbf{r}$ and $\sim \mathbf{p}$ (two clauses, and add them to our clause set, i.e.

$$\{\mathbf{p} \lor \mathbf{q}, \sim \mathbf{q} \lor \mathbf{r}, \sim \mathbf{p}, \sim \mathbf{r}\}$$

We then use the resolution principle repeatedly until we derive a null clause, if we can. We use * to denote the resolved literals, + to signify the resolvent, and [ ] to signify the null clause:

$$\{\mathbf{p} \lor \mathbf{q}, \sim \mathbf{q} \lor \mathbf{r}, \sim \mathbf{p}, \sim \mathbf{r}, \mathbf{q}\}$$
$$\;\;\;\;\; *\;\;\;\;\;\;\;\;\;\;\;\;\;\;\;\;\;\; *\;\;\;\;\; +$$

$$\{\mathbf{p} \lor \mathbf{q}, \sim \mathbf{q} \lor \mathbf{r}, \sim \mathbf{p}, \sim \mathbf{r}, \mathbf{q}, \mathbf{r}\}$$
$$\;\;\;\;\;\;\;\;\;\;\;\;\;\;\;\; *\;\;\;\;\;\;\;\;\;\; \mathbf{o}*\; +$$

$$\{\mathbf{p} \lor \mathbf{q}, \sim \mathbf{q} \lor \mathbf{r}, \sim \mathbf{p}, \sim \mathbf{r}, \mathbf{q}, \mathbf{r}, [\,]\}$$
$$\;\;\;\;\;\;\;\;\;\;\;\;\;\;\;\;\;\;\; *\;\;\;\; *\;\; +$$

Since [ ] has been derived, that means that the non-negated form of the introduced wff, i.e. $\sim \mathbf{r} \rightarrow \mathbf{p}$, is a theorem of our original axiom set.

The affirmation strategy, on the other hand, would look like this:

$$\{\mathbf{p} \lor \mathbf{q}, \sim \mathbf{q} \lor \mathbf{r}\} \text{ (original axiom set)}$$

The clause form of our alleged theorem, $\sim \mathbf{r} \rightarrow \mathbf{p}$, is

$$\mathbf{r} \lor \mathbf{p}$$

(after double negation). Resolution on the original set of axioms gives us

$$\{\mathbf{p} \lor \mathbf{q}, \sim \mathbf{q} \lor \mathbf{r}, \mathbf{p} \lor \mathbf{r}\}$$
$$\;\;\;\; *\;\;\;\;\;\;\;\;\;\; *\;\;\;\;\;\; +$$

$\mathbf{p} \lor \mathbf{r}$ is precisely what we want, since it is a commutated form of $\mathbf{r} \lor \mathbf{p}$, hence we have affirmed that $\sim \mathbf{r} \rightarrow \mathbf{p}$ is a theorem given the original axiom set.

Another way to represent the resolution mechanism is through a form of stepped proof. For instance, it may be clearer, for longer examples, to use the following format to describe the example of refutation above:

| | | |
|---|---|---|
| 1. | $p \lor q$ | given |
| 2. | $q \lor r$ | given |
| 3. | $p \lor r$ | 1,2 |
| 4. | $\sim p$ | given (part of the negation of $\sim r \rightarrow p$) |
| 5. | $r$ | 3,4 |
| 6. | $\sim r$ | given (part of the negation of $\sim r \rightarrow p$) |
| 7. | [] | 5,6 |

So far, our resolution principle has dealt with the PC. In order to deal with FOPC, we need to distinguish between two types of resolution procedure: *ground resolution* and *general resolution*. Ground resolution deals with *ground clauses*, and general resolution deals with *general clauses*. A ground clause is a clause in which all variables have been replaced by 'ground terms', i.e. variable-free terms. Let us have a look at an example of ground resolution.

    If the clause set is:

$$\{Pa \lor Qa, Pa \lor \sim Qa, \sim Pa \lor Qa, \sim Pa \lor \sim Qa\}$$

We can use ground resolution with this example, since only the constant letter **a** appears. We can describe the process by which [] is derived as follows:

| | | |
|---|---|---|
| 1. | $Pa \lor Qa$ | given |
| 2. | $Pa \lor \sim Qa$ | given |
| 3. | $Pa$ | resolvent of 1,2, and **Pa** $\lor$ **Pa** becoming **Pa** |
| 4. | $\sim Pa \lor Qa$ | given |
| 5. | $Qa$ | resolvent of 3,4 |
| 6. | $\sim Pa \lor \sim Qa$ | given |
| 7. | $\sim Pa$ | resolvent of 5,6 |
| 8. | [] | resolvent of 3,7 |

General resolution, on the other hand, deals with clauses that contain variables and uses *substitution*, or *unification* procedures. Such procedures, called θs, act as pattern matches on arguments of predicates and functions. In general, we can represent any substitution by a set of ordered pairs:

$$\theta = \{(t_1, v_1), (t_2, v_2), \ldots, (t_n, v_n)\}$$

The pair $(t_i, v_i)$ means that *term* $t_i$ is substituted for, or unified with, *variable* $v_i$ throughout the two resolved literals. In our examples, we shall also carry forward the substitution to the resolvent, in order to aid exposition. For example, let us present the above derivation of the null clause, this time using general resolution. If the clause set is:

$$\{Px \lor Qy, Pa \lor \sim Qa, \sim Px \lor Qy, \sim Pa \lor \sim Qa\}$$

where we have a mixture of variables and constants, the process is as follows:

| | | |
|---|---|---|
| 1. | $Px \lor Qy$ | given |

2. **Pa** ∨ ~**Qa**    given
3. **Pa**    resolvent of 1,2, θ = {(a,x),(a,y)}
4. ~**Px** ∨ **Qy**    given
5. **Qy**    resolvent of 3,4, θ = {(a,x)}
6. ~**Pa** ∨ ~**Qa**    given
7. ~**Pa**    resolvent of 5,6, θ = {a,y)}
8. **[ ]**    resolvent of 3,7

At line 3, for instance, **x** and **y** in line 1 are replaced by **a**, allowing resolution to take place. But $t_i$ stands for *term i*, hence we can replace a variable by any term we wish, where *term* means constant, variable, or function. For instance, here is another example, very similar to the two above:

$$\{Px \lor Qy, Pw \lor {\sim}Qz, {\sim}P(f(x)) \lor Qy, {\sim}Pz \lor {\sim}Qy)$$

1. **Px** ∨ **Qy**    given
2. **Pw** ∨ ~**Qz**    given
3. **Px** ∨ **Pw**    resolvent of 1,2, θ = {(y,z)}
3′. **Px**    simplify 3, θ = {(x,w)}
4. ~**P(f(x))** ∨ **Qy**   given
5. **Qy**    resolvent of 3′,4, θ = {(f(x),x)}
6. ~**Pz** ∨ ~**Qy**    given
7. ~**Pz**    resolvent of 5,6
8. **[ ]**    resolvent of 3′,7, θ = {(x,z)}

Formally, if a substitution θ is applied to every member of a set $\{L_i\}$ of literals, we denote the set of substitutions instances by $\{L_i\}_\theta$. We say that a set $\{L_i\}$ of literals is *unifiable* if there exists a substitution θ such that

$$L_{1\theta} = L_{2\theta} = L_{3\theta} = \ldots$$

In such cases, θ is said to be a *unifier* of $\{L_i\}$ since its use collapses the set to a singleton. For example,

$$\theta = \{(a,x),(b,y)\}$$

unifies

$$\{P(x,f(y),b), P(x,f(b),b)\}$$

to yield

$$\{P(a,f(b),b)\}$$

That is, two clauses have been reduced to a single clause which is not exactly like either of the two clauses but is in some sense a unifier of the two clauses. In automated theorem proving, it is highly desirable to use a *unification algorithm* which guarantees to find the simplest unifier for any unifiable set $\{L_i\}$. Such a unifier is commonly called the *most-general-unifier*. In our examples above, we did not use unification as such but only substitution. We shall not deal further with the unification algorithm; further references can be found in (Nilsson, 1971).

### 3.8   LOGIC AND KNOWLEDGE REPRESENTATION

Let us now provide an example of how the procedures we have introduced may be of help in problem solving and knowledge representation by computer. Consider the trivial problem (Nilsson, 1971): 'If Maria goes wherever John goes, and John is at school, where is Maria?' We can interpret the problem as consisting of two premises and a question whose answer can be deduced from the premises. We can translate the premises into FOPC formulae as follows:

1. $(\forall x)\{At(john,x) \rightarrow At(maria,x)\}$
2. $At(john,school)/?(\exists x)At(maria,x)$

Next, we translate the premises into a form that is compatible with mechanical resolution, and then start the resolution process:

1. $\{\sim At(john,x) \lor At(maria,x)\}$   given
2. $At(john,school)$                         given
3. $At(maria,school)$                        $1,2, \theta = \{(school,x)\}$

This is as far as we can go, since no more resolvents can be generated. At line 3, we have **At(maria,school),** which is the 'solution', in that the question, 'Is there somewhere that Maria is?', is answered not just by **At(maria,school)** but also by the $\theta$ that **x** has been replaced by **school.** Hence, if we return **x = school** as a way of describing the $\theta$, we also return the answer that 'School' is the response to the question, 'Is there somewhere that Maria is?'

Here is another example, of the type which can be found in many logic programming books:

> **Alan is the father of Mary, and Ken is the father of June.**
> **Mary is the mother of Albert and of Joan.**
> **Anyone who is the father of anyone who is a mother of anyone is a grandfather.**
> **Is someone the grandfather of Joan?**

In FOPC (with apologies logic purists!):

1. **Father(alan,mary)** $\land$ **Farther(ken,june)**
2. **Mother(mary,albert)** $\land$ **Mother(mary,joan)**
3. $(\forall x)$ $(\forall y)$ $(\forall z)$ $\{\{$**Farther(x,y)** $\land$ **Mother(y,z)**$\} \rightarrow$ **Grandfather(x,z)**$\}/?$ $(\exists x)$ $\{$**Grandfather(x,joan)**$\}$

After translation of the premises into clause form:

1. **Father(alan,mary)**
2. **Father(ken,june)**
3. **Mother(mary,albert)**
4. **Mother(mary,joan)**
5. $\sim$ **Father(x,y)** $\lor$ $\sim$ **Mother(y,z)** $\lor$ **Grandfather(x,z)**

Since we wish to show that $(\exists x)\{$**Grandfather(x,joan)**$\}$ is a theorem of the system, we should use the resolution process to head towards this goal, if possible. We see that at line 4, **joan** appears as the second argument in **Mother(mary,joan)**. That starts off the resolution process:

1. **Father(alan,mary)**          given
2. **Father(ken,june)**           given
3. **Mother(mary,albert)**        given
4. **Mother(mary,joan)**          given
5. **~ Father(x,y) ∨ ~ Mother(y,z) ∨ Grandfather(x,z)**     given
6. **~ Father(x,mary) ∨ Grandfather(x,joan)**     4,5,θ = {(joan,z),(mary,y)}
7. **Grandfather(alan,mary)**     1,6,θ = {(alan,x)}

We have now derived the theorem, with the last θ for **x** being **x = alan**. Hence, Alan is the grandfather of Joan.

From the last example, we can see how important it is for the resolution process to have a *strategy* of some sort, if the appropriate, or desired, theorems are to be derived. There are in fact several resolution strategies. The one that we have used in our examples is called *linear input resolution*, where the last-produced resolvent is used with any other clause to derive a new resolvent, which is then itself used with any other clause to derive a new resolvent, etc. Although such a strategy is fine for the purposes of exposition, it is not a desirable one, from a computational point of view, since there is vagueness about *which* clause should be used with the last resolvent. Obviously, we should choose a clause which is appropriate in the circumstances, but trying to program this notion of appropriateness will have problems of its own.

Linear input resolution is complete for *Horn clauses*. A Horn clause is a clause in conjunctive normal form with at most one unnegated (i.e. one positive) literal. This implies that all first-order predicate language formulae, if they are to be translated into Horn clauses, must be of the form:

**If p and q and . . . then r**

since, after translation,

$$\{p \wedge q \wedge \ldots \} \to r$$

and then during conversion,

$$\sim (p \wedge q \wedge \ldots \} \vee r$$
$$\sim p \vee \sim q \vee \ldots \vee r$$

Note that **r**, the consequent, is the only unnegated literal. Hence, a *logic programming language* based on Horn clauses, such as Prolog, will have to employ special procedures for dealing with negated conditions. For instance, if we had:

$$(\sim p \wedge q) \to r$$

this would be converted to:

$$p \vee \sim q \vee r$$

which is not in Horn clause form. There is nothing to stop a logic programming language using non-Horn clauses, except that the desirable property of completeness should be preserved. Horn clauses are preferred because there are several resolution strategies which ensure that, if a wff is indeed a theorem of the system, it can be derived, but only if the clauses are in Horn form. For example, *linear resolution with unrestricted selection function for Horn clauses* (LUSH) imposes an ordering (any ordering strategy can be used, hence the term *unrestricted*) on the way the resolution process is carried out. A typical ordering strategy is to work through the literals in the resolvent in a left-to-right way and pick complementary literals from anywhere in the clause set. For instance, if $\sim\!p \lor \sim\!q \lor \sim\!r \lor s$ is a resolvent, we find any clause which allows $\sim\!p$ to be resolved. If there isn't one, we find a clause that allows $\sim\!q$ to be resolved, and so on. LUSH resolution is only complete for Horn clauses. Another resolution strategy, *selected literal* (SL) resolution, however, is complete for Horn and non-horn clauses: SL resolution allows not just literals in the clause set to be used for resolving but also earlier resolvents (ancestor resolution). More information on resolution strategies can be found in (Frost, 1986).

That concludes our brief look at resolution-based theorem proving and its use in knowledge representation. There are now many books available which provide more information on the subject (for example, Frost (1986), Clocksin and Mellish, (1981)) but our purpose in this section was just to provide a brief introduction on how logic can be useful in knowledge representation.

In addition to resolution-based methods, there are non-resolution methods also, of which *natural deduction* and *matrix connection* are two popular ones. Frost (1986) provides more details on each of these, as well as others.

So far, we have dealt with FOPC as a knowledge representation language. During the 1970s and 1980s, much interest has been expressed in the use of 'alternative' logics for not only knowledge representation but also specifying, reasoning about, and veryifying computer programs. Logics with titles such as *many-sorted logic*, *situational logic*, *non-monotonic logic*, *many-valued logic*, *fuzzy logic*, *modal logic*, *temporal logic*, *epistemic logic* and *intensional logic*, to name just a few, have all been explored as far as their application to AI and computer science is concerned. Again, Frost (1986) provides a good introduction to these logics, as does Turner (1984).

## 3.9   META-THEORY

Having described the *mechanics* of formal systems, let us now summarize the salient points of such systems, but this time from a meta-theoretic point of view. We shall introduce second-order formal systems at this stage, as well as one or two more logical operators, to give a better idea of what a formal system looks like when used for computation purposes. Also, we shall clarify the links between logic and function theory.

First we re-introduce the basic notations of syntax and semantics. The syntax consists of the following symbols and rules (Manna, 1974):

(1) Truth symbols: **t,f**
(2) connectives: $\sim , \rightarrow , \wedge , \vee , \leftrightarrow$
(3) Operations: $=$
(4) quantifiers: $\forall, \exists$
(5) constants:

> $n$-ary function constants $\mathbf{f}_i^n$ ($i$ greater than or equal to 1, $n$ greater than or equal to zero), where $\mathbf{f}_i^0$ is an *individual constant* and is also denoted by $\mathbf{a}_i$ (i.e. a constant is a function of no arguments)

> $n$-ary predicate constants $\mathbf{p}_i^n$ ($i$ greater than or equal to 1, $n$ greater than or equal to zero), where $\mathbf{p}_i^0$ is called a *propositional constant*

(6) variables:

> $n$-ary function variables $\mathbf{F}_i^n$ ($i$ greater than or equal to 1, $n$ greater than or equal to zero), where $\mathbf{F}_i^0$ is called an *individual variable* and is also denoted by $\mathbf{x}_i$

> $n$-ary predicate constants $\mathbf{P}_i^n$ ($i$ greater than or equal to 1, $n$ greater than or equal to zero), where $\mathbf{P}_i^0$ is called a *propositional variable*

Using these symbols, we define, recursively, three classes of expressions: *terms*, *atomic formulae* (atfs) and *well-formed formulae* (wffs):

Terms
: Each individual constant $\mathbf{a}_i$ and each individual variable $\mathbf{x}_i$ is a term. If $\mathbf{t}_1, \mathbf{t}_2, \ldots , \mathbf{t}_n$ ($n$ greater than or equal to 1) are terms, then so are $\mathbf{f}_i^n(\mathbf{t}_1, \mathbf{t}_2, \ldots , \mathbf{t}_n)$ and $\mathbf{F}_i^n(\mathbf{t}_1, \mathbf{t}_2, \ldots , \mathbf{t}_n)$.

atfs
: **t** and **f** are atfs. Each propositional constant $\mathbf{p}_i^0$ and each propositional variable $\mathbf{P}_i^0$ are atfs. If $\mathbf{t}_1, \mathbf{t}_2, \ldots , \mathbf{t}_n$ ($n$ greater than or equal to 1) are terms, then $\mathbf{p}_i^n (\mathbf{t}_1, \mathbf{t}_2, \ldots , \mathbf{t}_n)$ and $\mathbf{P}_i^n (\mathbf{t}_1, \mathbf{t}_2, \ldots , \mathbf{t}^n)$ are atfs.

wffs
: Each atf is a wff. If **A**, **B** and **C** are wffs, then so are $\sim \mathbf{A}$, $\mathbf{A} \rightarrow \mathbf{B}$, $\mathbf{A} \wedge \mathbf{B}$, $\mathbf{A} \vee \mathbf{B}$, and $\mathbf{A} \leftrightarrow \mathbf{B}$. If $\mathbf{v}_i$ is a variable, and **A** is a wff, then $(\forall \mathbf{v}_i)\mathbf{A}$ and $(\exists \mathbf{v}_i)\mathbf{A}$ are wffs.

Note that $< \mathbf{wff} > \leftrightarrow < \mathbf{wff} >$ yields a wff, i.e. $\leftrightarrow$ is a connective, while $< \mathbf{term} > = < \mathbf{term} >$ yields an atf, i.e. $=$ is an operator. Also, we can simplify the notation for constants and variables to some extent, as we did in our examples. The superscripts for **f**, **F**, **p**, and **P** are used only to indicate the number of arguments: they can be omitted completely. The subscripts are used for enumerating the symbols and can be omitted whenever their omission causes no confusion. Also, we can use additional symbols: **a,b,c** for individual constants; **f,g,h** for function constants: **p,q,r,s** for predicate constants; **x,y,z** for individual variables; **F,G,H** for function variables; and **P,Q,R,S** for predicate variables. In addition, we use punctuation marks (), { }, and , where necessary.

  Having described two components of a formal axiomatic system — the list of symbols and the syntax, or *formation*, rules, we now have to specify a list of initial formulae and a list of inference, or *transformation*, rules. The list of initial formulae, the *axioms*, can change from system to system. Given a set of axioms, a proof consists of manipulating the initial formulae by means of transformation rules in order to show that a certain formula not in the list of initial formula is derivable from them. All 'new' formulae derived from the list of the initial formula according to the transformation rules are called *theorems*.

The transformation rules can also vary from system to system. Most systems of logic include the so-called 19 rules of inference (Modus Ponens, Disjunctive Syllogism . . . ), four quantifier negation rules, and four rules for instantiation and generalization (Copi, 1967).

Let us first consider the *quantifier-free PC*. The only symbols allowed to appear in such calculus are propositional constants $\mathbf{p}_i^0$, i.e. $\mathbf{A}, \mathbf{B}, \mathbf{C}$, etc. That is, only constants that have no arguments can be manipulated in the PC. A propositional constant is a symbol which denotes, or stands for, a particular proposition. For instance, 'John watches television' can be denoted by $\mathbf{J}$. Hence, the PC is restricted to propositional constants and those transformation rules not dealing with quantifiers.

If we extend the notation to include propositional variables $\mathbf{P}_i^0$ i.e. $\mathbf{P}, \mathbf{Q}$, etc., as well as $\mathbf{p}_i^0$, we derive the *quantified PC* (not considered in this chapter).

Since the notation of PC is restricted to propositional constants (and propositional variables in the case of quantified PC), PC can only be used in theories that have something to say about statements *as a whole*, and not about subparts of a statement. For instance, we saw earlier that the PC had nothing to say about the statement **The present King of France is bald,** which cannot be true since there is no King of France, but cannot be false either since by implication that would mean that the present King of France was not bald, i.e. had hair. We also saw how, through logical analysis using the FOPC, the statement was broken down into subparts, in the process in which we introduced the notion of some individual $\mathbf{x}$ having the *property of being*, or *belonging to the set*, **King of France.** To allow expression of these subparts, we replace our set of admissible symbols by the following set:

(1) *n*-ary (*n* greater than or equal to zero) function constants $\mathbf{f}_i^n$
(2) *n*-ary (*n* greater than or equal to zero) predicate constants $\mathbf{p}_i^n$
(3) individual variables $\mathbf{x}_i$
(4) individual constants $\mathbf{a}_i$

We now have the predicate calculus (FOPC), which allows us to analyse statements containing the words *some, any, all, every*, and so on.

Before continuing, it may be useful to consider a statement we made above, namely,

> The statement ['The present King of France is bald'] was broken down into subparts, in the process of which we introduced the notion of some individual $\mathbf{x}$ having the *property of being*, or *belonging to the set*, **King of France.**

In that statement, we appear to have made a major assumption, i.e. having a property is the same as belonging to a set. Let us look at that assumption more closely. Consider these two statements in the domain of integers:

x is greater than one and less than three
x is ten divided by five

Let us signify the first statement by **A(x)** and the second by **B(x)**. These two properties, **A** (being greater than one and less than three) and **B** (dividing ten by five), are true only of the number two. If it is argued that because these two properties are true of exactly the same number they are *identical* in some sense, we have as a necessary condition for two properties being identical that they refer, or apply, to the same set of objects. In other words, two properties cannot be identical if they refer, or apply, to different sets of objects. That much is uncontentious. But there is a problem in philosophical logic as to what counts as a *sufficient* condition for two properties to be identical. In our exposition above, we assumed that the necessary condition is also a sufficient condition, i.e. two properties are identical if and only if they refer, or apply, to the same set of objects. This assumption, which is widely held amongst logicians, is known as the *axiom of extensionality* and is axiomatic to most first order and higher order systems. We shall see why very shortly.

When applying logic to mathematics, it is usual to work in terms of relations which minimally must take two arguments (binary relation), and functions of one or more arguments, rather than predicates, or properties, of one argument.

We can define a *first-order theory* as follows:

A *first-order theory* is an axiomatic theory which includes *predicate logic* with the following *axioms of equality*:

**Equality axiom 1: x = x**
**Equality axiom 2: x = y→ {A(x)↔A(y)} for any formula A**

This seems an odd pair of axioms to include, and in explaining why they should be we shall tie up some loose ends left over from the previous chapter. According to Frege (1892), propositions have *sense* and *reference*: very roughly, the reference, or extension, of a predicate, say, **being between one and five** in the domain of natural numbers, is the set, or class, of such numbers, namely, **{2,3,4}**, but the *qualification requirement* for a number to be a member of this set is **being between 1 and 5.** That is, the sense, or *intension*, of a predicate is that property or those properties *in virtue of possessing which* a number is a member of the set or class: in the case of **being between one and five,** there are two properties, namely, **being greater than one,** and **being less than five,** and a number must possess both if it is to be a member of the set denoted by **being between one and five.** The *motivation* for such a distinction is not hard to find. Derek Partridge is Professor of Computer Science at Exeter University; now consider the statement: **The Professor of Computer Science is Head of Department.** If the only sort of meaning allowed is extensional, the two phrases, namely, **The Professor of Computer Science,** and **Head of Department,** denote the same individual, namely, Derek Partridge, and that is all there is to it. If that is the case, then the following statements should be exactly equivalent to the above: **Derek**

**Partridge is Head of Department, The Professor of Computer Science is Derek Partridge,** and **Derek Partridge is Derek Partridge,** since in all cases the reference of all the phrases is Derek Partridge. But it is clear that there is a difference in meaning in the sense of the two phrases, despite the two phrases having *co-reference*, i.e. denoting the same individual. The truth of **Derek Partridge is Derek Partridge** is a simple matter of logic: we need not go outside the sentence to realize that this statement is stating an obvious tautology. The truth of **The Professor of Computer Science is Derek Partridge** is one of fact: we need to look at the academic history of Exeter University to discover whether this is indeed the case, i.e. whether Derek Partridge was appointed Professor of Computer Science by Exeter University. We have asserted it, but that does not make the statement true. And finally, the truth of **The Professor of Computer Science is Head of Department** also depends on empirical fact, but of a different sort. It is possible that this statement is true, not because we know who the Professor of Computer Science is and who the Head of Department is, but because of some rule, or principle, that says that the Professor of Computer Science, no matter who it is, is always also the Head of Department. In this case, the reference of the two phrases is of no importance to us. It therefore follows that although two phrases are co-referential, that does not mean that they have the same sense.

This brings us back to the principle of identity. We stated above that first order theories contain these two axioms:

> **Equality axiom 1:** $x = x$
> **Equality axiom 2:** $x = y \rightarrow \{A(x) \leftrightarrow A(y)\}$ **for any formula A**

The motivation for these two axioms may now be clearer. The second axiom states that if **x** and **y** are identical, i.e. **x** and **y** have the same reference, then **x** can be substituted for **y**, and vice versa, in any sentence **A** in which **x** or **y** appears, **without changing the truth-value** of the sentence. This is known as the principle of *indiscernibility of identicals*. Hence, this axiom introduces the notion of extensions and references into the first-order system as a universal truth. If we want to talk about intensions and senses, we need to introduce a more powerful calculus: the FOPC can only generalize over **individuals,** not properties, and if we want to theorize on properties, say, on sets of properties in virtue of possessing which an individual qualifies for membership of sets, or classes, we need to be able to quantify over properties and predicates. But the symbolism of FOPC is restricted to function constants, predicate constants, individual variables, and individual constants. If we extend this symbolism to include function variables and predicate variables, $F_i^n$ and $P_i^n$, respectively, we obtain a second-order theory. FOPC has its quantification confined to individual variables. Second-order theories (SOTs) allow quantification of function and predication variables as well. For instance, the proposition **Simba has all properties** can be represented by

> $(\forall P)\ Ps$

and **Simba has some property** by

($\exists$P) Ps

By generalizing with respect to both the individual variable and the property variable, we obtain, for example,

($\forall$x) ($\forall$F) {Cx$\rightarrow$ Fx} **All cats (C) have every property F**

We have seen how it is not only individuals that have properties. Properties themselves can have properties (i.e. predicates themselves can have predicates, functions can themselves have functions). For instance, the property of being a football fan has the property of making its possessor unwelcome in motorway service stations. Properties can also be predicated of themselves. For instance, the property of being atractive may itself be attractive. A property that can be truly predicated of itself is called a *predicable* property. Thus, being predicable is a property that belongs to all those and only those properties that can be truly predicated of themselves. On the other hand, any property that cannot truly be predicated of itself will be said to be an *impredicable* property. Thus, being impredicable is a property which belongs to all those and only those properties that cannot truly be predicated of themselves.

Let us now ask whether the property of being impredicable can truly be predicated of itself or not. If the property of being impredicable can be truly predicated of itself, then it has the property of being impredicable, from which it follows by definition that it cannot be truly predicated of itself! On the other hand, if the property of being impredicable cannot be truly predicated of itself, then like all other properties which cannot be truly predicated of themselves, it has the property of being impredicable, which means that it can be truly predicated of itself! We thus have a contradiction.

It may be worth our while to provide another concrete, but artificial, example of this contradiction, since the sort of reasoning required to understand it recurs several times in this volume. Imagine that we ask for the set of all sets that contain exactly five elements. Imagine, further, that there are exactly five such sets, **A, B, C, D,** and **E,** each of which contains exactly five elements. Hence, our set of all five-element sets — let us call this set **V** — contains five sets. Now, is **V** to be included within itself? (Let us assume that **V** is not already in **V,** i.e. **V** is not one of **A** to **E.**) **V** is required to contain all sets with five elements, and **V** itself has five sets, **A, B, C, D,** and **E.** Since **V** is to contain *all* five-element sets, **V** should also go into **V.** But if it does, **V** now contains six elements, **A, B, C, D, E,** and **V.** Since **V** now contains six elements, **V** now should not be included within itself! If **V** is removed from **V, V** will again contain five elements, hence **V** should go back into **V,** and so on.

The best known method for avoiding such logical contradictions is Russell's *Simple Theory of Types* (Russell, 1908). The essential point to the Theory of Types is not just the separation of all entities into different logical types, e.g. 'The lowest type consists of individuals, such as **x, y,** and **z,** the next of properties of individuals, such as **P, Q,** and **R,** the next of properties of properties of individuals, such as **Some P are Q,** and so on,' but the restriction that any property which may be predicated of an entity of one logical type cannot be predicated of any entity of any other logical type. That is, the type of a property must be higher than the type of any entity of which it can be predicated. Consequently, it does not make any sense to affirm or to deny of any property that it belongs to itself. No property such as *impredicable* can be defined. In other words, our example using **V** cannot logically arise, since **V** will be defined to be of a type that contains **A, B, C, D,** and **E** as elements, but not **V**. If we want to include **V** as an element in any other set, we need to 'move up' the hierarchy and define, say, **VV,** which is allowed to have sets such as **V** as elements. But **VV** will itself be defined to be of a type that cannot be included within itself either. Computer scientists may notice some similarities with the notion of *typed* programming languages at this point.

In order to avoid ambiguity, one convention we can use is to symbolize properties of properties of individuals by underlined, capital letters, such as $\underline{A}$, $\underline{B}$, to prevent their being confused with properties of individuals **A** and **B**. For example, if we had **t** for 'Tanzy', **Mxy** for 'x is the mother of y', and $\underline{G}$ **P** for 'P is good', we can symbolize 'Tanzy has all of her mother's good qualities' as

$$(\forall P)\{(\exists x)\{Mxt \wedge (\forall y)\{Myt \rightarrow y = x\} \wedge Px \wedge \underline{G}\} \rightarrow Pt\}$$

We can now return to the question we posed some time ago. In FOPC, the domain for **x** is the set of individuals we may specify in any given case. What is the domain for **P** in SOT? An obvious answer is that it is the set of properties which we may specify in any given case. The further question then arises: How do we know when properties are identical or different? Most systems of higher-order logic contain an *axiom of extensionality* to overcome this problem. That is, two properties are identical if and only if they apply to the same set of objects.

And that concludes our brief introduction to meta-theory. ((Delong 1970) provides an excellent introduction to the notion of meta-theory.) To summarize, then, a logic which contains quantification over only one domain — the individuals — is called a FOPC. A logic which contains quantification with two types of variables — individual variables on the one hand and predicate and function variables on the other — is called a SOT.

## 3.10   GÖDEL'S THEOREMS

Let us now look at Gödel's findings (Gödel, 1931). Our exposition will be based closely on Nagel and Newman's introduction (1958) but will also contain some expansions of their material since, in various parts, even their proof is fairly condensed. The method, and 'toy' formal system, however, is theirs. It is worth looking at their exposition in some detail, for two reasons. First, Nagel and Newman provide undoubtedly the 'easiest' introduction to Gödel's findings. Secondly, it is only by obtaining a good understanding of Gödel's findings that we can be in a position to evaluate the Mathematical Objection thoroughly.

We need to introduce the notion of *Gödel numbers* (GNs), where each wff of an example axiomatic system can be assigned a unique GN based on the symbols present in the wff. Given a GN, we can reconstruct the wff by means of factorization. Let us restrict the symbols of our 'toy' formal system to the following:

$$\sim \ \lor \ \to \ \exists \ = \ 0 \ s \ ( \ ) \ ,$$

where the usual interpretations apply. **0** is the symbol for zero, and **s** is the symbol for the function **the immediate successor of.** For instance, **s(0)** is 1, and **s(7)** is 8.

We shall ascribe a GN from 1 to 10 to each of the above symbols. In addition, let us assign to each individual variable **x, y, z,** and so on, a *distinct* prime number greater than 10; to each propositional variable **p, q, r,** and so on, the *square* of a prime number greater than 10; and to each predicate variable **P, Q, R,** and so on, the *cube* of a prime greater than 10. So, for instance, the wff $(\exists x)(x = sy)$ would be coded as

$$
\begin{array}{ccccccccccc}
( & \exists & x & ) & ( & x & = & s & y & ) \\
\downarrow & \downarrow & \downarrow & \downarrow & \downarrow & \downarrow & \downarrow & \downarrow & \downarrow & \downarrow \\
8 & 4 & 11 & 9 & 8 & 11 & 5 & 7 & 13 & 9
\end{array}
$$

A GN for the above wff may be attained by *raising* a sequence of prime numbers to their GN code. If we start the sequence of primes from 2, 3, 5, 7, 11, 13, and so on, we shall obtain:

$$2^8 \times 3^4 \times 5^{11} \times 7^9 \times 11^8 \times 13^{11} \times 17^5 \times 19^7 \times 23^{13} \times 29^9$$

Thanks to the 'big number' facility available on Franz LISP, this works out to the 87-digit (!) number:

145 666 408 661 709 409 197 789 938 288 649 818 781 891 470 181 481 887 898 950 349 321 995 516 094 737 500 000 000

As we can see, even for simple wffs, very big numbers are being generated. Instead of reproducing this number every time we wish to refer to the GN of this wff, let us call this number **m**. That is, **m** is the value for the above wff, or expression. Now consider the wff

$(\exists x)(x = s0)$

which has the GN

$$
\begin{array}{ccccccccccc}
( & \exists & x & ) & ( & x & = & s & 0 & ) \\
\downarrow & \downarrow & \downarrow & \downarrow & \downarrow & \downarrow & \downarrow & \downarrow & \downarrow & \downarrow \\
8 & 4 & 11 & 9 & 8 & 11 & 5 & 7 & 6 & 9
\end{array}
$$

When these GNs are raised to a sequence of primes, we obtain:

$$2^8 \times 3^4 \times 5^{11} \times 7^9 \times 11^8 \times 13^{11} \times 17^5 \times 19^7 \times 23^6 \times 29^9$$

which evaluates to the 77-digit number

42 782 342 422 298 457 756 383 755 753 999 396 957

012 777 572 054 456 011 868 014 366 962 500 000 000

Let us call this GN **n**. Although these numbers are not important in themselves, what is important is that there is a mathematical relationship between **m** and **n**. That is, the two numbers are related by the fact that with the first number we raised 23 to the power 13 in the sequence of primes, signifying that the symbol **y** occurred in the ninth position, whereas in the second number we raised 23 to the power 6, signifying that the symbol **0** appeared in the same position. The logical fact that the second wff is derived from the first by simply substituting **0** for **y** is now reflected in a mathematical relationship: if we divide **m** by **n** we obtain as quotient with no remainder

3 404 825 447

which is 23 raised to the power 7. The result of dividing **m** by **n** is precisely the result of dividing 23 raised to the power 13 (for **y**) by 23 raised to the power 6 (for **0**), i.e. 23 raised to the power 7.

We can attach another GN, **k**, to this pair of wffs as before:

$$k = 2^m \times 3^n$$

which results in a 163-digit number! **k** now stands for the pair of formulae $(\exists x)\ (x = sy)$ and $(\exists x)\ (x = s0)$.

Given any GN, we can retrieve the original expression(s) by working backwards through the primes and factors. If a GN is less than or equal to 10, we know it is the GN of an elementary constant symbol, which can be identified. If the GN is greater than 10, it can be decomposed into its prime factors. If it is a prime greater than 10, or the second or third power of such a prime, it is the GN of an identifiable variable. If it is the product of successive primes, each raised to some power, it may be the GN either of a formula or of a sequence of formulas. For instance, if the GN of an expression is 243 000 000:

$$243\ 000\ 000 = 64 \times 243 \times 15\ 625$$
$$= 2^6 \times 3^5 \times 5^6$$
$$=> 6 \quad 5 \quad 6$$
$$\downarrow \quad \downarrow \quad \downarrow$$
$$0 \quad = \quad 0$$

i.e. **0 = 0**.

This process of working backwards is guaranteed to return a string, if the number we are given stands for a wff or even a badly formed string of vocabularly symbols. That is, the process will not loop forever trying to discover what the original string is. To see why this process will always stop with a string of symbols, or no string at all, we need only look at the sequence of primes. If we adopt the mechanical procedure that we start with the first prime number, 2, and raise it to successive powers 1,2,3, . . . , then we stop using 2 as the only prime number in our sequence once 2 raised to a certain power exceeds the number we are given. That is, either 2 raised to a certain power will equal the number we are given exactly, or else at some stage 2 raised to a certain powert will exceed the number we are given. If the latter situation arises, we then start examining the prime sequence 2 times 3, raising each of these to a sequence of powers (e.g. 1,1 followed by 2,1 followed by 3,1 etc., and then by 1,2 followed by 2,2 etc.). If again we reach the situation where 2 times 3, each raised to various powers, exceed our given number, we then try 2 times 3 times 5, and so on. If the number does stand for a wff, this mechanical process will certainly find the correct sequence of primes and their powers. If the number does not stand for a string, there will be a point in our sequence of primes where even raising all the primes to one and working out their product will give us a result that exceeds the number we are given. We can then conclude that the number we are given does not stand for a string at all.

The process of Gödel Numbering can be applied to statements of meta-theory as well. For instance, consider $(\mathbf{p} \vee \mathbf{p}) \rightarrow \mathbf{p}$, the GN of which is

$$2^8 \times 3^{11^2} \times 5^2 \times 7^{11^2} \times 11^9 \times 13^3 \times 17^{11^2}$$

i.e. a 326-digit number which we shall designate **a**. Consider the formula

$$(\mathbf{p} \vee \mathbf{p}),$$

the GN of which is

$$2^8 \times 3^{11^2} \times 5^2 \times 7^{11^2} \times 11^9$$

which results in a 174-digit number we shall designate **b**. We can now express the *meta-theoretical* statement that $(\mathbf{p} \vee \mathbf{p})$ is a part of $(\mathbf{p} \vee \mathbf{p}) \rightarrow \mathbf{p}$ by saying that GN **b** is a factor of GN **a**. In fact, if we multiply **b** by 13 raised to the power 3, then by 17 raised to the power 11 raised to the power 2, we shall obtain **a**. Hence, logical, *meta-theoretical* statements can also be expressed mathematically.

Let us consider the meta-theoretical statement: 'The sequence of formulas with GN **x** is a proof of the formula with GN **z**.' We introduce the notion of *proof-pair* at this point. A proof-pair is a pair of natural numbers **x** and **z** where **x** is the GN of a formal derivation (proof) whose bottom-line (i.e. conclusion) is the formula with GN **z**. For instance, if we had the proof:

1. $\sim \mathbf{p} \vee \sim \sim \mathbf{q}$ (given)
2. $\sim \sim \mathbf{q} \vee \sim \mathbf{p}$ (1) commutation)
3. $\mathbf{q} \vee \sim \mathbf{p}$ (2 double negation)

where the third line of the proof represents the conclusion of the proof, then GN **x** would consist of the GN of the sequence of formulas on all three lines of the proof, and GN **z** would represent the GN of the formula on the third line only. That is,

$$
\begin{array}{cccccc}
\sim & \mathbf{p} & \vee \sim \sim & & \mathbf{q} \\
\downarrow & \downarrow & \downarrow\ \downarrow\ \downarrow & & \downarrow \\
1 & 11^2 & 2\ \ 1\ \ 1 & & 13^2
\end{array}
$$

which, when raised to a sequence of primes, gives us

$$2^1 \times 3^{11^2} \times 5^2 \times 7^1 \times 11^1 \times 13^{13^2}$$

Let us call this number **a**. The second line of the proof is $\sim \sim q \lor \sim p$:

$$
\begin{array}{cccccc}
\sim & \sim & q & \lor & \sim & p \\
\downarrow & \downarrow & \downarrow & \downarrow & \downarrow & \downarrow \\
1 & 1 & 13^2 & 2 & 1 & 11^2
\end{array}
$$

After raising a sequence a primes, starting again from 2, to these powers, we obtain a second number, say, **b**. The third line is $q \lor \sim p$:

$$
\begin{array}{cccc}
q & \lor & \sim & p \\
\downarrow & \downarrow & \downarrow & \downarrow \\
13^2 & 2 & 1 & 11^2
\end{array}
$$

After raising a sequence of primes, against starting from 2, to these powers, We obtain a third number, say, **c**. The entire proof will therefore have the GN:

$$2^a \times 3^b \times 5^c$$

We call this **x**. The final line of the proof is **c**, which we call **z**. Hence, we have the pair of natural numbers **x** and **z** which stand in a certain mathematical relationship, this relationship being given by **Dem.** That is, the task of **Dem,** when given two numbers, can be intuitively described *at the meta-level* as follows. First, **Dem** unpacks **x**, its first argument, so that the original strings are recovered. If **x** does not code for a sequence of strings, **Dem** can halt straight away and return the value **false** to signify that **x** and **z** are not a proof-pair. After unpacking **x**, **Dem** can then check that all the strings are wffs, according to the syntax rules of the formal system. If a non-wff appears in **x**, again **Dem** can halt and return **false** at this stage. If all the strings are wffs, **Dem** then works through the wffs, one at a time, checking that each wff of the proof, apart from the first, follows logically from the previous wff. **Dem** will therefore require access to the rules of inference and other transformation rules that belong to the formal system. If at any stage **Dem** finds that a wff does not follow logically from the previous wff, it returns **false.** If all the wffs, apart from the first, follow from the previous wff, **Dem** can then check that the first wff is an axiom of the system, i.e. universally true, or is a theorem that is derived from another proof. **Dem** will therefore require access to a database of stored axioms, definitions, and theorems. Finally, **Dem** unpacks **z**, the second argument, and checks not only that **z** does code for a wff but also that the wff does indeed appear as the last line of the proof, as given by **x**. If all these checks are satisfied, **Dem** adds the wff to its theorem database and returns **true.**

The above account is an intuitive one at the meta-level: what will actually happen at the level of the formal system is that **Dem** will not appear as such, but what **Dem** stands for at the meta-level can be represented at the level of the formal system by means of relationships between numbers. In other words, well-formedness of strings will be expressed in mathematical terms (e.g. 'No GN must begin with a prime raised to the power 2', i.e. $\lor$ (the disjunction)), as will the various transformation and inference rules. This is a complex task, but that does not make the task impossible in principle, and it is this notion *in principle* that is important here.

Hence, *in principle*, there will always be a way to specify, mathematically, the meta-theoretic statement that a proof exists for a statement, as follows. The statement,

> The sequence of formulas with GN x is a proof of the formula with GN z,

is represented by a formula in the formal system which expresses a purely arithmetic relation between x and z. We write this relation between x and z as the formula

**Dem (x,z)**

but we must remind ourselves of the fact that **Dem** stands for a *meta-theoretical* statement, namely, **The sequence of formulas with GN x is a proof (or demonstration) of the formula with GN z.** Note that such a proof-pair **(x,z)** is true if and only if the GN of the alleged proof stands to the GN of the conclusion in the arithmetical relation here designated by **Dem.** In order to decide whether a meta-theoretical statement is true, we need only concern ourselves with the question as to whether **Dem** holds between the two numbers.

If two numbers do not stand in a relationship that we designate by **Dem,** then we can specify ~ **Dem(x,z)** to express the meta-theoretical statement

> **The sequence of formulas with GN x is not a proof for the formula with GNz.**

That is, when x and z are 'unpacked' to give us the original wffs (assuming they are wffs, and not just badly formed strings), we can say that the entire sequence of wffs as given by x is not a proof of the wff as given by z, since the mathematical relationship, as specified by **Dem,** does not hold between x and z. For example, if we had the following sequence:

1. ~p ∨ q
2. q ∨ ~p
3. ~q

the last line of the sequence does not follow from the earlier statements. In this case, x would be a number that coded for all three wffs, and z would code for the last wff, and the pair **(x,z)** would *not* stand in the relationship **Dem** to each other. That is,

> ~ **Dem(x,z).**

Hence, ~ **Dem(x,z)** is true when **Dem(x,z)** is false.

So far, we have introduced a simple formal system consisting of various symbols, a way of attaching distinct numbers to the symbols, a method of generating a GN for a wff, and a meta-level procedure, or predicate, called **Dem,** which will test whether a statement can be derived by means of a proof. We now introduce a meta-level function called **Sub.** Consider the formula

$$(\exists x)\ (x = sy)$$

That is, **There is some x such that x is the immediate successor of y.** Let us assume that this wff has **m** for its GN, while the variable **y** has the GN 13. Let us *substitute* in this formula for the variable with GN 13, i.e. for **y**, the numeral for **m**. The result is the formula

$$(\exists x)\ (x = sm)$$

which says that there is a number **x** such that **x** is the immediate successor of **m**. This new formula also has a GN which can be calculated. But instead of making the calculation, we can *identify* the number by saying that it is the GN of the formula that is obtained from the formula with GN **m**, by substituting for the variable with GN 13, the numeral for **m**. This meta-theoretical characterization uniquely determines a number which is a certain arithmetical function of the numbers **m** and 13, where the function itself can be expressed within the formal system. We have already seen that the GN of $(\exists x)\ (x = sy)$ is

$$2^8 \times 3^4 \times 5^{11} \times 7^9 \times 11^8 \times 13^{11} \times 17^5 \times 19^7 \times 23^{13} \times 29^9$$

i.e. **m**. To find the GN of $(\exists x)\ (x = sm)$, where we want to express the statement that there is an immediate successor of **m** which is an 87-digit number, we replace **y** with an appropriate notation for **m**. The only appropriate notation in our example system, since digits are not part of it, is to represent numbers as a sequence of successor functions on zero. Both sequence and zero are symbols of our system. For instance, three can be represented as **sss0,** i.e. the immediate successor of zero is one, and the immediate successor of one is two, and the immediate successor of two is three. Hence, any number, say, **i**, can be represented as a sequence of **s** occurring **i** times, followed by **0**. So, for instance, if we wish to represent the GN **m** (our 87-digit number) in our basic vocabulary, we replace **m** with a sequence of **s** occurring **m** times, followed by **0**.

Returning to the wff $(\exists x)\ (x = sm)$, we see that we can now represent **m** as follows:

$$(\exists x)\ (x = sssssss.\ .\ .s0)$$

where the letter **s** occurs **m** + 1 times: do not forget that the wff already contains one **s**. That is, **m** has been replaced by **m** occurrences of **s**. The wff $(\exists x)\ (x = ssssss.\ .\ .s0)$ contains only the basic vocabulary of our system and so will have its own GN. To calculate this GN, we first code for the elementary signs:

$$8,4,11,9,8,11,5,7,7,7,7,7,7,7,\ .\ .\ .\ ,7,6,9$$

in which each 7 occurs **m** + 1 times. We then calculate the GN of this formula:

$$2^8 \times 3^4 \times 5^{11} \times 7^9 \times 11^8 \times 13^{11} \times 17^5 \times 19^7 \times 23^7 \times 29^7 \times 31^7 \times \ldots$$
$$p_{k-2}^7 \times p_{k-1}^7 \times 9_k^9$$

where $p_k$ is the kth prime in order of magnitude in the sequence.

We introduce the function **Sub,** the task of which is to relieve us of the monotony of working out a new GN for such wffs. That is, **Sub(m,13,m)** will be a function, the working of which can be described intuitively at the meta-level as follows. First, **Sub** will take its first argument, **m,** and will unpack the GN for which **m** stands so that the original string is obtained in the vocabulary of our system. It will do this by trying out, methodically, a sequence of primes, raising each of them to a power, until either the product of a sequence of primes, even raised to the minimal power, one exceeds **m,** in which case **m** does not stand for a string at all, or until a certain product of primes and their powers are found which equal **m** exactly. The powers are then used to express the string in our basic vocabulary. If we like, we can also make **Sub** check whether the string of symbols constitutes a wff, according to the syntax rules of our system.

Next, **Sub** will scan the string of symbols, looking for the symbol which has the number as given by the second argument, namely, 13, which stands for **y.** The task of **Sub** is to replace every occurrence of **y** with a suitable representation for the third argument, namely, **m,** and it can do this by substituting, for **y, m** occurrences of s followed by **0.** Finally, **Sub** has the task of assigning a Gödel code to each symbol in the newly formed string and calculating a new GN for this string. The resulting GN is returned as the value for **Sub(m,13,m).**

We can imagine that **Sub** works not just for the one GN **m,** but for a variety of arguments. In general, the expression **Sub(y,13,y)** signifies the meta-theoretical characterization: **The GN of the formula that is obtained from the formula with GN y, by substituting for the variable with GN 13 the numeral for y.** That is, we allow **Sub** to work with any number **y,** where the task of **Sub** is to unpack **y,** to find all occurrences of the symbol for which the Gödel code is 13, and to replace all occurrences of this symbol with a suitable representation for the numeral **y,** and then to return a new GN for the resulting string.

We are now in a position to outline Gödel's main argument. Gödel showed the following:

(1) how to construct a formula **G** that represents the meta-theoretical statement **The formula G is not demonstrable** (that is, the formula says of itself that it is not demonstrable);
(2) that if **G** is demonstrable, then $\sim$ **G** is demonstrable, in which case the system is not consistent;
(3) that **G,** although not demonstrable, is nevertheless a *true* statement;
(4) since **G** is both true and not demonstrable, the axioms of the system (of arithmetic) are incomplete.

Let us examine these findings more closely.

The formula $\sim$ **Dem(x,z)** has already been introduced and means 'The

sequence of formulas with GN **x** is not a proof for the formula with GN **z**.'
We gave an example earlier of how a pair **(x,z)** would not stand in the
mathematical relationship **Dem** to each other. We now introduce, at the
meta-theoretic level, the statement,

$$(\forall x) \sim \textbf{Dem (x,z)}$$

which stands for the statement:

> **For every x, the sequence of formulas with GN x is not a proof for
> the formula with GN z.**

Another way to put this, using the existential quantifier which is part of the
basic vocabulary of our example formal system, is as follows:

$$\sim (\exists x) \textbf{ Dem (x,z)}$$

i.e. it is not the case that there is some **x** such that **x** is a GN for a sequence of
formulas which constitute a proof for the formula with GN **z**. That is, we
wish to talk about those **z** for which there does not exist a proof. Or, another
way to put this is to say that the above statement stands for 'No **x**
demonstrates **z**.' The truth of the statement, $(\forall x) \sim \textbf{Dem(x,z)}$, or $\sim$
$(\exists x)\textbf{Dem(x,z)}$, at the meta-theory level will obviously depend on what **z**,
which is *free* within the statement, actually is. What sort of wff can take the
place of **z** within our formal system?

Let us now provide a **z**. Consider the statement called **First**:

$$\textbf{First: } (\forall x) \sim \textbf{Dem (x, Sub (y,13,y))}$$

which states that

> For all **x**, the sequence of formulas with GN **x** is not a proof for the
> formula with a GN obtained by substituting for the variable with GN 13
> the numeral for **y**.

Hence, **z** has now been instantiated to be a GN that results after **Sub(y,13,y)**
operates, and what **Sub** will do here is to take a GN **y** (free), unpack it to a
wff, replace all occurrences of whatever 13 stands for with an appropriate
representation of **y**, calculate a new GN and return that as the value for **z**. In
other words, **First** belongs to the formal system in that **Dem** and **Sub** have
been given a grounding in the primitives of our formal system, but it also
represents a meta-theoretical statement. Also, notice that **y** is still free in the
statement. Hence, we are still not in a position to decide on the truth of the
statement **First** until such time as **y** is instantiated with a GN. In short, **First**
represents the meta-theoretical statement **The formula with GN that results
from Sub(y,13,y) is not demonstrable.** But since **First** belongs to our formal
system, it has a GN of its own. We have used the universal quantifier in **First**
(as did Nagel and Newman (Nagel and Newman, 1958)), which is not strictly
speaking part of the basic vocabulary, so let us switch to those symbols which
are basic:

$$\textbf{First': } \sim (\exists x) \textbf{ Dem(x, Sub (y,13,y))}$$

Suppose the GN of **First′** is **n**. That is, we first express all the symbols of **First′** in the basic vocabulary of our system. There is no problem with $(\exists x)$ and $\sim$. **Dem** was introduced at the meta-level but was based on a mathematical relationship between pairs of numbers at the level of the example formal system. **Sub** was also introduced at the meta-level, based again on mathematical relationships at the level of the formal system. Hence, we assign Gödel codes for all the symbols in **First′** and then calculate a GN for **First′**. We use **n** to refer to this GN.

We now substitute the numeral **n** for the variable with GN 13 (and this is the crux of the matter), that is, *for the variable* **y**, which is what GN 13 stands for, in the formula **First′**. We call the result of this substitution the **Gödel Formula G**:

**Gödel Formula G:  $\sim (\exists x)$ Dem (x, Sub (n,13,n) )**

That is, all occurrences of **y** have been replaced with **n**, and the **y** which was previously free is now instantiated with respect to an actual GN. It may appear that we are finally in a position to be able to decide on the truth of **G**, which now has the following interpretation: **It is not the case there exists a proof for the formula that results when, given a formula with GN n, all occurrences of y are replaced with an appropriate representation of n, and a new GN is worked out for the resulting formula.**

Now, this formula, since it belongs to the formal system, must also have a GN. But its GN is **Sub(n,13,n)**. Recall that **Sub(n,13,n)** is the GN of the formula that is obtained from the formula with GN **n** by substituting for the variable with GN 13 — for the variable **y** — the numeral **n**. But **Gödel Formula G** has been obtained from the formula with GN **n** (i.e. from **First′** above) by substituting for the variable **y** occurring in it the numeral for **n**. Hence, the GN of **G** is in fact whatever is returned by **Sub(n,13,n)**, yet we are told by **G** that this GN, or rather the formula that the GN represents, cannot stand as a **z** in a proof-pair (**x,z**), that is, there is no sequence **x** of wffs that provides a proof for **z** as a bottom line.

At the meta-theory level, the interpretation of

**G:  $\sim (\exists x)$ Dem (x, sub (n,13,n))**

is: **The formula with GN sub(n,13,n) is not demonstrable.** Since the formula with GN **Sub(n,13,n)** is **G** itself, **G** can be construed as asserting of itself that it is not demonstrable.

Let us summarize the process, this time being faithful to Nagel and Newman's notations and procedures (Nagel and Newman, 1958).

(1) We presented the theoretical formula $(\exists x)\,(x = sy)$ and gave it a GN **m**.
(2) We formulated a new expression $(\exists x)\,(x = sm)$ where the GN of the formula in (1) is substituted for variable **y**. This new expression has another GN.
(3) From (1) and (2) we derive the function **Sub(m,13,m)**, the value of which is the GN obtained by replacing, in the formula whose GN is **m**, variable **y** by GN **m**.

(4) We generalize **Sub(m,13,m)** to, say, **Sub(y,13,y)**, which is the GN obtained by substituting for the variable with GN 13, i.e. **y**, the GN of **y** in the formula with GN **y**.

(5) We introduce the formula $(\forall x) \sim$ **Dem(x,z)**, which states that for all **x**, the sequence of formulas with GN **x** is not a proof for the formula with GN **z**.

(6) We replace **z** with **Sub(y,13,y)**:

**First:** $(\forall x) \sim$ **Dem(x,sub(y,13,y))**

This formula states that for all **x**, the sequence of formulas with GN **x** is not a proof for the formula with a GN obtained by substituting, in the formula with GN **y**, for the variable whose GN is 13, i.e. **y**, the numeral for **y**. Let us call **First's** GN **n**.

(7) We now substitute, in **First**, for the variable with GN 13, i.e. for **y** in **Sub(y,13,y)** the numeral for **n**, to obtain

**G** $(\forall x) \sim$ **Dem(x,Sub(n,13,n))**

That is, we substitute **First's** own GN for **y** in **First** to obtain **G**. Thus, **G's** GN must be the value of **Sub(n,13,n)**, since we have substituted **n** for **y** in **Sub(y,13,y)**, and **y's** GN is 13.

Formula **G** above can be construed as asserting of itself that it is not demonstrable. That is, it is asserting of itself:

**I am not a theorem of the formal system.**

Now, is **G** a theorem of the formal system? If so, it must assert the truth. But if it is a theorem, **G** is asserting that it is not a theorem. Therefore we have a contradiction. So is **G** not a theorem? If **G** is not a theorem, then the proposition it is asserting, that it is not a theorem, is true. There now exists (at least) one true statement which is not a theorem. Thus, the formal system is incomplete.

The contradiction, quite simply, is that both **G** and $\sim$ **G** are demonstrable in the system. We now have an inconsistency in the system. Should we wish to keep our theoretical apparatus consistent, we reject the contradiction. That is, we reject the idea that **G** is demonstrable. But then we must accept that the system is not complete, since **G** asserts a truth, that it is not demonstrable. So we have a consistent, but incomplete, system.

Nagel and Newman go on to examine the contradiction in more detail, and we shall just sketch out their views for the sake of completeness. One way that may be suggested to make the formal system complete would be to include **G**, not as theorem, but as an axiom of the system, since the incompleteness of the system rests on the incompleteness of the axioms. However, this suggestion overlooks the crucial fact that the axioms of a system such as the arithmetic system are essentially incomplete. Even if **G** were added as an axiom, the augmented set would still not be sufficient to yield all arithmetical truths, since another true, but undecidable formula could be constructed in the enlarged system merely by repeating in the new system the procedure for deriving an undecidable but true formula in the initial system. By *undecidable formula* we mean a formula **G** such that neither **G** nor its contradictory is demonstrable. In the logical calculus of arithmetic, the implication of the above result is that it will not be possible to set down once and for all a set of axioms from which every true arithmetical statement can be formally derived.

We must conclude that if the formal system is consistent, its consistency cannot be established by any meta-theoretical reasoning that can be represented within the formal system itself. However, this does not exclude the possibility of a meta-theoretical proof of the consistency of the formal system. What is excluded is the possibility of representing such a proof within the formal system itself.

Let us examine the idea of making the set of axioms complete by introducing another formula. We have already stated that adding **G** to the axioms does not result in a complete system, since we can repeat the construction of another formula like **G** — say, **G'** — within the new system. So what would happen if we added $\sim$ **G** as a new axiom? The negation of G would be

$$\sim \mathbf{G:} \ \sim \ \sim (\exists x) \ \mathbf{Dem} \ (x, \ \mathbf{Sub} \ (n,13,n))$$

$\sim$ **G** can be interpreted meta-theoretically as

> **There does exist some number x such that the sequence of formulae with GN x is a proof for the formula with a GN obtained by substituting, in the formula with GN n, for the variable with GN 13 the numeral for n.**

That is, $\sim$ **G** appears to state that at least one proof-pair **Dem(a,Sub(n,13,n))** exists. But the proof-pair cannot exist at the same level as the formal system, as we have seen. Nor can it exist at the next higher level, since it will be at a higher level than that, at which level again the proof-pair cannot exist without going up one more level, which will still not contain the proof-pair without a higher level, and so on. That is, an infinity of levels suddenly opens up if we wish to instantiate the **x** to a particular **a**.

One escape route here would be not to instantiate the **x** to a particular GN but to keep it general. Thus, $(\exists x)\mathbf{Dem(x,Sub(n,13,n))}$ is to be interpreted as meaning **There is some generalized number such that** . . . rather than **There is a number such that** . . . The generalized number refers not to a number within the formal system but to a meta-theoretical number. A meta-theoretical number can be an infinitely large number. So, even although $\sim$ **G** is an axiom which asserts that its negation has a proof, **G** and $\sim$ **G** will never collide in the system if we construct only finite proofs in the system. If we construct only finite proofs, we will never prove **G**. Hence **G** and $\sim$ **G** can never be combined to form a contradiction. This, very roughly, is the procedure most frequently adopted in logic programming, where all proofs must be finite.

We now state Gödel's two theorems, *from the point of view that we have adopted*. His first theorem states that any axiomatic system *sufficiently rich in power* (powerful enough to contain elementary arithmetic) is incomplete in the sense that there will be some formula **G** which states a truth but which is not derivable in the system. If **G** is derivable, so is ~ **G**; hence the system is complete but inconsistent, at the same time.

Gödel's second theorem states that if an axiomatic system *of a sufficiently powerful kind* is consistent, then **G** is not provable in that system. If the system is inconsistent, **G** is provable in that system (since every formula is provable).

That is, one cannot show both consistency and completeness in such a system, at the same time. We should say at this point that we have assumed a semantic notion of completeness (see Section 3.6), whereas Gödel was originally concerned with **deductive completeness**, which is that a system is deductively complete if for every formula **A** of the system, either **A** or ~ **A** is a theorem of the system. For our purposes, the semantic notion of completeness was used to make the exposition more intelligible, but let us conclude this section with a quote from McCawley (1981, p. 76):

> The most celebrated result regarding deductive completeness is Gödel's incompleteness theorem, which shows that any axiomatization of the arithmetic of positive integers either is deductively incomplete or inconsistent; that is, if your supposed axioms for arithmetic are consistent (that is, they don't allow you to deduce any contradictions), then there are [formulae] of arithmetic that are 'undecidable' relative to those axioms: [formulae] A such that neither A nor ~ A can be proven from those axioms.

And that concludes our version of Nagel and Newman's exposition of Gödel's findings. We should now see that 'Gödelizing' is a complex process, and that it relies on the manipulation of extremely large (some may say 'impossibly large') numbers. But that should not detract from the importance of what is being claimed.

## 3.11   AI AND LOGIC

So there we have it. We have finally presented the foundations of the Mathematical Objection. Let us re-state the Mathematical Objection, according to both Turing (as we described in Chapter 1) and Lucas (1961), and perhaps the exact force of the argument will now be clear.

Gödel's theorems show that mechanism is wrong. Every sufficiently powerful formal system will contain, if consistent, formulae which cannot be proved in the system but which we humans can see are true. That is, if we switch on the machine and ask it to produce all the theorems of the system, it will never produce the one that we humans know is a theorem, namely, that formula which is obtained by Gödelizing. This is because the machine is given a concrete instantiation of a formal system. Thus, a machine which is capable of doing sufficiently complicated tasks (e.g. arithmetic) will not be able to produce a formula which we know to be true. Program and wiring determine the behaviour of the machine. One day we shall build machines that model human behaviour and human cognitive processes. However, it will never be able to do everything that a human mind can do. Hence, the machine will never provide an adequate model of the mind. 'Thanks to Gödel's theorem, the mind always has the last word' (Lucas, 1961, p. 48).

One of the crucial steps in the above argument, of course, is **A machine is given a concrete instantiation of a formal system.** By means of this phrase, Lucas manages to tie up a proven 'limitation' of a formal (paper) system with an attack on the possibility of AI. That is, the Mathematical Objection, and Lucas' version of it, would have no relevance to AI if it were not for this crucial, bridging step. Interestingly, it is also a crucial step for Searle, whose Chinese Room Argument we examined in the last chapter. According to Searle, *Strong* AI is characterized by the claim that '. . . instantiating a formal program with the right input and output is a sufficient condition of, indeed is constitutive of, intentionality' (Searle, 1980, p. 296). In fact, the assertion that a computer is nothing more than an instantiation of a formal system has been variously used as a criticism of the AI approach and of the attempt to ascribe mental and cognitive qualities to computers.

There might be a sense in which it is correct to say that a computer is an instantiation of a formal system, and this is where the material in the earlier part of this chapter comes in useful. If the system contains variables, as most first-order systems would do, then when the program which embodies the formal system is running — let us say that the formal system is expressed in the programming language Prolog — it could then be argued that this is a case of a formal system being 'instantiated' with respect to a particular computer in that actual values are being substituted for variables in the program at run time by means of various substitutions, or θs. In this sense, 'instantiation' is being interpreted in a strict, logical sense. This sense will not do, however, because if a formal system did not contain variables but constants only, we could not then say that the corresponding Prolog program, when running, is being 'instantiated' on the computer. Therefore, Lucas and Searle, as well as other proponents of the Mathematical Objection, must mean something more by 'instantiation' than the strict logical interpretation of replacing variables with substitution instances.

This is where the debate becomes interesting. If we look for further clues as to what may be meant by 'instantiation', we find the following reference. At the end of his exposition of the Chinese Room Argument (which, it should be remembered, Searle claims takes the strong AI position to its logical conclusion), Searle states:

> As far as Chinese is concerned, I simply behave like a computer; I perform computational operations on formally specified elements. For the purposes of the Chinese, *I am simply an instantiation of the computer program*. (Searle, 1980, p. 285) (his italics)

It therefore appears that, in the context of the Chinese Room Argument, it is possible for humans to be instantiations, this time not of formal systems but of computer programs. But this is a different claim that needs to be argued for separately. That is, if Lucas wants his arguments to stick he needs to demonstrate that a formal system can be translated into a formally equivalent computer program so that the machine runs a computer program that is in all respects equivalent to the formal system on paper. We are not claiming that this cannot be done; only that Lucas needs to be careful on this point. That is, if the formal system is of a sufficiently powerful kind, then its translation into computer language statements must also be of exactly the same power. Ideally, there should be a one-to-one correspondence between the formally specified elements of the formal system and the constructs of the computer program. This is an interesting side-issue that we shall not pursue here.

Interestingly, Searle and Lucas take separate routes with regard to what they consider to be 'machines'. According to Searle, in response to the question, 'Could a machine think?', his view is that

> . . . *only* a machine could think, and indeed only very special kinds of machines, namely brains and machines that had the *same causal powers* as brains. And that is the main reason why strong AI has had little to tell us about machines. By its own definition it is about programs, and programs are not machines. (Searle, 1980, p. 305) (his italics)

Hence, Searle is adopting the view that computers are not the sort of 'machine' that is sufficiently powerful for thought. Programs run on computers, and programs are not computers or any other sort of machine. Since (as we saw in the last chapter) a program provides formal rules for manipulating uninterpreted objects, not even a machine that runs such a program has the power of a brain. Thus, for Searle, it appears that by definition 'brain' is 'something which is not programmed'.

Strong AI researchers could at this point raise the question of whether a brain, although not *programmed*, is nevertheless *programmable*. If it is not, then how can the brain have any causal powers, since the notion of 'cause' implies some degree of logical representation (see Chapter 1), and anything which can be expressed in such terms can be programmed? If it is, then strong AI researchers could claim that it is the *programmable* aspect of the brain that they are interested in, since it is by providing programs at the level of the brain that *mental* concepts, such as understanding, can be defined, in the same way as computer scientists are interested in the *programmable* aspects of abstract machines so that various definitions of computability can then be provided. That is, strong AI researchers may well claim that their task is to demonstrate that programs give rise to understanding in the same way that computer scientists demonstrate that quintuples give rise to looping. This is not to justify, or defend, the strong AI position, but only to point out that Searle and Lucas need to provide a clearer account of exactly what they see the relationships being between 'formal system', 'computer programs', 'brains', and 'minds'.

We shall examine Searle's reliance on the notion of 'same causal power as brains' in the next volume. Our only task here has been to point out that, in the case of both Searle and Lucas, the crucial bridging step between, on the one hand, what is formally specified on paper by means of axioms, definitions and rules, together with the limitations that go with formal

systems, and, on the other, what takes place in a computer, requires further
clarification. It may be perfectly possible for strong AI researchers to claim
that they are concerned with an idealized study of the mind (Beardon, 1988),
in the same way that Chomsky claimed that linguistic theory was all about
the study of a native speaker's *competence*:

> Linguistic theory is concerned primarily with an ideal speaker–listener,
> in a completely homogenous speech-community, who knows its lan-
> guage perfectly and is unaffected by such grammatically irrelevant
> conditions as memory limitations, distractions, shifts of attention and
> interest, and errors (random or characteristic) in applying his knowledge
> of the language in actual performance. (Chomsky, 1965, p. 3)

We are not claiming here that this is indeed what strong AI is claiming: we
shall return to this point in Volume 2, when we discuss AI as a science. What
the above quote is intended to show in this context is that whereas Searle
automatically associates 'instantiation' with *performance* on formally specified elements, this should not be assumed to be so. As we have seen in these
last two chapters, much can be said of formal systems, logic and computation
without necessarily bringing a running program into it.

Let us assume that it is not important to be absolutely clear on what the
connection between a formal system and a machine is, or on what the
connection between a mind and computer program is. (In fact, we shall pick
up these strands in the next volume.) Is not Lucas onto something when he
states that '. . . it is of the essence of being a machine, that is should be given
a concrete instantiation of a formal system'? (Lucas, 1961, p. 44). That is, is
it not the case that machines are indeed limited in what they can do, and that
Gödel's theorems demonstrate that this must be so? If they do, then it
appears to follow that mechanism is indeed false: our human minds will
always be one step ahead.

Hofstadter (Hofstadter, 1979), in what is probably the most comprehensive examination of Gödel's theorems and their relevance to AI, makes the
point that it is of the essence of the Gödelizing process that we can have no
algorithm for it. At first, this may seem to consolidate the Lucas view, and
therefore the Mathematical Objection. But if there is no algorithm, that
means that we humans have no algorithm for Gödelizing also. That means
that, in principle, each (sufficiently powerful) formal system will have its
own unique Gödel formula that has to be worked out 'by hand'. Given the
difficulty that we humans may have in understanding Gödelizing in the first
place (and if in this chapter you yourself faced difficulties when we presented
the Gödelizing process you will understand the conceptual elusiveness of the
process) then it is conceivable that for some formal systems we may never
find the Gödel formula, simply because it is to difficult. We may know that
such a formula exists, but cannot find it. Hence, if the mathematical
Objection is simply a question of **knowing that** such a formula exists, that too
can, if necessary, be put into a computer, and the computer and human will
now have the same amount of knowledge. That is, if the Mathematical
Objection rests on there *being* a Gödel formula, then knowledge of such

existence can be shared with a computer. On the other hand, if the Mathematical Objection depends on such a Gödel formula *being found*, i.e. knowing *how* to find it, then we humans cannot guarantee to find it for every formal system if there is no mechanical procedure for discovering this Gödel formula. And if it is claimed that a procedure does exist that guarantees to find a Gödel formula for any formal system, we can then express this procedure in computational terms and therefore the computer can find the Gödel formulae for us!

Another point that can be made is that Gödel showed that it is not possible for a formal system (of a sufficiently powerful kind) to be both complete and consistent *at the same time*. That does not mean that a formal system is not both complete and consistent; only that if it is required that completeness and consistency be demonstrated simultaneously, this cannot be done. Just as we humans may not be able, when confronted with a Gödel formula, 'I am not provable in the system', to consider the consistency and completeness of this formula at the same time, since we need to concentrate on one or the other but cannnot concentrate on both concepts simultaneously, so it may be possible for a computer to regard a Gödel formula from the viewpoint of completeness, ignoring consistency, for one moment, and then switch to viewing the formula in its consistency aspects, this time ignoring completeness.

The third point, and another that Hofstadter makes, is that although the Church–Turing thesis states that mental processes of any sort can be simulated by a computer program, the underlying representation of which is of a power equal to FOPC, or partial functions, or Type-0 languages, or TMs, the *AI version* of this thesis is that currently we know very little about intelligence and how to program it on computers. That is, we are nowhere near reaching the point at which the Mathematical Objection, even if it were true, becomes relevant. As the intelligence of machines evolves, its underlying mechanisms will gradually converge to the mechanism underlying human intelligence.

Other AI researchers not so much respond to Lucas as *by-pass* him. According to Minsky (1968), the Mathematical Objection, and Lucas' version of it, demonstrates clearly that the 'logistic approach', i.e. the approach based on logic, is the wrong one for AI to adopt. If the Mathematical Objection lies across the path of AI because AI has adopted the logic-based approach, then this shows that it is not AI which is 'wrong', but the logic-based approach being applied to AI. In fact, there is a lot to be gained if AI researchers rejected their dependence on the notions of 'propositions', 'inference', 'axioms', 'deduction', and so on, and instead concentrated on the essentially human notions of handling conflicts and paradoxes, learning from one's mistakes, planning a route, and so on. In fact, Minsky, whose argument demonstrating the unsolvability of the halting problem we presented in the previous chapter, probably did more than any other researcher in AI during the late 1960s to forge a new path for AI — a path that led to the formulation of knowledge representation techniques that were preferably *in*formal so that the Mathematical Objection, which applies to formal systems, could not be leveled against such research. Frames (Minsky, 1975) and scripts (Schank and Abelson, 1977) are just a couple of examples of such knowledge representation techniques which are informal, from a logical point of view.

In summary, we can say that the main contribution that AI has made to logic is this: if the Mathematical Objection demonstrates that AI is not possible, then that shows that the use of formal systems and theories, which the Mathematical Objection assumes, is not the most appropriate way to approach the concept of a thinking, or intelligent, machine. There is, however, another contribution that AI can make, and that is to interpret the question, 'Can machines think?', and the Mathematical Objection to it, as follows: 'What precisely is the relationship between formal system or theory, on the one hand, and the computer or program that is supposed to be an instantiation of it, on the other hand, and are the formal constraints of formal systems and theories necessarily also constraints of the computer or program?' Additional questions concern the interrelationships between 'brain, 'program' and 'mind'. We shall carry forward this reformulation question to the next volume.

## REFERENCES

Baker, G. P. and Hacker, P. M. S. (1984) *Language, sense and nonsense*. Basil Blackwell.

Beardon, C. (1988) Explanations in cognitive science, *Artificial Intelligence Review*, **2,** (3) 181–193.

Chomsky, N. (1965) *Aspects of the theory of syntax*. MIT Press.

Clocksin, W. F. and Mellish, C. S. (1981) *Programming in Prolog*. Springer Verlag.

Copi, I. M. (1967) *Symbolic logic*, third edition, Macmillan.

Delong, H. (1970) *A profile of mathematical logic*. Addison-Wesley.

Frege, G. (1970) On sense and reference, first published in *Zeitschrift für Philosophie und philosophische Kritik*, **100** 25–50. Translated and reprinted in Geach, P. T. and Black M., *Philosophical writings of Gottlob Frege*. Basil Blackwell.

Frost, R. A. (1986) *Introduction to knowledge base systems*. Collins.

Gödel, K. (1931) Uber formal unentsheidbare Satze der *Principia mathematica* und verwandte systeme, *Monatshefte für Mathematik und Physik*, **38** 173–198. Translated and reprinted in Gödel, K. (1982) *On formally undecidable propositions*. Basic Books.

Hofstadter, D. R. (1979) *Gödel, Escher, Bach: an eternal golden braid*. Harvester Press.

Lucas, J. R. (1961) Minds, machines and Gödel, *Philosophy*, **36** 1961, pp. 112. Reprinted in Anderson, A. R. (ed.) (1964) *Minds and machines*, Prentice-Hall, from which the page references are taken.

McCawley, J. D. (1981) *Everything that linguists have always wanted to know about logic (but were ashamed to ask)*. Basil Blackwell.

Manna, Z. (1974) *Mathematical theory of computation*. McGraw-Hill.

Minsky, M. L. (1968) mather, minds and models, in Minsky, M. L. (ed.) *Semantic information processing*. MIT Press.

Minsky, M. L. (1975) A framework for representing knowledge, in Winston, P. H. (ed.), *Psychology of computer vision*. McGraw-Hill.

Nagel, E. and Newman, J. R. (1958) *Gödel's proof*. New York University Press.

Nilsson, N. J. (1971) *Problem-solving methods in artificial intelligence*. McGraw-Hill.

Robinson, J. A. (1965) A machine-oriented logic based on the resolution principle, *Journal of the Association for Computing Machinery*, **12** (1) 23–41.

Russell, B. (1905) On denoting, *Mind* **14** 479–493. Reprinted in Marsh, R. C. (ed.) (1968) *Logic and knowledge* (fourth impression), George Allen and Unwin.

Russell, B. (1908) Mathematical logic as based on the theory of types, *American Journal of Mathematics*, **30** 222–262. Reprinted in Marsh, R. C. (ed.) (1968) *Logic and knowledge* (fourth impression), George Allen and Unwin.

Schank, R. C. and Abelson, R. P. (1977) *Scripts, plans, goals, and understanding*. Lawrence Erlbaum.

Searle, J. R. (1980) Minds, brains, and programs, *The Behavioral and Brain Sciences*, **3,** 417–424. Reprinted in Haugeland, J. (ed.) (1981) *Mind design* pp. 282–386. MIT Press (from which the page references are taken).

Turner, R. (1984) *Logics for artificial intelligence*. Ellis Horwood.

# 4

# Semantics

## 4.1 INTRODUCTION

Our approach consists of describing, first, *truth conditional theory*, followed by *model theory*, and finally by *possible-world semantics*. Tense and modal logics will be covered on the way. We shall adopt the method of exposition of Dowty, Wall and Peters (1981) to a large extent in our exposition, but shall expand on various topics where necessary. Whereas these authors go on to describe the semantic theory known as *Montague's Intensional Logic*, we shall follow them only as far as an extended model theory. At the end of the chapter, we should be in a good position to examine the Argument from Informality of Behaviour, which states that the behaviour of a machine is determined by instructions and rules that it must follow; we humans are not governed by such rules; therefore, we cannot be machines. The point of this chapter is to show that there is a well-accepted branch of philosophy that deals with meaning and understanding in a formal way, and before we tackle the Objection we need to know exactly what is being claimed by this branch of philosophy.

We have already mentioned Montague once. Let us mention him again, this time as the author of a quote which succinctly summarizes the reason why many logicians and formalists believe that it is worth their while researching into the area of logical semantics:

> I reject the contention that an important theoretical difference exists between formal and natural languages. (Montague, 1970, p. 188)

That is, for Montague and many other logicians, insights can be gleaned as to how natural language works through the study of artificial, or formal, languages. We shall remain faithful to the spirit of this quote in our exposition, but shall raise some objections to this 'axiom' of logical semantics in the second volume. For instance, we may well use the terms 'sentence' (a natural language term) and 'wff' (a formal term) interchangeably in this chapter.

Montague's concern was with the *semantics* of language, and here we encounter our first problem. What is *semantics*? Logicians themselves appear reluctant to state explicitly what they take semantics to be. In most textbooks on logic, and among the many pages devoted to symbols, syntax rules, transformation rules, inference rules, theorems, and so on, we may find one or two brief reference to semantics. Perhaps the most concise statement of what logicians take semantics to be, and therefore its relation to syntax, is provided not by a logician but by the theroretical linguist, McCawley, who writes:

> A logician is doing 'syntax' when he is constructing RULES OF INFERENCE, that is, general principles that specify what conclusions may be inferred from what premises, or is investigating the implications of particular rules of inference. He is also doing 'syntax' when he is constructing FORMATION RULES, that is, rules that specify the class of propositions he is dealing with. A logician is doing 'semantics' when he is setting up the conditions on what the TRUTH VALUES of the various propositions under consideration can be (McCawley, 1981, p. 14)

Setting up the condition on what the truth values of various propositions can be leads us nicely to the idea that, for logicians, semantics is *truth conditional*. That is, to know the meaning of a declarative sentence is to know what the world would have to be like for the sentence to be true. In other words, to give the meaning of a sentence is to specify its truth conditions, to give necessary and sufficient conditions for the truth of the sentence.

For example, the sentence **Simba is next to Freya** is true if and only if a certain physical entity named by **Simba** and another entity named by **Freya** stand in a certain spatial and temporal relation named by the words **is next to**. We can make a distiction between *object language* and *meta-language*. The sentence

**Simba is next to Freya**

is part of the object language, in this case, English, whereas the sentence

> **Simba is next to Freya** is true if and only if a certain physical entity named by **Simba** and another entity named by **Freya** stand in a certain spatial and temporal relation named by the words **is next to**

is part of the meta-language, also English, and specifies the *conditions* for the object language sentence to be true. Since confusion can arise if the same language is used for expressing sentences in the object language and for expressing truth conditions in the meta-language, logicians prefer to use notations and symbols that make it clear whether we are dealing with an object or a meta-language expression.

Truth conditions by themselves do not tell us very much except that the sentence as a whole is true or false. We may want to know more about **why** a sentence is true or false. How is it that one particular combination of words, such as **Simba is chasing Freya** gives rise to a true sentence, whereas another, say, **Freya is chasing Simba** is false? What is it about one particular combination of words that leads to a satisfaction of the necessary and sufficient truth conditions, whereas another does not? This leads us to the notion of *model theory*. That is, logical semantics is *model-theoretic* if it involves the construction of abstract mathematical models of those things in the world making up the semantic values of expressions in the object language.

Let us try to clarify exactly what model theory is. In the previous two chapters, we constructed some 'toy' formal systems and theories. We have said that a formal system becomes a theory only when some non-logical axioms are added to the formal system. Also, we have said that truth-conditional semantics deals with the necessary and sufficient conditions, expressed in a meta-language, for sentences, or wffs, to be true. Given a theory on paper, we made various *interpretations* of the symbols, e.g. 'Let **F(alan)** stand for **Alan is a father**.'

Such interpretations of formulae are possible only because, even before axioms are added to a formal system, the basic vocabulary had to be spelled out. That is, we had to declare the various constant letters, function letters, predicate and property letters, and so on. For a theory to have meaning, or, come to that, for a formula to have meaning, there must exist, logically prior to formula meaning and theory formulation, a *model* of the language in which the theory is couched. We need an account of how the primitive vocabulary items are related to, or mapped onto, objects or structures in the world under examination.

Two implications now present themselves. First, if providing a model for the logical symbols of the formal language is logically prior to the addition of axioms, does that not mean that we can have different relationships between logical symbols and objects, on the one hand, and the same set of axioms, on the other? For instance, **F(x)** might mean 'x is a father' according to one model, and 'x if frightened' in another, but the theory remains the same. This can not only be the case, but also, from a methodological point of view, is highly desirable. That is, one of the main reasons for using logic for theory construction is that it is the hallmark of a good theory that it should have different models, but nevertheless still be true with respect to each 'world' that the symbols are modelled in. We can safely say that some conceptual structure has been captured in our theory when all models of a theory reveal the same conceptual structure. Model theory therefore tells us not only what a theory means, but also what a theory could not mean.

The second implication is that it may be possible to have the same model but with different theories, i.e. with different axioms. How do we decide which of the various theories is the correct one of the one world being described? One answer is to say that theory construction is a two-way process: that axioms will demonstrate the inadequacies of the model, and the model will constrain the type of axioms we want to introduce into the theory. The formal properties of completeness and consistency will help us in this two way process in theory construction. For instance, one way to demonstrate soundness of a formal theory is to specify a model, or an *interpretation*. The model will provide a world of objects that satisfy the axioms. In an FOPC-based theory, variables and constants are interpreted as denoting objects and entities in the world under consideration, and the predicate symbols as denoting relations in that world, the point being that if it can be shown that the axioms of the formal theory are satisfied by the objects and entities in the interpreted world, all theorems derivable from the axioms will also be satisfied. Hence, once again, model theory is a useful methodological tool.

A practical effect of adopting a model-theoretic approach is that the meaning of a complex expression is somehow a function of the meaning of sub-expressions, since it is the sub-expressions which, logically, first have meaning, or 'semantic value', ascribed to them because of the relationship they have with the entities, i.e. because of the model of the formal language. Hence, a *syntax rule* can be interpreted as a statement that certain input expressions combine in a certain way to produce an output expression. That is, associated with every syntax rule which provides the necessary constraints for words, or sub-expressions, to be joined together syntactically, there will be a corresponding semantic rule that provides the necessary constraints for words, or sub-expressions, to be joined together semantically. As as we shall see later, these constraints are provided with the help of various relations and functions.

Finally, we have *possible-world semantics*. We have already seen in our brief introduction to truth-conditional semantics above that to know the meaning of a declarative sentence is to know what the world would have to be like for the sentence to be true. Notice that we said 'would have to be like', which gives rise to the interpretation that we are dealing with a necessary condition. If we relaxed the phrase *would have to be like* to include *possibility*, so that we now had:

> To know the meaning of a declarative sentence is to know how the world would have to be, as it might be, or might have been, not just as it is

we are entering the domain of possible-world semantics. That is, we move away from the idea that a world is to be thought of as set of circumstances that would have to be the case in order for our statements to be true, and instead we start thinking of a world as a set of circumstances that might have been the case, or might be the case, as well as would have to be the case. Notice that we are not concerned with models as such. A model provides a mapping between logical symbols and entities in a world. Possible-world semantics is essentially an investigation into theories of things being other than they actually are, irrespective of model difference. That is, if we had one model with many different theories, possible-world semantics would evaluate each of these theories with respect to not only all those worlds that would have to be the case, but also worlds that might be the case.

There is much disagreement amongst logicians as to whether possible-world semantics is required, and what expressive power one gains by adopting possible-world semantics. According to many logicians, a possible world is to be interpreted as a row of truth values in a truth table. For instance, if we had

$$(P \wedge Q) \to (\sim P \vee Q)$$

we would have, as a full truth table,

$$(P \wedge Q) \to (\sim P \vee Q)$$

| t | t | t | t | | f | t | t | t |
|---|---|---|---|---|---|---|---|---|
| t | f | f | t | | f | t | f | f |
| f | f | t | t | | t | f | t | t |
| f | f | f | t | | t | f | t | f |

If we examine one row of the truth table, say, the second, the possible world being described is one in which **P** is true, and **Q** is false, and that is all there is to it. But possible world semantics is concerned with more than this *extensional* view of possible worlds. For instance, possible-world logicians would like to say not only that a world is possible but also that the world is possible *in relation to other worlds*, something which cannot be analysed in the extensional view of possible worlds above. We shall see later what else possible world logicians want to introduce.

## 4.2 BRIEF HISTORICAL NOTE

Before continuing, it may be fruitful to provide a brief history of the subject, since in our exposition which follows we have collapsed the views of many logicians into one in order to present a unifying view of the subject. From our point of view, logical semantics began with Frege in 1879 who regarded statements as being composed not of subject and predicate but of function and argument. The important aspect of his work, from our point for view, is that he willingly accepted that functions could take anything as an argument, whereas until his work mathematicians had accepted that functions were purely mathematical and so took only mathematical 'entities' and mathematical 'objects' as arguments. Also, Frege accepted that functions could return any sort of entity as a value. With the apparatus of function theory, he was the first logician to propose a definition of quantifiers and hence of general statements. It is due to Frege that we have the idea of a concept (called 'predicate', in our exposition) as a function returning truth values, and this idea was applied to various logical connectives. This provided the extensional view of meaning. Frege, once he had proposed the distinction between sense and reference, also applied this approach to the sense of concepts. It is generally accepted that Frege's only motive in adopting this functional approach was to reduce arithmetic to logic.

Russell also had this motive but built on top of the Frege's approach a whole philosophy called 'logical atomism'. The key to logical atomism lay in the provision of a logically perfect language in which there would be only one word for each simple object, and objects that were not simple would have a combination of words, the combination being made up of words for the simpler objects that the complex object consisted of. The important point here, that a logical language ideally consisted of words which, when suitably structured according to syntax rules, displayed the structure of the object, led to the notion that to interpret such combinations of words only required an assignment of entitites to the simple words. The structure of the word combination would do the rest. Such an idea drove Russell to conclude that languages which did not have the structure of an ideal language, such as his logical language (FOPC), would contain ambiguities and would not be adequate for philosophical or scientific analysis.

Logic as a discipline came of age with the publication of Wittgenstein's *Tractatus* (1921), where the view was expressed that every *compound proposition* was a *truth function* of simple, or elementary, propositions, and that the sense of compound proposition was given by its set of *truth conditions*, which, for Wittgenstein, was an expression of agreement or disagreement with the different truth possibilities of simple propositions. Hence, the meaning of logical constants, such as ∧ (**and**) and ∨ (**or**), were provided by means of truth tables. Logical properties, such as logical truth, or logical consequence, could now be explained simply as a function of the truth possibilities of the individual propositions that made up the complex proposition. These functions could be mechanically realized, in that clear procedures could be adopted (e.g. assigning different truth values to the simple propositions, calculating the resulting truth values of the connectives between the simple propositions) for working out the final truth value of complex proposition. Perhaps the most important part of Wittgenstein's work lay in the way he demonstrated that logical laws could be expressed by means of truth tables: prior to his work, the general consensus of opinion was that a statement represented a logical law if and only if it could be derived from the axioms and definitions of a logical system. This had the immediate effect during the 1930s of allowing logicians and mathematicians to formulate *meta-logical* properties or laws, the truth of which could be demonstrated in isolation from any axiomatic system. Completeness and consistency of axiomatic systems could not now be demonstrated in truth-functional form, as well as rule-governed form.

Also during the 1930s, some logicians began to make explicit reference to the similarities between natural language and artificial languages. Carnap, for instance, expressed the view that there was no difference in principle between formalized languages and natural languages, and that therefore mathematical techniques could be used fruitfully in the description of natural languages. But the founding father of logical semantics is generally considered to be Tarski (1935), who proposed a *theory of truth* for a formal language, such as the FOPC. Quite simply, according to Tarski, *a true sentence of a language* is defined in a metalanguage where conditions were specified for a sentence to be true. Logical constants were explained by truth tables, but the truth of atomic formulae, such as **Is_sleeping(j)**, is provided by a meta-rule of the form, '**Is_sleeping(j)** is true if and only if the object correlated with **j** has the property correlated with **Is_sleeping**.' Although Tarski saw this sort of meta-rule as complementing the function of truth tables, in that the rules specified *how* truth values could be attached to atomic formulae so that the truth values of individual formulae could be combined to produce a truth value for a complex sentence, Carnap and other logicians interpreted the meta-rule as a way of providing the meaning of individual, atomic sentences, i.e. sentences with no complexity. Hence, the notion of truth condition was extended to encompass not only the view that a truth table provided truth conditions of complex formulae but also the view that the truth conditions of a simple, or non-complex, formula could be expressed by means of a meta-language.

Another important aspect of Tarski's work was his use of *models*, which were to be used to study the relationship between symbols of a formalized calculus and their interpretation. Current views now consider models to be of use in studying the relationship between any language (natural or artificial) and the world.

The final historical development of importance to us is the introduction of *intensional logic*. The origins of possible-world semantics can be found in a book by Carnap (1947), where he introduced the concept of the intension of a sentence being a determination of its truth value in every possible world. Roughly, he was prompted into this because there appeared to be no way of specifying the logical, or necessary, truth of an individual sentence by means of a meta-language statement. For instance, consider the sentence. **Two is even**. The semantics of this sentence could be expressed in a meta-language sentence, or *T-sentence*, as 'Two is even is true if and only if two is even', which we may call $T_1$. But if we wanted to express the necessity of **Two is even**, we would have to go up one further level, say, to the meta-meta-language sentence, $TT_1$: '$T_1$ is necessarily true'. In order to overcome the requirement that a meta-meta-language was needed before necessary truth could be specified, Carnap introduced necessity into the $T_1$, i.e. the meta-language, sentence itself, so that $T_1$ was now: '**Two is even** is necessarily true if and only if two is even.' Once the notion of necessity was introduced into a sentence this way, the door was open for other modalities, including possibility, to be introduced into **T-sentences**. From there, it was a short step for some logicians to study logics where necessity and possibility were built into object language sentences. Baker and Hacker (1984) provide a critical overview of the development of formal, or logical, semantics. Tense logic is a relative newcomer to logic, being explicitly examined by Prior (1955, 1967). Galton (1987) provides a comprehensive overview of tense logic and its relation to philosophy and computer science. Problems in possible-world semantics, and in philosophical logic in general, are discussed by Carr (1987) and Grayling (1982).

With these introductory remarks out of the way, let us now provide an exposition of logical semantics.

## 4.3 TRUTH CONDITIONAL THEORY

Let us introduce a 'toy' formal theory, very similar to the one proposed in Dowty *et al.* (1981). Although the following exposition may seem difficult at first, mainly because of the complexity of the notation, you'll soon get the hang of it. You should always remember that the basic ideas are quite simple, but formalizing these ideas, and understanding the notation used in the formalization, can be quite difficult for the beginner.

We first declare a language which we call $L_1$ and which consists of names, one-place predicates, and two-place predicates:

names                                  **j, t, b, p**
one-place predicates        **S**
two-place predicates        **B**

We now specify the syntax of **L₁**:

If δ is a one-place predicate and α is a name, then δ (α) is a formula.

If γ is a two-place predicate and α and β (beta) are names, the γ (α, β) is a formula.

If Φ is a formula, then ~Φ is a formula.

If Φ and Ψ are formulae, then Φ ∧ Ψ, Φ ∨ Ψ, Φ → Ψ, Φ ↔ Ψ are formulae.

We now provide some semantics for **L₁**. We use the special brackets ⟦ ⟧ around a symbol to signify **the semantic value of** the symbol. We have four names, and their semantic values are as follows:

⟦**j**⟧ = Judy                              ⟦**p**⟧ = Petri
⟦**t**⟧ = Tanzy                            ⟦**b**⟧ = Barney

That is, the four names have, as semantic values, four dogs that frequently roam around the Department of Computer Science at Exeter University. We assume that the world we are concerned with contains just these four dogs, or *individuals*, according to the terminology of logic. Diagramatically, we have the situation shown in Fig. 4.1, where each of the names is mapped

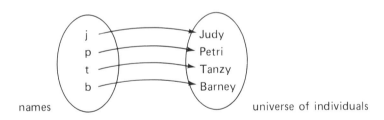

Fig. 4.1.

onto an individual in the world. Hence, we need a *total* function from the names of the language into a set of individuals in the domain of discourse. Note that the semantic value of a name is the entity itself, and not another symbol. That is ⟦**j**⟧ results not in the symbol 'Judy'; rather, ⟦**j**⟧ returns, as its semantic value, Judy herself. We signify this as:

⟦**judy**⟧ = Judy

We now provide the semantics of the one-place predicate, **S**:

$[\![S]\!]$ = the set of all individuals which are sable.

Hence, for one-place predicates, such as 'is sable', the denotation is a set of individuals that are sable. So,

S(j) is true if and only if $[\![j]\!]$ ∈ (is a member of) $[\![S]\!]$

In other words, the formula S(j) is true if and only if the individual referred to by j — the real Judy — is in the set of entities which are sable. If the only sable individual is Judy, $[\![S]\!]$ = {Judy}. That is, the denotation of S, which is shorthand for 'is sable', is a set containing only one individual in our domain of discourse, namely, Judy. Hence, S(j), which stands for 'Judy is sable', is true, since $[\![j]\!]$ ∈ $[\![S]\!]$, i.e. Judy ∈ {Judy} (individual Judy is a member of the set containing Judy).

Similarly, S(p) is false, since $[\![p]\!]$ ∉ $[\![S]\!]$, i.e. Petri is not a member of the set of sable individuals. The important point to note here is that the semantic value of a name is an *individual*, whereas the semantic value of a predicate is a *set of individuals*. By tying up sematic values with sets, formal logicians can now use the mathematical preciseness and power of not only set theory but also function theory. (We described the relationship between set theory and function theory in Chapter 2.)

Generally speaking, then, for a formula using a one-place predicate, that formula is true if and only if the semantic value of the argument is contained in the set which is the semantic value of the predicate, i.e.

δ(α) is true if and only if $[\![\alpha]\!]$ ∈ $[\![\delta]\!]$

and this statement provides, in a meta-language, the necessary and sufficient conditions for an object language statement containing a one-place predicate to be true.

We now provide the denotation of the two-place predicate, **B** ('barks at'):

$[\![B]\!]$ = the set of pairs in which the first barks at the second

That is, the denotation of this predicate is provided, not by a set of individuals, as we had with a one-place predicate, but by *pairs* of individuals such that the first individual of the pair is barking at the second. We have the general rule that, if γ is a two-place predicate and α and β are names, then

γ (α, β) is true if and only if ⟨$[\![\alpha]\!]$, $[\![\beta]\!]$⟩ ∈ $[\![\gamma]\!]$

That is, a formula containing a two-place predicate is true if and only if the two semantic values of the arguments to this predicate are in the ordered relationship to each other and this ordered relationship is in the set of ordered relationships which is the semantic value of the predicate.

For example, imagine that the denotation of **B** is the set: {⟨Judy,Petri⟩, ⟨Petri,Tanzy⟩}. That is, in our world, Judy is barking at Petri, and Petri is barking at Tanzy. Then, **B(j,p)** is true, since

⟨$[\![j]\!]$, $[\![p]\!]$ ⟩ ∈ $[\![B]\!]$

That is,

$$\langle Judy, Petri \rangle \in \{ <Judy, Petri>, \langle Petri, Tanzy \rangle \}$$

Let us summarize the two semantic rules we have introduced so far:

> If $\delta$ is a one-place predicate and $\alpha$ is a name, $\delta(\alpha)$ is true if and only if $[\![\alpha]\!] \in [\![\delta]\!]$

> If $\gamma$ is a two-place predicate and $\alpha$ and $\beta$ are names, $\gamma(\alpha,\beta)$ is true if and only if $\langle [\![\alpha]\!],[\![\beta]\!] \rangle \in [\![\gamma]\!]$.

These two semantic rules in their own way capture the essence of logical semantics. The relationship between a sentence and the world is expressed by means of the 'set-theoretic' concept 'is a member of'.

We should now see how the concepts of truth and meaning are tied up in truth-conditional semantics: to know the meaning of a *sentence* is to know the conditions under which it is true, and to know the meaning of a **word** is to know what that word can be used to refer to. Notice how the two semantic rules above, which are meta-level and provide the necessary and sufficient truth conditions ('necessary and sufficient' because of the biconditional nature of the meta-level sentence — see Chapter 2) for formulae to be true, mirror exactly two syntax rules of $L_1$, namely,

> If $\delta$ is a one-place predicate, and $\alpha$ is a name, then $\delta(\alpha)$ is a formula; and

> If $\gamma$ is a two-place predicate, and $\alpha$ and $\beta$ are names, then $\gamma(\alpha,\beta)$ is a formula.

In $L_1$, there are five other syntax rules, and there will correspondingly be five other semantic rules which also provide necessary and sufficient conditions and which will therefore also be expressed as biconditionals (i.e. using 'if and only if'):

If $\Phi$ is a formula, then $\sim\Phi$ is true if and only if $\Phi$ is not true.

If $\Phi$ and $\Psi$ are formulae, then $\Phi \wedge \Psi$ is true if and only if both $\Phi$ and $\Psi$ are true.

If $\Phi$ and $\Psi$ are formulae, then $\Phi \vee \Psi$ is true if and only if either $\Phi$ or $\Psi$ is true.

If $\Phi$ and $\Psi$ are formulae, then $\Phi \rightarrow \Psi$ is true if and only if either $\Phi$ is false or $\Psi$ is true.

If $\Phi$ and $\Psi$ are formulae, then $\Phi \leftrightarrow \Psi$ is true if an only if either $\Phi$ and $\Psi$ are both true, or else they are both false.

Here is another language, $L_2$:

| | |
|---|---|
| names | **judy, tanzy, barney, petri** |
| one-place predicate | **Is_sleeping, Is_hungry** |

We assume the same syntax as with $L_2$, except that the rule dealing with two-place predicates does not apply. Here are the semantic values for the names:

$[\![\textbf{judy}]\!]$ = Judy          $[\![\textbf{petri}]\!]$ = Petri
$[\![\textbf{tanzy}]\!]$ = Tanzy          $[\![\textbf{barney}]\!]$ = Barney

Note again that **judy** is a name, whereas Judy is an individual. We now declare the semantic values of the one-place predicates, but this time we use **1** and **0** to signify **true** and **false**, respectively. Also, instead of providing semantic values as a set, we shall provide, as a semantic value, a *function* that maps an individual onto **1** and **0**. The predicate **Is_sleeping** has as its sematic value the function shown in Fig. 4.2; that is, the semantic value of

Fig. 4.2.

**Is_sleeping** is a function that takes, as an argument, an individual, e.g. Judy and not **judy**, and returns either **1** or **0**. The value **1** can be interpreted as claiming that the individual which is mapped onto **1** by the function is in the set of individuals which is the semantic value of **Is_sleeping**. The set of mappings which go to make up the function is the semantic value, i.e. meaning, of **Is_sleeping**. We shall sometimes use this notation rather than the previously introduced notation '$[\![\textbf{Is\_sleeping}]\!]$ = {Judy}'.

Fig. 4.3 shows the semantic value of **Is_hungry**, again expressed as a

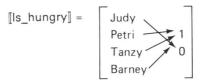

Fig. 4.3.

function; that is, $[\![\textbf{Is\_hungry}]\!]$ = {Petri, Tanzy}.

The semantic rules of $\textbf{L}_2$ are the same as for $\textbf{L}_1$, except that the semantic rule for two-place predicates will not apply. We can now 'compute' the semantic values of the following formulae:

**Is_sleeping(judy)**

          **Is_sleeping(petri)**
          **Is_hungry(judy)**
          **Is_hungry(tanzy)**

That is, if the one-place predicates are interpreted as standing for functions which take individuals as arguments, we have:

          **Is_sleeping(judy)** = [[**Is_sleeping**]]([[**judy**]]) = 1
          **Is_sleeping(petri)** = [[**Is_sleeping**]]([[**petri**]]) = 0
          **Is_hungry(judy)** = [[**Is_hungry**]]([[**judy**]]) = 0
          **Is_hungry(tanzy)** = [[**Is_hungry**]]([[**tanzy**]]) = 1

since [[**is_sleeping**]] = {Judy} and [[**Is_hungry**]] = {Petri, Tanzy, Barney}.

    Thus, '[[**Is_hungry**]]([[**tanzy**]]) = 1' expresses the information that, when the function which is the semantic value of **Is_hungry** is applied to the semantic value of the argument name, the function is evaluated. If the function is total, there will be a value returned for the argument. If the value is **1**, that means that the individual is in the set denoted by the predicate. If **0**, that means that individual is not in the set denoted by the predicate.

    There are some advantages in moving over to interpreting predicates as standing for functions, rather than denoting sets. For instance, by using functions, we can provide a principled way of generating the values **1** and **0**. Also, through the use of functions, we can add to the expressive power of our theory by being able to talk at a more abstract level about sets of individuals. For instance, consider the next language, $L_3$:

        names                **judy,tanzy,barney,petri**
        two-place predicates     **Barks_at**

The semantic values of the names are:

        [[**judy**]] = Judy          [[**petri**]] = Petri
        [[**tanzy**]] = Tanzy      [[**barney**]] = Barney

We take the value of a two-place predicate to be a function which yields other functions as its output (see Fig. 4.4). We shall provide an example in a moment, but first let us re-introduce the semantic rule dealing with two-place predicates:

        If $\gamma$ is a two-place predicate and $\alpha$ and $\beta$ are names, $\gamma(\alpha,\beta)$ is true if and only if $\langle [[\alpha]],[[\beta]] \rangle \in [[\gamma]]$

We can express this rule in functional form as follows:

        If $\gamma$ is a two-place predicate and $\alpha$ and $\beta$ are names, $\gamma(\alpha,\beta)$ is true if and only if

$$[\, [[\gamma]]\,([[\beta]]\,)\,]\,([[\alpha]]) \;=\; 1$$

In other words, **Barks_at(barney, petri)** is true if and only if the following computes to **1**:

        [ [[**Barks_at**]] ( [[**petri**]] ) ]( [[**barney**]] )

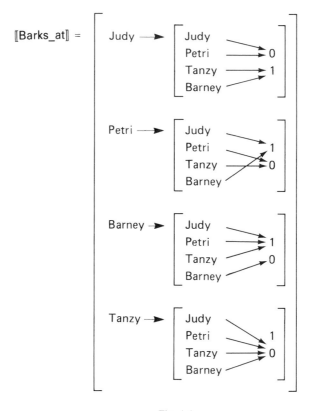

$[\![Barks\_at]\!] =$

Fig. 4.4.

First,

$$[[\![\mathbf{Barks\_at}]\!]([\![\mathbf{petri}]\!])]$$

is worked out, and rather than a single value being returned, as happened with a one-place predicate, another function is returned, as shown in Fig. 4.5.

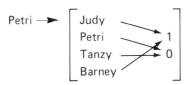

Fig. 4.5.

When this function is applied to ($[\![\mathbf{barney}]\!]$), **1** is returned, i.e. the formula **Barks_at(barney,petri)** is true.

Notice that we worked out the value of the predicate being applied to the value of the *second* argument, first of all, then applied this value to the value of the first argument. That is, we handed over the semantic value of **petri** to **Barkes_at** first, although the form of the sentence is **Barks_at(barney,petri)**. We then applied the resulting function to **barney** in order to obtain the value. **1**. We might be tempted to apply the value of the predicate to the first argument before applying the resulting function to the value of the second argument, and change the semantic rules accordingly. However, such a change of order would not always be desirable. For instance, in Chapter 2, we saw how a function could be regarded as a mapping between elements in a domain and elements in a co-domain. But it is possible that an element in the domain has no corresponding element in the co-domain if the mapping is undefined for a particular domain element. We then have the problem of deciding whether this is because the mapping is not comprehensive enough, or whether in fact there is no mapping between that domain element and a co-domain element. However, we can stipulate that an element appears in the co-domain because there *is* some mapping from an element in the domain onto it. Hence, to keep our semantic system within the realms of computability, it is more desirable to work from the co-domain element back to the domain element, with the guarantee that at least one such domain element will exist. This is another way of stating the *closed-world assumption* namely, any mapping not explicitly defined or not derivable from some rule is assumed not to exist. Therefore, a member of the co-domain is by definition one which has one or more elements in the domain, and the existence of a mapping between domain and codomain elements defines what the elements of the domain are also, under the closed-world assumption.

Returning to our 'toy' language, the connectives of $L_2$ can also be expressed as functions (see Fig. 4.6). Although we have not provided concrete examples of how these connectives work on the semantic values of individual formulae, the mechanism should now be clear. Connectives take as arguments, not functions or individuals, but the resulting values of whole formulae. For instance, in $L_2$, **Barks_at(tanzy, judy)** $\land$ **Barks_at(petri,judy)** is false, since **Barks_at(tanzy,judy)** is true but **Barks_at(petri,judy)** false. Hence, the conjunction of these two formulae is false.

That concludes our introduction to truth conditional semantics. The two main essential ingredients are

(1)  a set of entities, objects, or individuals which can be assigned as semantic values, as well as various functions constructed out of these entities, objects, or individuals; and
(2)  a set of semantic rules specifying how the semantic value of any complex expression is determined in terms of the semantic values of its components.

## 4.4  MODEL THEORY

The second aspect of logical semantics concerns *model theory*, or, the notion of *truth relative to a model*. In our 'toy' languages, **judy** was a name

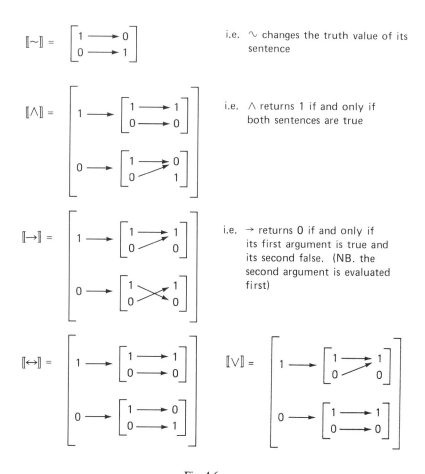

Fig. 4.6.

and **Is_sleeping** a predicate. But the formula **Is_sleeping(judy)** might receive a different semantic value if **judy** referred to, say, Judith, our secretary, or if **Is_sleeping** referred to a different set of sleeping individuals.

We follow our practice of providing a formal description of *model* first, before discussing the description in more detail.

Formally, a *model* is an ordered pair:

$$\langle A, F \rangle$$

where **A** is a set of individuals, and **F** is a function which assigns semantic values of the appropriate sort to the basic expressions. We now say that formula **S** is true with respect to a particular model **M**. More generally,

$$[\![\alpha]\!]^M = \text{the semantic value of } \alpha \text{ with respect to model } M$$

In our examples of 'toy' languages in the previous section, various semantic values were given for a particular language, with there being no mention of any relationship between the different sets of values provided. The essential idea of model theory is to provide a methodology whereby such relationships can be described and analysed.

For instance, let us assume the following language $L_4$:

|                    |                                  |
|--------------------|----------------------------------|
| names              | **judy,tanzy,barney,petri**      |
| one-place predicates | **Is_sleeping, Is_hungry**     |
| two-place predicates | **Barks_at**                   |

We assume the usual syntax rules.

Model $M_1$ for $L_4$ can be described as follows:

$$M_1 = \langle A_1, F_1 \rangle$$

where

$A_1$ = the set of dogs in the Department

= {Judy, Petri, Tanzy, Barney}

$F_1$ is defined as follows and is the *union* of all the following sets of semantic values for the names:

|                           |                            |
|---------------------------|----------------------------|
| ⟦**judy**⟧=Judy           | ⟦**petri**⟧=Petri          |
| ⟦**tanzy**⟧=Tanzy         | ⟦**barney**⟧=Barney        |

The predicates have the functions shown in Fig. 4.7 as semantic values. The semantic values of the connectives $\land$, $\lor$, $\sim$, $\rightarrow$, and $\leftrightarrow$ are not included since their values are assumed to be constant across all models.

$M_1$ provides one set of mappings for various language symbols. But now consider $M_2$ and $M_3$. First, here is $M_2$:

$$M_2 = \langle A_2, F_2 \rangle$$

where

$A_2$={Judith, Petri, Tanzy, Barney}

|                           |                            |
|---------------------------|----------------------------|
| ⟦**judy**⟧=Judith         | ⟦**petri**⟧=Petri          |
| ⟦**tanzy**⟧=Tanzy         | ⟦**barney**⟧=Barney        |

See also Fig. 4.8. Notice that ⟦**judy**⟧ is Judith, our Secretary, and no longer Judy, the dog. Also, notice that $M_2$ no longer defines a dog barking at itself as being false: it's now undefined.

And here is $M_3$:

$$M_3 = \langle A_3, F_3 \rangle$$

where

$A_3$=the set of all non-negative integers

|                      |                       |
|----------------------|-----------------------|
| ⟦**judy**⟧=1         | ⟦**petri**⟧=2         |
| ⟦**tanzy**⟧=3        | ⟦**barney**⟧=4        |

See also Fig. 4.9. $M_3$ is not a desirable model, given the symbols, but

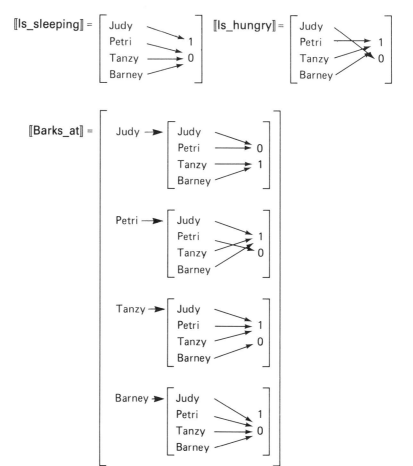

Fig. 4.7.

nevertheless it is a model which maps names onto numbers and predicates onto mathematical relations. An intuitive interpretation of **Barks_at** in $M_3$ is 'is greater than', for **Is_hungry** 'is an odd number' and for **Is_sleeping** 'is an even number'. Hence, in $M_3$, **Is_hungry(judy)** means '1 is an odd number', which is true. Also in $M_3$, **Barks_at(petri,tanzy)** means '2 is greater than 3', which is false.

Given $L_4$ and $M_1$, $M_2$, and $M_3$, the formula:

**Barks_at (tanzy, petri)**

is **true** with respect to, or in, all three models, because the semantic rule for computing the value of two-place predicates just happens to return 1 for this one formula in all three models. However,

**Barks_at (judy, tanzy)**

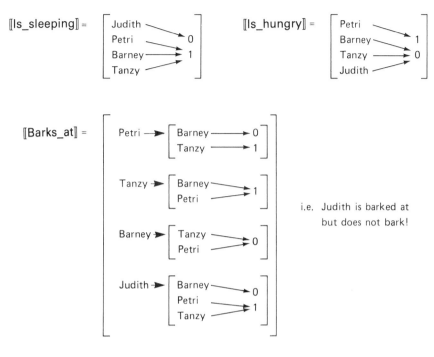

Fig. 4.8.

is **true** with respect to $M_1$, **undefined** in $M_2$, and **false** with respect to $M_3$.

Given this basic introduction to model theory, we can now redefine some terms introduced in the previous chapter.

(1)  A formula of a language **L** is *valid* if and only if it is true with respect to every possible model for **L**.

That is, validity applies to formulae of a language if and only if they are true no matter what denotations the primitives of the language are assigned. At first, this seems to be an impossible condition to meet. After all, just as we did above, all we need to do is assign different denotations to names and predicates so that the semantic value of a formula changes from model to model. If a formula does turn out to be true in all the models so far constructed, it will surely be possible to construct a new model in which that formula will be false?

This objection fails to take into account the fact that a formula of, say, $L_4$ consists not only of an *atomic* formula, i.e. where only one predicate occurs, but also of a complex formula, such as

**Is_sleeping(judy)** ∨ ~**Is_sleeping(judy)**

or

((**Is_sleeping(judy)** → ~**Barks_at(petri,tanzy)**) →

(~**Is_sleeping(judy)** ∨ ~**Barks_at(petri,tanzy)**)

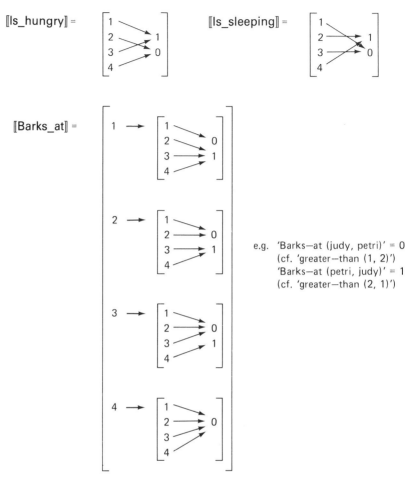

Fig. 4.9.

which, *because of their logical form*, will be true in all possible worlds (provided that undefined semantic values are taken care of). Hence, we have a semantic definition of *validity*, which contrasts with the syntatic definition introduced in the previous chapter, namely, that a statement of a theory is a *theorem* if and only if there is a proof of it from the formal system alone.

(2) A formula of a language **L** is *contradictory* if and only if it is false with respect to every possible model for **L**.

For instance, **Is_sleeping(judy)** $\wedge$ **~Is_sleeping(judy)** is a contradictory formula of **L₄**. The syntactic version of this was: a statement of a theory is a contradiction if and only if its negation is a theorem also.

(3) Two formulae of a language **L** are *logically equivalent* if and only if the first is true in exactly the same models in which the second is true, and in no others.

For instance, the formula, **Is_sleeping(judy)** $\wedge$ **Is_hungry(barney)** is equivalent to **Is_hungry(barney)** $\wedge$ **Is_sleeping(judy)**. The syntactic version looks like this: a statement of a theory is deducible (provable) from a set of other statements if it is the last statement of a sequence of statements which are either axioms, or follow from a previous statement by a rule of inference.

(4) A formula $\Phi$ of a language **L** is a *logical consequence* of a set of formulae $\Gamma$, or $\Gamma$ *logically entails* $\Phi$, if and only if every model in which all the formula of $\Gamma$ are true is a model in which $\Phi$ is true also.

For instance, if $\Gamma$ is the set

{**Is_sleeping(judy)** $\rightarrow$ **~Is_hungry(barney)**, **Is_hungry(barney)**},

and if $\Phi$ is

**~Is_sleeping(judy)**,

$\Phi$ is a logical consequent of $\Gamma$. That is, if $\mathbf{p} \rightarrow \mathbf{q}$ and $\mathbf{\sim q}$, then $\mathbf{\sim p}$.

So far, our 'toy' languages have not used quantifiers. It is time to consider a language which looks more like a first-order language than the ones we have been considering. Here is $\mathbf{L_5}$:

| | |
|---|---|
| names | **j,p,t,b** |
| individual variables | **x,y,z**, . . . |
| one-place predicates | **Is_hungry**, **Is_sleeping** |
| two-place predicates | **Barks_at** |

The syntax rules are the same as before, except we add the following two rules:

If $\Phi$ is a formula and u is a variable, then $(\forall u)\Phi$ is a formula.

If $\Phi$ is a formula and u is a variable, then $(\exists u)\Phi$ is a formula.

What would the corresponding semantic rules look like? If we had, say, **Barks_at(x,y)** as a formula, we could, according to the syntax rules, construct $(\exists y)$**Barks_at(x,y)**. It is not difficult to construct a semantic rule that would define this formula to be true if and only if **y**'s semantic value was such that there was some pair of values in the set denoted by **Barks_at** where **y**'s value was the second of the pair. But we now need to introduce into our definition of *model* the concept of *assigning* semantic values to variables. Such value assignment will again be carried out by functions. These assignments are the semantic equivalents of the substitution θs we introduced in the previous chapter. Whereas substitutions were concerned with *lexical* substitution of terms for variables, semantic assignment, which we shall refer to by **g** (the standard way of doing so), is concerned with value assignment.

We should note the difference between the meaning, or denotation, of a name, on the one hand, and the use of a variable, on the other. A variable can stand for many *individuals*, but a name can only have one value, its referent, as given in the **F** part of a model definition or specification. Once this denotation is set up between a non-logical constant and its value, it cannot be changed by anything else within the model. That is, different values can be assigned to variables, but not to names: a name has a *constant* value and so cannot be assigned different values at all. Hence, any **g** will be a function of semantic assignment for variables only.

Before we look at some examples, here is a formal definition of *model*, this time taking into account a first-order language.

> A model for a language such as $L_5$ is an ordered pair $\langle A, F \rangle$ such that **A** is a non-empty set of entities or individuals and **F** is a function assigning a semantic value to each non-logical constant of $L_5$ (names, one-place predicates, and two-place predicates). The set of possible semantic values for names is **A**. The set of possible semantic values for one-place predicates is a set of functions from **A** to the semantic values **1** and **0**, which we signify by $\{1,0\}^A$. The set of possible semantic values for two-place predicates is a set of functions from **A** to another set of functions from **A** to the values **1** and **0**, which we signify by $(\{1,0\}^A)^A$. A *value assignment* **g** is any function assigning a member of **A** to each variable of $L_5$. We abbreviate 'the semantic value of a formula or sentence $\alpha$ with respect to **M** and **g**' as
>
> $[\![\alpha]\!]^{M,g}$

Let us provide some semantic rules for assigning values to variables.

> If **u** is an individual variable of $L_5$, then $[\![u]\!]^{M,g} = g(u)$.
>
> If $\alpha$ is a non-logical constant of $L_5$, then $[\![\alpha]\!]^{M,g} = F(\alpha)$.

For example, we have the following functions **F** for the non-logical constants of $L_5$:

> **F(j)** = Judy   **F(p)** = Petri   **F(b)** = Barney   **F(t)** = Tanzy
>
> **F(Is_sleeping)** = {Judy,Petri}
> **F(Is_hungry)** = {Tanzy,Barney}
> **F(Barks_at)** = {⟨Judy, Petri⟩,⟨Petri,Judy⟩}

One **g** is as follows:

> **g** = x → **Judy**,
>      y → **Barney**,
>      z → **Barney**,
>      $x_1$ → **Petri**,
> . . .
> .
> .
> .

That is, according to this assignment, **x**'s value is Judy, **y**'s value is Barney, **z**'s value is Barney also, $\mathbf{x_1}$'s value is Petri, and so on. If our language contains an infinite number of variable letters, **g** is infinite! This need not concern us unduly, since we provide a **g** that is appropriate for the formula or sentence at hand, and within that formula or sentence it will be obvious which variables need values assigned to them. Nevertheless, if a syntax for a language allows a theoretically infinite number of variable letters, our semantics must reflect that.

We can provide the truth conditions for formulae and sentences of $\mathbf{L_5}$, corresponding to the syntax rules. We shall work through these rules in some detail with a couple of examples soon.

(1) If $\delta$ is a one-place predicate and $\alpha$ is a term, then $[\![\delta(\alpha)]\!]^{\mathbf{M},\mathbf{g}} = [\![\delta]\!]^{\mathbf{M},\mathbf{g}}([\![\alpha]\!]^{\mathbf{M},\mathbf{g}})$.
(2) If $\gamma$ is a two-place predicate and $\alpha$ and $\beta$ are terms, then $[\![\gamma(\alpha,\beta)]\!]^{\mathbf{M},\mathbf{g}} = [[\![\gamma]\!]^{\mathbf{M},\mathbf{g}} ([\![\beta]\!]^{\mathbf{M},\mathbf{g}})] ([\![\alpha]\!]^{\mathbf{M},\mathbf{g}})$.
(3) If $\Phi$ is a formula, then $[\![\sim\Phi]\!]^{\mathbf{M},\mathbf{g}} = 1$ if and only if $[\![\Phi]\!]^{\mathbf{M},\mathbf{g}} = 0$.

Similar rules can be provided for $\wedge$, $\vee$ $\rightarrow$, and $\leftrightarrow$, though we shall not do so here.

(4) If $\Phi$ is a formula and **u** is a variable, then $[\![(\forall\mathbf{u})\Phi]\!]^{\mathbf{M},\mathbf{g}} = 1$ if and only if for *every* value assignment **g**′ such that **g**′ is exactly like **g** except possibly for the individual assigned to **u** by **g**′, $[\![\Phi]\!]^{\mathbf{M},\mathbf{g}'} = 1$.
(5) If $\Phi$ is a formula and **u** is a variable, then $[\![(\exists\mathbf{u})\Phi]\!]^{\mathbf{M},\mathbf{g}} = 1$ if and only if for *some* value asssignment **g**′ such that **g**′ is exactly like **g** except possibly for the individual assigned to **u** by **g**′, $[\![\Phi]\!]^{\mathbf{M},\mathbf{g}'} = 1$.

Given these truth conditions, we can now define truth for formulae in $\mathbf{L_5}$ *relative* to **M**:

(6) For any formula $\Phi$ of $\mathbf{L_5}$, $[\![\Phi]\!]^{\mathbf{M}}$ is valid (i.e. $\Phi$ is valid with respect to **M**) if $[\![\Phi]\!]^{\mathbf{M},\mathbf{g}} = 1$ for *all* value assignments **g**. That is, a formula is valid in a model if it is true for all possible variable assignments.
(7) For any formula $\Phi$ of $\mathbf{L_5}$, $[\![\Phi]\!]^{\mathbf{M}}$ is contradictory (i.e. $\Phi$ is contradictory with respect to **M**) if $[\![\Phi]\!]^{\mathbf{M},\mathbf{g}} = 0$ for all value assignments **g**. That is, a formula is contradictory in a model if it is false for all possible variable assignments.

We have introduced a lot of formalisms, notations and definitions in the last couple of pages, and the best way to understand what is happening is to present a couple of examples, both assuming $\mathbf{L_5}$ to be the language.

We have the model **M** consisting of the pair $\langle\mathbf{A},\mathbf{F}\rangle$, where **A** is the set {Judy, Petri, Tanzy, Barney} and **F** is described below. Consider the formula $(\forall\mathbf{x})\mathbf{Is\_sleeping(x)}$. This formula was constructed according the the syntactic rules:

(a) If $\delta$ is a one-place predicate (e.g. **Is_sleeping**) and $\alpha$ is a term (e.g. **x**) then $\delta(\alpha)$ is a formula (e.g. **Is_sleeping(x)**).
(b) If $\Phi$ is a formula and **u** is a variable, then $(\forall\mathbf{u})\Phi$ is a formula:

$$(\forall x)\text{Is\_sleeping}(x)$$

Imagine we have the following value for **Is_sleeping**:

$$[\![\text{Is\_sleeping}]\!] = \{\text{Judy, Barney, Petri}\}$$

Let us assume an initial set of value assignments **g**:

$$\mathbf{g} = \begin{aligned}&x \rightarrow \textbf{Judy}\\&y \rightarrow \textbf{Barney}\\&z \rightarrow \textbf{Tanzy}\\&w \rightarrow \textbf{Petri}\end{aligned}$$

The semantic analysis will first examine the semantic rule associated with the syntactic rule (a) above. The semantic rule for (a) is

(a') If $\delta$ is a one-place predicate and $\alpha$ is a term, then $[\![\delta(\alpha)]\!]^{\mathbf{M,g}} = [\![\delta]\!]^{\mathbf{M,g}}([\![\alpha]\!]^{\mathbf{M,g}})$

That is, **Is_sleeping(x)** is true with respect to **M** and **g** since **g(x)** is Judy and $[\![\text{Is\_sleeping}]\!] = \{\text{Judy, Barney, Petri}\}$, i.e. **Is_sleeping(x)** is true where **x**'s value assignment is Judy.

The second semantic rule is

(b') If $\Phi$ is a formula and **u** is a variable, then $[\![(\forall\mathbf{u})\Phi]\!]^{\mathbf{M,g}} = 1$ if and only if for every asignment **g'** such that **g'** is exactly like **g** except possibly for the individual assigned to **u** by **g'**, $[\![\Phi]\!]^{\mathbf{M,g'}} = 1$

That is, to determine the semantic value of $(\forall x)\textbf{Is\_sleeping(x)}$, we must determine the value of **Is_sleeping(x)**, not just with respect to **g** but also with respect to all value assignments like **g** except for the value originally assigned to x. We can now see that $(\forall x)\textbf{Is\_sleeping(x)}$ is false, because there is one assignment, namely, $x \rightarrow$ Tanzy, which results in the semantic value of $(\forall x)\textbf{Is\_sleeping(x)}$ being false, since Tanzy is not in the set of sleeping individuals, according to our model, **M**, and functions, **F**.

With the same model **M** and functions **F**, now consider the formula $(\exists x)\textbf{Is\_sleeping(x)}$. Syntax rule (a) above still applies, but (b) is replaced by the syntax rule:

(c) If $\Phi$ is a formula and **u** is a variable, then $(\exists\mathbf{u})\Phi$ is a formula:

$$(\exists x)\text{Is\_sleeping}(x)$$

This syntax rule for the existential quantifier has the associated semantic rule:

(c') If $\Phi$ is a formula and **u** is a variable, then $[\![(\exists\mathbf{u})\Phi]\!]^{\mathbf{M,g}} = 1$ if and only if for some value assignment **g'** such that **g'** is exactly like **g** except possibly for the individual assigned to **u** by **g'**, $[\![\Phi]\!]^{\mathbf{M,g'}} = 1$.

That is, to determine the semantic value of $(\exists x)\textbf{Is\_sleeping(x)}$, we must determine the value of **Is_sleeping(x)** with respect to *some* value assignment such as **g**. Since our **g** has $x \rightarrow$ Judy and Judy is a member of the set of sleeping entities according to our model, $(\exists x)\textbf{Is\_sleeping(x)}$ is true.

Formulae using a combination of ∃s and ∀s will use a combination of these semantic rules, the ordering of the combination depending on the syntactic structure of the formula. Notice also that it does not matter which **g** we pick initially, since we are concerned that there should be *some* **g** that does return the semantic value 1 (for ∃), or *all* **g** that must return 1 (for ∀).

More examples, as well as detailed analyses, can be found in Dowty *et al.* (1981).

## 4.5   POSSIBLE-WORLD SEMANTICS

We now consider the third aspect of logical semantics — that of possible worlds. The notion of possible worlds is intrinsically bound up with the notion of *intension* and with *tense operators*. In our exposition so far, we have assumed that once the truth of a formula is determined with respect to a particular model, that truth value is identified permanently with that formula. For instance, **Barks_at(judy,petri)**, once assigned a value such as **1**, for **true**, is forever true in that model. But in the real world, the truth value of sentences and formulae changes as the world changes. **Barks_at(judy,petri)** may be true one moment, but false the next, and true again at some later time. Adding tense operators to our toy language should allow us to identify the time at which the sentence, if true, is true and, if false, is false. Also, by adding these operators, we should be able to provide denotations for expressions not just for a single state of affairs, where a moment in time is associated with a state of affairs, but for many possible states of affairs. And this is where *intension* comes in.

First, though, let us try and clarify the notion of possible worlds further. Let us concentrate on the word *world* first of all. In the previous section, we defined a model as follows:

> A model **M** is a pair ⟨**A,F**⟩ where **A** is a set of individuals, e.g. {Judy,Barney,Tanzy,Petri}, and **F** is a set of functions which assign semantic values to each non-logical constant of the language **L₅**.

If we assume that the set of individuals, **A**, remains the same, then, *very roughly*, a *world* is one set of such assignments. For instance, if **F** consists of the following functions:

$$f_1(\textbf{judy}) = \text{Judy} \qquad f_2(\textbf{barney}) = \text{Barney} \qquad f_3(\textbf{tanzy}) = \text{Tanzy}$$
$$f_4(\textbf{petri}) = \text{Petri}$$
$$f_5(\textbf{Is\_sleeping}) = \{\text{Judy, Barney}\}$$
$$f_6(\textbf{Is\_hungry}) = \{\text{Petri,Tanzy}\}$$
$$f_7(\textbf{Barks\_at}) = \{\langle \text{Petri,Tanzy} \rangle\}$$

we have described a world in which Judy and Barney are sleeping, Petri and Tanzy are hungry, and Petri is barking at Tanzy. Let us call this world, $w_1$. Now consider a different set of assignments:

$$f_1(\textbf{judy}) = \text{Judy} \qquad f_2(\textbf{barney}) = \text{Barney} \qquad f_3(\textbf{tanzy}) = \text{Tanzy}$$

$$f_4(\textbf{petri}) = \text{Petri}$$
$$f_5(\textbf{Is\_sleeping}) = \{\text{Petri},\text{Tanzy}\}$$
$$f_6(\textbf{is\_hungry}) = \{\text{Judy},\text{Barney}\}$$
$$f_7(\textbf{barks\_at}) = \{\langle \text{Judy},\text{Barney}\rangle\}$$

We have described a world in which it is now Petri and Tanzy who are sleeping, Judy and Barney who are hungry, and Judy who is barking at Barney. Let us call this world, $w_2$.

Now, we *could* claim that we have presented two different *models* here, that $w_1$ and $w_2$ represent two different, and separate, states of affairs which need to be modelled differently; formulae of $L_5$ will be true or false with respect to one or other of these models, because a particular state of affairs assigns truth values to the propositions of the language being modelled. Relationships *between* states of affairs, for instance, that one state of affairs chronologically occurs before another, can then be unpacked in terms of an ordering amongst the different models. Proponents of the 'worlds' approach, however, would contend that there are some advantages in being able to express relationships amongst states of affairs within the model itself, so that we have one model within which the appropriate relationships between states of affairs, or worlds, can be expressed.

For instance, *counterfactual conditionals*, such as 'If Judy had not been hungry, she would not have barked at Barney', might be more easily managed within a model that could represent different states of affairs so that such counterfactuals could be evaluated with respect to different worlds within the same model, i.e. with the same semantic assignments for the primitive, non-logical constants, such as **judy** and **barney**. If Judy had not been hungry, what else would follow? And is it true that if Judy had not been hungry, she would not have barked at Barney? What justification is there for that statement? The interpretation of counterfactuals for proponents of the 'worlds' approach, in other words, would be: 'In some world of the model, in which things are like *this*, what would happen if things were like *that*?' Opponents of the 'worlds' approach, however, would probably interpret counterfactual conditions as constitutive of a different model that needs constructing with different semantic values being assigned to the non-logical constants. Both opponents and proponents of the 'worlds' approach may claim that they have logical intuition on their side. In both cases, there would be agreement that states of affairs determine the truth or falsity of statements; however, there would be disagreement as to whether an assignment of truth values was with respect to a model, or with respect to a world *of* a model.

Let us now look at the word 'possible', in 'possible worlds'. We have already stated that a proposition is necessarily true if it is true in all states of affairs. A proposition is contradictory if it is false in all states of affairs. A proposition is contingent if it is true in some state of affairs and false in others. In our introduction to PC, we saw how a state of affairs was represented by one row of a truth table. A state of affairs, roughly, can be interpreted as an assignment of truth values, **t** and **f**, to individual propositions. Hence, we have the following family of terms. A proposition which has to be, or is bound to be, true is a *necessarily true* proposition. One which is bound to be false is an *impossible* proposition. One which is neither necessary nor impossible is a contingent proposition. A proposition which is not impossible is *possible*. Possible propositions, therefore, include all true propositions, i.e. those that are necessarily true as well as contingently true. If a proposition is possibly true, that must be because there is possibly a state of affairs that makes the proposition true. If a proposition is necessarily true, that is because it is true in all possible states of affairs. Hence, the logic of possibility is the study of both necessity and of possibility. The term *modal logic* is usually used to refer to such a logic. Proponents of modal logic would claim that by building into their logic the notion of possibility, they are in a better position to analyse the notion of *possible states of affairs*. In PC, a state of affairs either is, or it is not. The totality of rows in a truth table gives rise to the concept *all possible states of affairs*, where each row represents an assignment of truth values by a state of affairs. In modal logic, however, a state of affairs is possible *in relation to other states of affairs*. For instance, one state of affairs may be more or less like another state of affairs. Modal logic can be described, roughly, as the study of this relationship amongst states of affairs and the relationship between the notions of possibility and necessity.

We may now see a difference between the phrases *state of affairs* and *possible world*. Very roughly, *state of affairs* refers to one row of a truth table, or one assignment of truth values, in isolation from others. *Possible world*, on the other hand, assumes that states of affairs are related in some way.

We have only scratched the surface of various differences between traditional logicians and modal logicians, however. A good summary of the modal position is given by Lewis (1973):

> I believe that there are possible worlds other than the one we happen to inhabit. If an argument is wanted, it is this. It is uncontroversially true that things might be other than they are. I believe, and so do you, that things could have been different in countless ways. But what does this mean? Ordinary language permits the paraphrase: there are many ways things could have been besides the way they are ... [T]aking the paraphrase at face value, I therefore believe in the existence of entities that might be called 'ways things could have been'. I prefer to call them 'possible worlds'.

'Possible world' proponents do not have things their own way, by any means, and there are some profound metaphysical objections to their approach. But let us now tie up 'possible worlds' with 'intensions', so that the motivation for the use of a modal logic when dealing with an *intensional language* becomes clear. We saw in the previous chapter how logicians distinguished between the intension and the extension of an expression. Briefly, the extension is the referent, or denotation, of the expression, whereas the intension is the sense, or meaning, of the expression. The distinction is required so that co-referentiality of expressions, as in *The Professor of Computer Science is Derek Partridge*, did not automatically mean equivalence of meaning. If it did, the sentence, *The Professor of Computer Science is Derek Partridge*, would not be saying anything meaningful, whereas the sentence does convey some useful information to those people who did not know that Derek Partridge was Professor of Computer Science (at Exeter University). Before we go on to look at intension, we should remember that, for *extension*, there were few problems in its formal specification. In a logical system, the extension of an expression is given explicitly. For instance, various assignments of individuals to constant names are provided when a model is declared. These assignments are given by various functions that make up the **F** part of the $\langle \mathbf{A}, \mathbf{F} \rangle$ pair of a model **M**, where **A** is a set of individuals. These assignments are provided for constant names as well as predicates. Also, the extension of variables is provided by various **g**s, and the truth of a formula, or sentence, in a logical system will be determined by these assignments and various semantic rules that operate in conjunction with the rules of syntax. We saw how a formula, or sentence, is true with respect to, or in, a particular model **M**.

We can now say that the *intension* of an expression is also a function, this time associating to each world the *extension* of that expression in that world. This is so deceptively simple that a few words are in order!

Consider the one-place predicate **Is_sleeping**. The denotation of this predicate varies from world to world, depending on who is sleeping. For instance, we may have:

$\mathbf{w_1}$  $[\![\text{Is\_sleeping}]\!]$ = {Judy, Tanzy}

$\mathbf{w_2}$  $[\![\text{Is\_sleeping}]\!]$ = {Judy, Petri}

$\mathbf{w_3}$  $[\![\text{Is\_sleeping}]\!]$ = {Petri, Barney, Tanzy}

That is, we have three worlds where different individuals are sleeping. We introduced a functional notation for representing this information, namely,

$[\![\text{Is\_sleeping}]\!]([\![\text{x}]\!])$ = 1 if the denotation of
x, after value assignment, is
in the set denoted by **Is_sleeping**;

= 0 otherwise.

The general semantic rule for one-place predicates was:

If $\delta$ is a one-place predicate and $\alpha$ is a term, then $[\![\delta(\alpha)]\!]^{\mathbf{M,g}} = [\![\delta]\!]^{\mathbf{M,g}}([\![\alpha]\!]^{\mathbf{M,g}})$.

Hence, the extension of **Is_sleeping** is provided for one world of the model. The *intension* of **Is_sleeping**, however, is the set of functions that assign semantic values for **Is_sleeping** in each world. Hence, given the denotations of **Is_sleeping** in the three worlds $\mathbf{w_1}$, $\mathbf{w_2}$, and $\mathbf{w_3}$, we have the collected set:

$[\![\text{Is\_sleeping}]\!]$ = {Judy, Tanzy}

$[\![\text{Is\_sleeping}]\!]$ = {Judy, Petri}

$$[\![\text{Is\_sleeping}]\!] = \{\text{Petri, Barney, Tanzy}\}$$

Given our definition of *intension*, namely, that it is a function associating to each world the *extension* of that expression in that world, we now signify the *intension* of **Is_sleeping** by means of the following notation:

$$\|\text{Is\_sleeping}\| = \text{the set of sleeping individuals in different worlds}$$

Note that '$[\![\ ]\!]$' around a symbol name signifies its *extension*, whereas '$\|\ \|$' around a symbol name signifies its *intension*. So,

$$\|\text{Is\_sleeping}\| = [\![\text{Is\_sleeping}]\!]^{w_1} = \{\text{Judy, Tanzy}\}$$
$$[\![\text{Is\_sleeping}]\!]^{w_2} = \{\text{Judy, Petri}\}$$
$$[\![\text{Is\_sleeping}]\!]^{w_3} = \{\text{Petri, Barney, Tanzy}\}$$

Better still would be to provide $\|\text{Is\_sleeping}\|$ in functional form, with the worlds acting as argument values to decide which denotation to return (see Fig. 4.10).

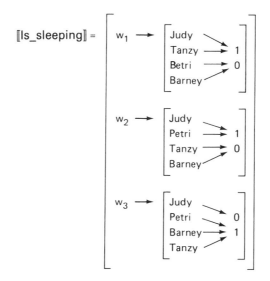

Fig. 4.10.

We can then include the intension of non-logical names (constants and predicates) as functions within the set **F** of functions that we specify every time we declare a model of a language. The notation

$$\mathbf{F}(\mathbf{w}_i, \alpha)$$

will be used to signify the denotation of a symbol $\alpha$ in a particular world, $\mathbf{w}_i$.

The set of denotations for a symbol for all the different worlds of a model is therefore the *intension* of that symbol in that model.

We have assumed that the set of assignments for the constant names **judy**, **petri**, **tanzy**, and **barney** remain the same in each world, although there is nothing in possible-world semantics, or in our definition of *intension*, to prevent us from changing the semantic values of these constants, e.g. ⟦**judy**⟧ = Petri, in another world. However, once a semantic values is assigned to a constant name in a world, that semantic value is associated permanently with that name in that world and therefore cannot be changed within that world. Also, once a set of values is assigned to a constant predicate for a world, those values must remain associated with that predicate in that world. It is only by specifying another world that we can change these constant semantic values. Only variables can have a variety of semantic assignments in a world.

Before going on to define a toy model for some possible worlds, there are some general observations we can make. The definition of *intension* provided above has the intuitive appeal that to know the meaning of, say, a predicate is to know what would count for that predicate to be true in different worlds. Hence, intension now appears to be a higher-order concept than extension. It is not the task of logic to specify how, or why, the predicate means what it does, only that if we are to claim that we know the intension of a predicate, that implies that we know how to apply that predicate in different worlds, i.e. we can identify true instances of that predicate in different worlds.

Secondly, if intension is to be defined in this way, to talk about intensions is going to require a second-order language. For instance, to ask what it is that all one-place predicates share in meaning is going to require quantification over functions, where the functions provide other functions as values.

Thirdly, the intension of a *sentence* can be described as what makes it true or false (sense) rather than as its truth value (reference). The intension of a *predicate* can be described as what makes the predicate refer to a set of individuals (sense) rather than as the set to which it refers (reference). The intension of a *name* can be described as what makes the name refer to an individual (sense) rather than as the individual to which it refers (reference). Hence, the intension of a sentence is what the world *would be like if the sentence were true*, and a sentence is true *if the world is in fact like that* (Stillings *et al.* 1987, p. 405). And this is where the notion of possible worlds comes in. If the intension of a sentence is what the world would be like if the sentence were true (not 'what the world *would have* to be like, notice), and if that sentence is true if the world is in fact like that, the argument for possible worlds claims that to be able to study intensions properly and to relate intensions to extensions, we need to have a logical device which allows us to describe states of affairs that are other than they actually are, since it is not until the extension is computed that we know whether a sentence, by virtue of it being true, is true because of an actual state of affairs. Roughly, before we can conclude that a sentence is true, we must know what to look for, and intension is used to identify what states of affairs are possible such that one or more (or sometimes none) make the sentence true.

It is time to provide some concrete examples of possible-world systems. Our exposition is based on the *indexical* approach to possible worlds, since such an approach satisfies several of our objectives.

We define a *temporal model* for a language **L** as an ordered quadruple:

$$\langle \mathbf{A}, \mathbf{I}, <, \mathbf{F} \rangle$$

such that **A** and **I** are any non-empty sets, $<$ is a *linear ordering* on **I**, and **F** is a function assigning to each pair consisting of a member of **I** and a non-logical constant of **L** an appropriate denotation, i.e. **F** includes the intension of non-logical symbols.

Intuitively, **I** is meant to represent a series of moments of time, i.e. a set of moments linearly ordered by $<$. The linear ordering is such that the following relations are axiomatic to any *temporal language* that is *linear*:

$\quad$ i $\not<$ i (i does not occur before itself)

$\quad$ i $<$ j $\land$ j $<$ k $\rightarrow$ i $<$ k (if i is before j and j is before k,

$\qquad\qquad\qquad\qquad\qquad\qquad\qquad\qquad$ then i is before k)

$\quad$ i $<$ j $\lor$ i $=$ j $\lor$ j $<$ i (for any two moments i and j, i is

$\qquad\qquad\qquad\qquad\qquad\qquad\qquad$ before j, or i is at the same time

$\qquad\qquad\qquad\qquad\qquad\qquad\qquad\qquad$ as j, or j is before i)

When we provide denotations of the basic expressions, we must add a time value, e.g. **F(20,b)**, which is to be interpreted as: 'the denotation of **b** at moment in time 20'. Typically, names denote the same individual at all times in a model, whereas predicates change in their denotation.

Given our previously introduced semantic rules, we now add a further *index* to our notation. Instead of $[\![\alpha]\!]^{M,g}$, i.e. the denotation of $\alpha$ in model **M** and with value assignment **g**, we now have

$$[\![\alpha]\!]^{M,i,g}$$

i.e. the denotation of $\alpha$ relative to model **M**, time **i**, and value assignment **g**. For instance, imagine that our temporal model on the language **L₅** is as follows:

$$\mathbf{TM_1} = \langle \mathbf{A}, \mathbf{I}, <, \mathbf{F} \rangle$$

where

$\quad$ **A** = {Judy, Petri, Barney, Tanzy},

$\quad$ **I** = {$t_1$, $t_2$, $t_3$},

$\quad$ $<$ = {($t_1$,$t_2$),($t_2$,$t_3$),($t_1$,$t_3$)}

and **F** includes the following values:

$\quad$ **F($t_1$,j)**=Judy $\quad$ **F($t_2$,j)**=Judy $\quad$ **F($t_3$,j)**=Judy

$\quad$ **F($t_1$,p)**=Petri $\quad$ **F($t_2$,p)**=Petri $\quad$ **F($t_3$,p)**=Petri

$\quad$ **F($t_1$,b)**=Barney $\quad$ **F($t_2$,b)**=Barney $\quad$ **F($t_3$,b)**=Barney

$$\mathbf{F(t_1,t)}=\text{Tanzy} \quad \mathbf{F(t_2,t)}=\text{Tanzy} \quad \mathbf{F(t_3,t)}=\text{Tanzy}$$

i.e. the names are constant across all times, and

$$\mathbf{F(t_1,Is\_sleeping)}=\{\text{Judy,Petri}\}$$

$$\mathbf{F(t_2,Is\_sleeping)}=\{\text{Judy,Petri}\}$$

$$\mathbf{F(t_3,Is\_sleeping)}=\{\text{Judy}\}$$

$$\mathbf{F(t_1,Barks\_at)}=\{\langle\text{Tanzy,Barney}\rangle,\langle\text{Barney,Tanzy}\rangle\}$$

$$\mathbf{F(t_2,Barks\_at)}=\{\ \}$$

$$\mathbf{F(t_3,Barks\_at)}=\{\langle\text{Petri,Tanzy}\rangle,\langle\text{Tanzy,Barney}\rangle\}$$

That is, at $\mathbf{t_1}$, Judy and Petri are sleeping, Tanzy is barking at Barney and Barney is barking at Tanzy. At $\mathbf{t_2}$, Judy and Petri are still sleeping but no dogs are barking, and at $\mathbf{t_3}$ Judy has slept through it all whilst Petri is barking at Tanzy and Tanzy is barking at Barney.

Hence, **Is_sleeping(j)** is true, or *satisfiable*, at $\mathbf{t_1}$ since

$$[\![\textbf{Is\_sleeping}]\!]([\![\textbf{j}]\!])^{\mathbf{M},t_1,\mathbf{g}}$$

is in our temporal model. Also, **Barks_at(x,b)** is satisfiable, since at $\mathbf{t_3}$

$$[[\![\textbf{Barks\_at}]\!]([\![\textbf{b}]\!])]([\![\textbf{x}]\!])^{\mathbf{M},t_3,\mathbf{g}}$$

where **g** is the assignment $\mathbf{x} \to \textbf{Tanzy}$. Notice also that whereas **Is_sleeping(j)** is true at all three times, this does not make **Is_sleeping(j)** true at all possible times, since we can imagine a time, say, $\mathbf{t_4}$, where Judy is no longer sleeping.

With these basic concepts, we can introduce *tenses* into our language. We use **F** to signify a *future* tense operator (not to be confused with functions **F** which return denotations for expressions — the context will make clear which **F** is meant), and **P** to signify a *past* tense operator. Here are the syntax and semantic rules for **F** and **P**.

(1) If $\Phi$ is a formula, then $\mathbf{F}\Phi$ is a formula

(2) If $\Phi$ is a formula, then $\mathbf{P}\Phi$ is a formula.

(3) If $\Phi$ is a formula, then $[\![\mathbf{F}\Phi]\!]^{\mathbf{M},i,\mathbf{g}} = 1$ if and only if there is some $i'$ in $\mathbf{I}$ such that $i < i'$ and $[\![\Phi]\!]^{\mathbf{M},i',\mathbf{g}} = 1$; otherwise $[\![\mathbf{F}\Phi]\!]^{\mathbf{M},i,\mathbf{g}} = 0$.

(4) If $\Phi$ is a formula, then $[\![\mathbf{P}\Phi]\!]^{\mathbf{M},i,\mathbf{g}} = 1$ if and only if there is some $i'$ in $\mathbf{I}$ such that $i'<i$ and $[\![\Phi]\!]^{\mathbf{M},i',\mathbf{g}} = 1$; otherwise $[\![\mathbf{P}\Phi]\!]^{\mathbf{M},i,\mathbf{g}} = 0$.

Returning to $\mathbf{TM_1}$, we should now see that

**F Is_sleeping (j)**

is true at $\mathbf{t_1}$ and $\mathbf{t_2}$, since, for $\mathbf{t_1}$,

$$[\![\textbf{F Is\_sleeping}]\!]([\![\textbf{j}]\!])^{\mathbf{M},t_1,\mathbf{g}} = 1$$

because there is some $t'$ in $\mathbf{I}$, i.e. $\mathbf{t_2}$, such that $\mathbf{t_1} < \mathbf{t_2}$, and

$$[\![\textbf{Is\_sleeping}]\!]([\![\textbf{j}]\!])^{\mathbf{M},t_2,\mathbf{g}} = 1$$

i.e. Judy will be sleeping at some moment in time after $t_1$, namely, at $t_2$ (and, incidentally, at $t_3$).

For $t_2$,

$$[\![F\ \textbf{Is\_sleeping}]\!]([\![j]\!])^{M,t_2,g} = 1$$

because there is some $t'$ in $\mathbf{I}$, i.e. $t_3$, such that $t_2 < t_3$, and

$$[\![\textbf{Is\_sleeping}]\!]([\![j]\!])^{M,t_3,g} = 1$$

Similarly, **F Is\_sleeping(p)** is true at $t_1$, but not at $t_2$, since there is no $t'$ in $\mathbf{I}$ such that $t_2 < t'$ and $[\![\textbf{Is\_sleeping}]\!]([\![p]\!])^{M,t',g} = 1$, i.e. Judy is not sleeping at $t_3$.

Similar considerations apply for formulae that use the **P** tense, but this time the procedure involves searching for moments of time before the current one for a certain state of affairs to hold. For instance, **P Barks\_at(x,t)** at time $t_3$ (and at $t_2$) is true since there is some $t'$ before $t_3$, namely, $t_1$, where

$$[[\![\textbf{Barks\_at}]\!]([\![b]\!])]([\![x]\!])^{M,t',g} = 1$$

for value assignment **g** being $x \rightarrow$ **Barney**.

Notice that no **F** formula uttered at $t_3$ can be true in $\mathbf{TM_1}$, since our model only contains three time instants. Also, no **P** formula at $t_1$ can be true, for the same reason. The real world cannot be constrained like this, but if the answer is to extend time instants indefinitely in both directions so that our model more closely resembles the real world we may have problems concerning computability. For example, how far back does one need to go to show that a **P** formula containing an existential quantifier only, such as $(\exists x)\{\mathbf{P}\ \textbf{Barks\_at(x,j)}\}$, is true? Bearing in mind that value assignments can also be infinite, we now appear to have two dimensions of infiniteness concerning possible world semantics, both of which will have implications for the computability of expressions.

By means of these basic tense operators, more tenses can be introduced into our language, $\mathbf{L_5}$:

> $FF\Phi$ it will be the case that it will be the case that . . .
>
> $PP\Phi$ it has been the case that it has been the case that
>         (or, it had been the case that) . . .
>
> $FP\Phi$ it will have been the case that . . .
>
> $PF\Phi$ it has been the case that it will be the case that . . .

$FF\Phi$ at $t_i$ is true if and only if $\Phi$ is true two instants, or more, *after* $t_i$. $PP\Phi$ at $t_i$ is true if and only if $\Phi$ is true two instants, or more, *before* $t_i$. $FP\Phi$ and $PF\Phi$ at $t_i$ both imply the disjunct $F\Phi \vee \Phi \vee P\Phi$.

Two new operators can now be introduced for the sake of completeness of exposition namely, **G** and **H**.

$$G\Phi \leftrightarrow \sim F \sim \Phi$$

$$H\Phi \leftrightarrow \sim P \sim \Phi$$

G signifies 'it *will always be* the case that', whereas **H** signifies 'it *has always been* the case that'. Referring back to **TM₁**, we should now see that the following formulae are true with respect to **TM₁**:

**FBarks_at(p,t)** at $t_1,t_2$

**FFBarks_at(p,t)** at $t_1$

**PBarks_at(t,b)** at $t_2,t_3$

**PPBarks_at(t,b)** at $t_3$

**FPBarks_at(t,b)** at $t_1,t_2$

**PFBarks_at(p,t)** at $t_2,t_3$

**F~Barks_at(p,t)** at $t_1$ (since at $t_2$ no dogs bark)

**GIs_sleeping(j)** at $t_1,t_2$ (since there are only three instants)

**(∃x)GIs_sleeping(x)** at $t_1,t_2$ (for x → **Judy**)

**~(∀x)HIs_sleeping(x)** at $t_2,t_3$ (for x → **Barney** and x → **Tanzy**, respectively).

The approach we have adopted to providing an exposition of modal logic requires us to present the above exposition of tense logic first. Remember that the whole point of the exercise is come up with a formalism to express *intensions* which does not require us to go 'outside' a model, i.e. to come up with a *model*-based approach, rather than a *models*-based approach. So far, we have introduced tenses as a way of showing how denotations change with time and how time instants can be ordered. Nothing in what we have stated so far allows us to specify denotations *other than the way they actually are*. That is, whilst our tense model allows us to describe variations in denotations (and our examples have used variations of predicate denotations only), the assumption has been that the denotations nevertheless correspond to the way things actually are. Modal logic, on the other hand, is used to allow logicians to specify changes of denotations that correspond to not only how things actually are but also how things might have been, or if things had been different from the way they actually are. As we stated earlier, not all logicians accept that there is any benefit to be gained from adopting the latter approach, and we leave you to judge towards which side of the debate your inclinations lie.

We add two new operators to the language, **L₅**:

□ — standing for 'it is necessarily the case that'

◇ — standing for 'it is possibly the case that'

The syntax and semantic rules for these two operators can now be provided:

(1) If Φ is a formula, then □Φ is a formula.

(2) If Φ is a formula, then ◇Φ is a formula.

(3) If Φ is a formula, then $[\![□Φ]\!]^{M,i,g} = 1$ (Φ is necessarily true with respect to **M**) if and only if for all **i′** in **I**, $[\![Φ]\!]^{M,i′,g} = 1$ (i.e. if Φ is true at all moments

in time in a temporal model).

(4) If $\Phi$ is a formula, then $[\![\Diamond\Phi]\!]^{M,i,g} = 1$ is and only if for some $i'$ in $I$, $[\![\Phi]\!]^{M,i',g} = 1$ (i.e. if $\Phi$ is true at some moment in time in a temporal model).

The important point to note is that the semantic rules reinterpret $I$ not as an ordered set of moments in time but as a set of unordered indices signifying possible worlds. For instance, imagine we have the following modal model $MM_1$, without the temporal precedence operator being included in the language $L_5$:

$$MM_1 = \langle A, I, F \rangle$$

where

$$A = \{Judy, Petri, Tanzy, Barney\}$$
$$I = \{i_1, i_2, i_3\}$$

F includes the following values:

$$F(i_1, j) = Judy \quad F(i_2, j) = Judy \quad F(i_3, j) = Judy$$
$$F(i_1, p) = Petri \quad F(i_2, p) = Petri \quad F(i_3, p) = Petri$$
$$F(i_1, b) = Barney \quad F(i_2, b) = Barney \quad F(i_3, b) = Barney$$
$$F(i_1, t) = Tanzy \quad F(i_2, t) = Tanzy \quad F(i_3, t) = Tanzy$$
$$F(i_1, Is\_sleeping) = \{Judy, Petri\}$$
$$F(i_2, Is\_sleeping) = \{Judy, Petri\}$$
$$F(i_3, Is\_sleeping) = \{Judy\}$$
$$F(i_1, barks\_at) = \{\langle Tanzy, Barney \rangle, \langle Barney, Tanzy \rangle\}$$
$$F(i_2, Barks\_at) = \{\ \}$$
$$F(i_3, Barks\_at) = \{\langle Petri, Tanzy \rangle, \langle Tanzy, Barney \rangle\}$$

Hence, $\Box$**Is_sleeping(j)** is true for all possible worlds in $MM_1$. Similarly, $\Diamond$**Barks_at(p,t)** is true with respect to $MM_1$ since there is some possible world, i.e. $i_3$, in which **Barks_at(p,t)** is true. We assume that $MM_1$ contains only these three possible worlds.

Because there are no precedences specified amongst the $i$, each $i$ signifies an atemporal *world* in which denotations may change. Hence, the intension of a predicate can still be described as the set of functions, $F$, which assign to each world the denotations that apply in that world. One of these worlds we can define to be the actual one, say, $i_1$, whilst the other two worlds, $i_2$ and $i_3$, represent worlds that are possible but which are different from the real world. By specifying possible-world semantics in this way, modal logicians claim that they now are now able, *within* a model, to specify not only necessary and possible truth of formulae (by means of the semantic rules above) but also the relation of one world to another. For instance, in the above model, it could be argued that world $i_1$ is related more closely to world

$i_2$ than world $i_3$ is to world $i_2$, since between $i_1$ and $i_2$ the only difference is that two dogs are not barking at each other, whereas between $i_3$ and $i_2$ there is a significant difference between Petri sleeping and Petri barking at Tanzy. Any specification of the relative similarity, or difference, between worlds is called an *accessibility relation*. For instance, if one world is possible with respect to another and if that world is possible with respect to a third world then the first world is possible with respect the third world, the accessibility relation would be specified as follows:

**if $R(w_1,w_2)$ and $R(w_2,w_3)$ then $R(w_1,w_3)$**

where **R** is some specified relation. Then, for instance, the truth of counter-factual statements, such as 'If Judy were not sleeping she would be barking at Petri', could be unpacked in terms of how *close* or *far* one world (say, the actual world) is from another in which Judy is not sleeping. That, at any rate, is the theory!

There are various properties of the two, recently introduced, modal operators:

$$\Box\Phi \to \Phi$$

$$\Phi \to \Diamond\Phi$$

That is, if $\Phi$ is necessarily true in all possible worlds, then it is true for any of them. Also, if $\Phi$ is true, then there must be some possible world in which $\Phi$ is true. There are also some equivalences, similar in operation to quantifier negation rules:

$$\Box\Phi \leftrightarrow \sim\Diamond\sim\Phi$$

$$\Diamond\Phi \leftrightarrow \sim\Box\sim\Phi$$

$$\sim\Diamond\Phi \leftrightarrow \Box\sim\Phi$$

$$\Diamond\sim\Phi \leftrightarrow \sim\Box\Phi$$

If we combine both tense *and* modal operators, we have *coordinate semantics*, where we combine the operators both of time and of possibility. If **T** is used to signify a set of time instants, a coordinate semantics model can be defined as follows:

$$\langle \mathbf{A, W, T}, <, \mathbf{F} \rangle$$

where **A**, **W** and **T** are non-empty sets, $<$ is a linear ordering of the set **T**, **W** is the set of worlds, and **F** assigns an appropriate denotation to each pair $\langle \mathbf{w,t} \rangle$ for **w** in **W** and **t** in **T**. A necessary statement then is one which is true with respect to not only all worlds but also all time instants within a world. A possible statement is one which is true in at least one world and at least at one moment in time. The future and past tenses have the same semantic rules as before, but the rules only apply to one world. That is, $F\Phi$ is true if and only if at some later time *in the same world* $\Phi$ is true, and similarly with respect to the past tense. Hence, tense operator semantics do not 'cross' worlds.

Denotations of non-logical symbols will now be expressed in terms of two-dimensional matrices, where one dimension stands for the different worlds, and the other dimension stands for different moments in time. For instance,

| Barks_at | $w_1$ | $w_2$ |
|---|---|---|
| $t_1$ | $\{\langle \text{Tanzy,Barney}\rangle,$ $\langle \text{Barney,Tanzy}\rangle\}$ | $\{\langle \text{Tanzy,Barney}\rangle\}$ |
| $t_2$ | $\{\ \}$ | $\{\ \}$ |
| $t_3$ | $\{\langle \text{Petri,Tanzy}\rangle\},$ $\langle \text{Judy,Tanzy}\rangle\}$ | $\{\langle \text{Petri,Tanzy}\rangle\}$ |

Here are some properties of tensed modal languages, according to the way we have defined them:

$$\Box\Phi \to F\Phi$$

$$\Box\Phi \to P\Phi$$

$$F\Box\Phi \leftrightarrow \Box\Phi$$

$$P\Box\Phi \leftrightarrow \Box\Phi$$

$$\Box\Phi \to \Box F\Phi$$

$$\Box\Phi \to \Box P\Phi$$

$$F\Phi \to \Diamond\Phi$$

$$P\Phi \to \Diamond\Phi$$

There is no reason why we should stop at two dimensions of semantic space, namely, tense and modality. We could, logically, add more dimensions, such as utterer of sentence, place of utterance, and so on.

## 4.6 'CAN MACHINES THINK?' OR 'WILL MACHINES THINK?'

At this stage, it may be useful to use the mechanisms and representations of a tensed modal logic to unpack the relationships between *can* and *will* which were described in Chapter 1. We have the property

$$F\Phi \to \Diamond\Phi$$

That is, 'If $\Phi$ will be the case, then $\Phi$ is possibly the case.' Let us replace $\Phi$ with **machines think**. That is, let us adopt the position, which may be dubious, that the words 'can' and 'will' signify modality and tense, respectively, just to see what happens. We now have:

**If in future machines think, then machines can think**.

The truth of this statement will depend, first, on there being, at some future time in a model, and in the same world, a state of affairs in which machines think, which will then allow us to have, as a semantic consequence, the statement that machines can think, and, secondly, on there being *no* machine that will ever think, since the conditional is vacuously true even if the conclusion is false. In the case of the former, we could, of course, set up various denotations (i.e. intension of 'think') in such a way that there is some possible world in which machines will think, but this would be circular. What is required here is to have a world which is as close as possible as to ours — one in which machines do not currently think — and then to examine time-instants in the future to see whether machines will think. If a model is specified in which the intension of 'think' is defined to contain a future state in which machines think, we can then conclude, with respect to that world in that model, that machines can think. Perhaps this is what Turing had in mind when he wrote:

> I believe that at the end of the century the use of words and general educated opinion will have altered so much that one will be able to speak of machines thinking without expecting to be contradicted. (Turing, 1950), p. 442)

That is, Turing may have believed that the meaning, or intension, of 'think' is such that the predicate will be applied to entities, such as computers, some time in the future. Notice that the model only reflects this belief and does not generate it: it is still possible for the conditional statement to be true even if at no future time does a machine think.

In Chapter 1, if we recall, we tried to reformulate Turing's argument logically. We stated there that one interpretation, called $L_1$, goes like this:

**L1: If machine X can pass the imitation game (C2) then it can think (E2). Machine X can pass the imitation game. Therefore, Machine X can think.**

The argument can now be expressed (with constant **a** replacing **X**) as follows:

$$\Diamond(Ma \wedge Pa) \rightarrow \Diamond Ta \quad \text{where} \quad Ma = \mathbf{a} \text{ is a machine,}$$
$$Pa = \mathbf{a} \text{ passes the imitation game,}$$
$$\text{and} \quad Ta = \mathbf{a} \text{ thinks}$$

We have the following sequence of symbolic manipulations:

$$\sim\Diamond(Ma \wedge Pa) \vee \Diamond Ta$$

$$\Box\sim(Ma \wedge Pa) \vee \Diamond Ta$$

$$\Box(\sim Ma \vee \sim Pa) \vee \Diamond Ta$$

$$\sim\Diamond Ta \rightarrow \Box(\sim Ma \vee \sim Pa)$$

$$\Box\sim Ta \rightarrow \Box(\sim Ma \vee \sim Pa)$$

That is, 'If necessarily **a** doesn't think, then necessarily either **a** is not a machine or **a** doesn't pass the imitation game'.

Our other reformulation was as follows:

> Only if Machine X can pass the imitation game can it think. It cannot pass the imitation game. Therefore it cannot think.

In modal terms, this becomes

$$\Diamond(\mathbf{Ma} \wedge \mathbf{Ta}) \rightarrow \Diamond\mathbf{Pa}$$

After some manipulation, this is transformed into:

$$\Box\sim\mathbf{Pa} \rightarrow \Box\sim\mathbf{Ma} \vee \Box\sim\mathbf{Ta}$$

i.e. 'If it is necessarily the case that **a** cannot pass the imitation game, then either it is necessarily the case that **a** is not a machine or it is necessarily the case that **a** does not think.'

Translating these versions of **L1** and **L2** into terms of 'impossibility', we have:

> L1: If it is impossible for **a** to think, then it is impossible for **a** to be a machine and to pass the imitation game.

> L2: If it is impossible for **a** to pass the imitation game, then it is impossible for **a** to be a machine or it is impossible for **a** to think.

Criticisms of Turing's reformulation of the question, 'Can machines think?', can now be categorized according to which of the above interpretations is accepted. (Both interpretations in terms of modal logic can be accepted if we assume the third logical formulation, **L3**: 'A machine thinks if and only if it passes the imitation game.') Also, it is important to note that, according to our way of providing an exposition of tensed and modal logics,

$$\text{F Machines think} \rightarrow \Diamond \text{ Machines think}$$

is a an axiomatic property. That is, if it is the case that in the future machines think, then it is the case that it is possible that machines think. However, we have not claimed that the relationship between future and possibility also goes the other way, namely,

$$\Diamond \text{ Machines think} \rightarrow \text{F Machines think}$$

That is, it is not an axiomatic property of any tensed, modal logic that we have described that if it is possible that machines think, then it follows that there will in the future be thinking machines. Our own interpretation, in other words, is that ordered moments of time can be interpreted individually as possible worlds, but that possible worlds cannot be interpreted as ordered in any temporal sense. That is, from a tensed logic we can derive a modal logic (as our exposition demonstrated), but from a modal logic we cannot derive a tensed logic. This interpretation is to be contrasted with the following quote from Hofstadter that we presented in Chapter 1:

> [Turing's article] is really about . . . 'Can a machine think?' — or rather, 'Will a machine think?' (Hofstadter, 1982, p. 70)

That is, Hofstadter's comment can, from the viewpoint of logic, be interpreted as claiming that we can derive at least a future tensed logic from a modal logic.

The above translations were made on the supposition that 'can' and 'will' express modality and tense, respectively, and we would not want to press this claim very far. What has been shown in the above translations is that modal and tense logics may have a role to play in unpacking the structure of expressions containing 'can' and 'will', but in any case the translations only provide us with alternative ways of expressing the original interpretations and may not help us substantially to identify how to answer the original question, 'Can machines think?'

## 4.7  AI AND SEMANTICS

We can now re-assess one of the concepts central to many objections to the idea that AI is impossible. Roughly speaking, the Argument from Informality of Behaviour is the objection that machines, by their very nature, have no choice but to follow the instructions of a program. Because they have no choice, and because of the nature of the rules, machines cannot be said to 'understand' what they are doing. Therefore, no matter how well a machine appears to simulate the behaviour of a human being, because they have no choice but to follow the rules, they cannot be said to think or be intelligent.

Turing's answer to this objection was to say that it is not possible to determine the circumstances under which we would stop looking for laws of behaviour regulating a person. That is, in principle it is possible that we humans also are governed by laws of various sorts, and that what appears to be freedom of choice is really law-governed. In a sense, Turing is appealing to a scientific hypothesis that, given enough time and effort, human behaviour may well be explained, or described, by a set of laws, or rules. This explanation, or description, may well be in terms of laws of behaviour, as it was for Turing (and which we examined in Chapter 1), or of lower-level laws dealing with the action of molecules — 'reductionism' — which we shall discuss in the next volume, or to *logical* rules, and this is what we have examined in this chapter. We have concentrated on the narrow area of logic which deals with logical rules of meaning and understanding of sentences, logical semantics.

Logical semantics appears to offer some hope for Turing. If it is claimed that to give the meaning of a sentence is to provide truth conditions for that statement to be true, then this is something a computer can be programmed to do. That is, we would expect it to be uncontroversially true that a computer, when fed a sentence, say, **S**, could produce the meta-language sentence: '**S** is true if and only if **W**', where **W** is a description of what the world would be like for the sentence to be true. For instance, if given the sentence **Simba is hungry**, the computer could reply with '**Simba is hungry** is true if and only if the entity named **Simba** is in the set of entities that is denoted by the expression **is hungry**'. This may not get us very far, except that it could be accepted that there is nothing impossible about a computer *providing* truth conditions.

Now, what if it is claimed that to *understand* a sentence is the same as to know what would be the case if the sentence were true, and that this also could be programmed into the computer? The crucial bridge between *giving* the truth conditions, which a computer can do, and *understanding* a sentence, which a computer may not, rests on the phrase '*knowing* what would be the case if the sentence were true'. That is, we have replaced one problematic word, 'understand', with another, 'know'. Can computers 'know' anything?

There are three issues involved here. First, there is the issue of the psychological reality, or plausibility, of such rules. Is it the case that there is a one-to-one correspondence between formal rules of meaning and under- standing, on the other hand, and cognitive structures, on the other? We shall leave this question until the next volume. The second issue is this: under what circumstances is it logically correct, or justified, to ascribe mental predicates of various sorts to humans? And are there circumstances in which we could ascribe such predicates to machines? Logical semantics, as we have seen, describes the extension of a predicate as the set of entities that have the property associated with that predicate. The intension, or sense, of a predicate is what counts for that predicate to be true in different worlds. We need to ask the question of what counts for mental predicates, such as 'know', 'understand', 'feels', 'thinks', and so on, to be true in different worlds. That is, why is 'thinks' true of humans but perhaps not true of machines?

The third issue is whether the characterization of understanding as provided by logical semantics, namely, that to understand a sentence is to know what would be the case if the sentence were true, is a correct or even useful one. This issue is concerned with the relationship that logical semantics has with other branches of philosophy and is not relevant to the relationship between AI and logical semantics as such, and so we shall not discuss it here. (Baker and Hacker (1984) provide a comprehensive critical analysis of logical semantics and its relationship to philosophy of language.) If it is argued that understanding a sentence consists of more than knowing what would be the case if the sentence were true, this is an argument against logical semantics and not against AI.

So, let us assume as a working hypothesis that logical semantics is correct in its portrayal of sentence understanding so that we can examine under what circumstances a human as well as a computer can be said to under- stand, or know, anything. More generally, let us examine whether, and if so how, mental predicates of various types can, logically, be *ascribed* to computers and to humans. The underlying assumption, of course, is that the *intension* of mental predicates is the same in the case of their ascription to humans as well as to computers (McCarthy, 1979). That is, we shall try and construct a language model and an associated logical world where the sense of mental predicates is the same so that both humans and computers fall in the set of entities referred to by a mental predicate. In other words, let us try to unpack the notion of a predicate's intension, or sense, where this is described as what would count for that predicate to be ascribed truthfully to individuals of a domain, in more detail.

Let us assume that there is such a sense, i.e. there is a language model and world in which the sense of mental predicates is the same no matter whether they are ascribed to computers or humans. The argument in favour of such a model and world runs like this:

(1)  we ascribe mental qualities to another person on basis X;
(2)  the computer fulfils the same requirements as a person given basis X;
(3)  hence we ascribe mental qualities to the computer on basis X.

At the heart of basis X will usually lie a view concerning the concept of a person, since it is this view which is invoked when examining how it is that we ascribe mental qualities to each other. The traditional theories which deal with the concept of a person are dualism and behaviourism, and we examined these in Chapter 1. A more useful theory, for our purposes, is found in Strawson (1959).

Strawson's theory, although more complicated than either dualism or behaviourism, has the big advantage that it allows for differences between types of mental predicate. Strawson bases his concept of a person on the distinction between *P-predicates* and *M-predicates*. If we split up the predicates of languages which can be ascribed to entities in the world into these two sorts, M-predicates signify physical or material characteristics (e.g. 'is six feet tall', 'weighs ten stone', 'has black hair') and P-predicates signify the possesion of consciousness on the part of that to which they are ascribed (e.g. 'is hungry', 'is in pain', 'intends going for a walk'). M-predicates are ascribed to others and to oneself purely on the basis of observation. For Strawson, the concept of a person is that of a type of entity such that both M-predicates and P-predicates are equally applicable to an individual entity of that type. In other words, states of consciousness could not be ascribed at all unless they were ascribed to persons.

P-predicates can be divided roughly into three types: those of assessment of character, those of thoughts and feelings, and those of action which imply intention, a state of mind, or at least consciousness in general.

(1)  An assessment P-predicate (e.g. 'is clever', 'its dogmatic' . . .) is ascribed to others on the same basis as it is ascribed to oneself. In other words, behaviour on the part of another person or on the part of oneself constitutes a logically adequate basis for the ascription of such predicates to others and oneself.
(2)  A feeling or thought P-predicate (e.g. 'is in pain', 'is wondering' . . .) is ascribed to others on the basis of observation but not to oneself on this basis. We experience thoughts and feelings and do not need to observe them to ascribe such P-predicates to ourselves. For Strawson, it is essential to predicates having one kind of meaning that they have two ways of being ascribed — one on the basis of behaviour, the other not on this basis.
(3)  A 'doing' or action predicate (e.g. 'is going for a walk', 'is writing a letter' . . .) is ascribed to others on the basis of behaviour and not generally to onself on this basis. But such predicates differ from feeling or thought processes in that there is a marked absence of any experience

of feeling. Thus, we have knowledge of bodily movements without the need for observation or experience.

So, Strawsons's theory implies that a person is no longer to be thought of as consisting primarily of a mind and a body, where the mind acts causally on the body, and where the body acts causally on the mind. Moreover, for Strawson, the concept of a person is such that we see others as self-ascribers, not on the basis of observation, of what we ascribe to them on this basis. We can represent Strawson's theory diagrammatically as follows:

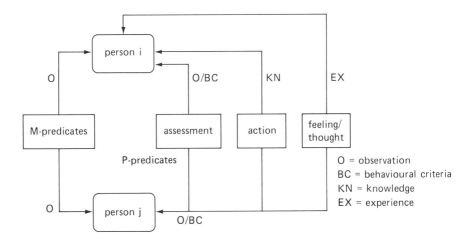

In this diagram, person **i** is myself or the possessor of this conceptual framework, and person **j** is some other person. But for Strawson, the essence of the concept of a person consists of person **i** accepting that in person **j**'s own 'conceptual scheme', person **j** is person **i**.

Strawson's theory, then, incorporates the better points of dualism with those of philosophical behaviourism. We do not intend to become involved in arguments concerning the correctness or incorrectness of Strawson's views at this point, as such considerations will be covered in Volume 2, but merely wish to show how his concept of M-predicates and P-predicates can be applied to computational philosophy in order to provide a logical basis for the ascription of such predicates to a computer.

There is obviously no problem with M-predicates, or material predicates, since we ascribe such predicates to computers (e.g. 'is four feet tall', 'has a dual-drive floppy disc unit') on the basis of observation, and a computer could ascribed M-predicates to us (e.g. 'has black hair', 'has two legs') if it could be provided with an observation mechanism, such as a camera, and a physical-attribute recognition routine. Also, the computer could ascribe M-predicates to itself on the basis of observation, just as we ascribe M-predicates to ourselves on the basis of observation (e.g. using a mirror).

Now let us examine P-predicates. Let us first consider assessment P-predicates such as 'is clever', 'is dogmatic', and so on. Such predicates are ascribed to others on the same basis as they ascribed to ourselves, i.e. on the of behaviour. We would ascribe such predicates to a computer on the basis of its behaviour, and this is essentially the Turing test. A computer could ascribe such predicates to us if it had an observation mechanism. Also, it could ascribe such predicates to us if a description of our behaviour were to be input. In both cases, the computer would need a set of assessment-evaluation routines which would provide a logically adequate basis for the ascription of such predicates to others. Also a description of the computer's own behaviour (e.g. results of computations, time taken to execute a task, details of problem-solving methods used) could be fed back into the computer in order to allow the computer to come to some assessment concerning its own behaviour by means of a similar set of assessment-evaluation routines. Obviously, the computer will have to look for slightly different details when assessing its own behaviour as opposed to a person's behaviour, but it is the basis of ascription which remains the same. That is, behaviour on the part of another person or on the part of itself (or on the part of other computers) constitutes a logically adequate basis for the computer to ascribe such predicates.

Next, let us consider action P-predicates such as 'is going for a walk', 'is writing a letter', 'is performing a task', and so on. According to Strawson, we apply such predicates to others on the basis of behaviour and not generally to oneself on this basis. That is, we could ascribe such predicates to a computer, again through observing the computer's behaviour (e.g. 'is retrieving data', 'is editing a file', 'is compiling a program'). We might have difficulty coping with the speed with which the computer performs its actions, but in principle our ascription of such action predicates is based on behaviour. We do not observe or experience our own actions: we just know what we are doing. A computer could ascribe such predicates to us on the basis of observing our behaviour and using a set of action-evaluation routines. Again this 'observation' could be made by means of a camera or by feeding in a description of our behaviour. Now, can a computer have knowledge of its own action without depending on observation or experience? Let us try to imagine a world where it can.

If asked to state what it is doing at any particular moment, the computer can *display*, or provide, the contents of current registers, program-counter, and so on, and continue with its task without having to observe or experience the contents of its register, program-counter, and so on. Also the computer's operating system keeps track of the processes invoked and the order in which they were invoked. Thus a computer's reply to the question 'What are you doing?' would consist of outputting information which describes the last process or state entered for the human to see. At the very least, the computer could produce a logical semantic rule, such as ' "I am in state x" is true if and only if . . .', which provides the necessary and sufficient conditions for it to be in state x. Notice that there is no question of the computer, when asked to specify what it is doing, monitoring or observing its own actions and behaviour in order to make an action-ascription. Namely, we can imagine that the computer has not only quintuples that are its program but also a description of these quintuples with appropriate responses if asked to describe what it is doing at any given moment.

So, we seem to have presented a model which is consistent with the Srawsonian framework adopted. Strawson's concept of a person is such that we see others as self-ascribers, not on the basis of observation, of what we ascribe to them on this basis.

Now, let us examine feeling and thought predicates, such as 'is in pain', 'is wondering', 'is depressed' and so on. We ascribe such predicates to ourselves by experiencing thoughts and feelings, and we ascribe them to other persons on the basis of observation.

Now, is there a possible world in which we ascribe thought predicates (e.g. 'is thinking') to a computer on the basis of behaviour? Consider the following scenario. If we ask the computer to perform a certain task and there is a pause between entering the request and receiving the answer during which time nothing seems to be happening, it is quite natural for us to say that the computer 'has gone off to have a think about it', or 'has decided to take its time'. We do not notice any oddity in these remarks and make them quite naturally. A frequent reply to such remarks is to say that we authropomorphize in these cases, that we attribute a human form or personality to the computer and therefore we *personify* in such cases. In fact, we appear to be adopting what Dennett calls the 'intentional stance' (Dennett, 1981, Chapter 12), an examination of which we shall leave until the next volume.

Hence, this imagined world is one in which personification takes place. In other words, 'Can we ascribe mental qualities to machines?' is synonymous with 'Can we provide a sound basis for anthropomorphizing (personifying) computers?' and 'Is there an area of overlap between the categories of computers and persons?', in the world under consideration. However, we now come to two important points.

First, many people would, within the Strawsonian framework, find it unnatural to say that a computer ascribes such thought predicates to itself by experiencing thoughts of various sorts. In the case of another person, they would not find such self-ascription unnatural, whereas in the case of computers there is doubt on this point. It is Strawson's point of course that it is logically necessary to regard other persons as being self-ascribers not on the basis of observation, of that which we ascribe to them on that basis.

Secondly, again within the Strawsonian framework, many people would have great reluctance in ascribing feeling predicates to computers, no matter how much the computer behaves in a way which conforms to the criteria for ascribing such predicates. For instance, they do not make such ascriptions because they believe that the computer is not a person but a machine which has been programmed to behave in this way, programmed to model or simulate human behaviour. Nor is it a mere machine; rather it is a machine to which two-thirds of P-predicates, those of assessment and of action, can be applied, as well as half of the remaining predicates, those of thought.

So, given a Strawsonian framework, it appears that we can construct a world in which the computer is regarded not as a complete person, nor as a mere machine or physical object, but somewhere in between. That is, we seem to have provided a mechanism which makes some degree of personification possible. This should not be surprising, since there are examples of degrees of personification all around us. The category 'pets' is on the whole more highly personified than the category 'wild animals'. Within the category 'pet', cats tend to be more highly personified than tortoises. The category 'robots' (of the Star Wars ilk) tends to be more highly personified than 'manual typewriters'. The important point to note here is that Strawson's theory does provide us with a logical mechanism which is consistent with our original assumption; that ascribing mental qualities to a computer expresses the same information about the computer that is expresses about a person. That is, it is consistent with respect to just those qualities that can be ascribed to a computer, no more and no less. But Strawson's framework does not provide us with a mechanism for ascribing all mental predicates to a computer, so we are in effect not ascribing total person-status to it.

Now, the question arises as to whether it is in principle possible to use quintuples, logic and semantics to add to the Strawsonian framework so that we can construct a world in which a computer can ascribe thought predicates and feeling predicates to itself in a manner which is consistent with the way we ascribe such predicates to ourselves. Let us make a brief attempt at doing so.

When dealing with action or doing predicates, quintuples were used to present an alternative but equivalent description of the way a computer (and a person) could ascribe such predicates to itself (himself/herself). This was possible because we introduced as an input a question that asked for a description of the system itself. Now, can we introduce similar inputs for thought and feeling? Let us examine thought predicates ('thinking', 'wondering' . . .) first of all.

If we were to introduce a question such as 'What are you thinking?', it might appear that we could use the same model as before for allowing the system to utter, in response, descriptions of itself which, if true, are true in virtue of the system being in the state it was in when it produced the description (Thomas, 1978). So for instance, if the system were asked to describe what it is thinking, it could utter such responses as 'I am thinking that the problem I am working on is difficult', or 'I am puzzled', or even the response 'Nothing', all of which , if true, are true in virtue of the system being in the state it was in when it produced these responses. Just as before, it is not necessary for the response to use a predicate which contains a precise description of the state itself. A general predicate would suffice.

This model is unsatisfactory for two reasons. First, such a model (and associated world) fails to distinguish adequately the difference within the Strawsonian framework between the basis for ascribing an action predicate and that for ascribing a thought predicate to oneself. According to Strawson, we have knowledge of our actions which is generally marked by an absence of feeling or experience, whereas we do experience thoughts and feelings. By introducing the same formal basis for self-ascription of both types of predicates to oneself, we are in effect nullifying this distinction and therefore rejecting it.

Secondly, applying the model for self-ascription of action predicates to self-ascription of thought predicates does not correspond closely with our intuition as to what happens when we do ascribe thought predicates to ourselves. When we say that we are puzzled or that we are finding a problem difficult, we seem to be making a meta-remark of some sort which attempts to describe our view of the state or situation we are in. That is, when we do ascribe such thought predicates to ourselves, we do not seem to be confining our remarks to one particular state but to a whole sequence or set of states. For instance, 'I am perplexed' would, if true, not only be true of the system that uttered the decription in virtue of the system being in the state it was in when it uttered the description, but also be true in virtue of the system *having been* in a certain state (or set of states) that it had been prior to it having uttered the description (Thomas, 1978). Now, if this is indeed the case, a straightforward application of our earlier model would fail to represent adequately the nature of self-ascription of thought predicates. In the earlier model, a description using an action predicate could be true of more than one state that the system finds itself in. But a description, if true, is true in virtue of the system being in a particular state (or being in a particular set of states) that it is in when it produces the description. The 'power' of thought predicates, on the other hand, appears to lie in a system being able to ascribe such thought predicates to itself which describe the sequence of events or states, or even the very last state, that it was in prior to its present state. But such a description, if true, is not true solely in virtue of the state the system is in when it produces the description. Rather, it seems as if we are making a meta-description, after the utterance of which we may return to the state we were in prior to our utterance of the description, that is, return to the state table to 'pick up our train of thought', or 'resume where we left off'.

If we assume that the above comments are correct in their portrayal of thought predicates, proponents of claims that machines can be ascribed mental predicates with the same sense as when these mental predicates are applied to humans will need perhaps to resort to a form of tensed logic within the modal framework. We shall not discuss such a model further. Our only objective was to shed some light on why it is that some AI philosophers are actively pursuing logic notations and semantic models in their search for some world in which it is possible for machines to think.

The whole enterprise of searching for possible worlds and a suitable language model has ignored the major objection that ascription of mental predicates to computers is logically impossible, simply because the ascription of mental predicates to any entity implies, or presupposes, that the entity in question has consciousness. Strawson himself makes this point when he characterizes P-predicates as implying consciousnes on the part of that to which they are ascribed. The claim here is that if the entity to which mental predicates are being applied does not possess consciousness in the first place, then our endeavours above are futile. Of course, this claim requires that there be a characterization of consciousness that does not appeal to mental predicates, otherwise circularity will arise: an entity is conscious if mental predciates can be ascribed to it, and mental predicates can be ascribed to an entity if it is conscious. Namely, although such a *definition* of consciousness and mental predicates in terms of each other may be intuitively appealing, it does not get us very far, since it is open to AI researchers to claim, simply, that computers are conscious because we can ascribe mental predicates to them, as happened in the personification world.

One way of unpacking the notion of consciousness in terms other than mental predicates is to argue that a necessary condition of an entity having consciousness is that the entity be alive. Although, strictly speaking, a machine cannot be said to be dead, it can be said strictly and necessarily that a machine is not alive. Hence, a necessary condition for an entity to be a machine is that the entity be not alive. Since being alive is a necessary condition for having consciousness, an entity cannot meet both the conditions for being a machine and the conditions for having consciousness, at the same time. Thus, the phrase 'conscious machine' fails for the same logical reasons as such phrases as 'childless parent' (Sayre, 1968).

The proponent of such an argument then has the task of specifying the conditions under which we would say that an entity was 'alive' in order to provide a sound basis for his or her argument. Since such conditions are attempting to provide a sound logical basis for the ascription of such terms as 'consciousness', 'feeling' and all the other mental predicates of language, these conditions cannot themselves use such terms when being formulated, otherwise, as we saw above, circularity arises. The force of this argument is to question the entire approach of constructing a world in which computers and humans can be equally ascribed with mental predicates of various sorts. But if, as Strawson claims, P-predicates imply the possession of consciousness on the part of that to which they are ascribed, computers, being machines, cannot possibly fall in the same sets of individuals as those denoted by various P-predicates. If the proponent of the above argument can claim that machines, specifically computers, cannot possess consciousness then it makes no sense to ascribe any mental predicates to computers at all. That is, there is no such possible world.

Since all above objection rests on there being a clear definition of what it is to be alive, it may be in order for AI researchers to call for this definition to be made explicit. One way to formulate the conditions which allow us to say an entity is 'alive' may be to specify the structural properties of an entity. If we wish to detemine whether an entity is alive or not, we do not use its behaviour as a criterion. Rather we examine its internal structure in order to determine whether the entity is made out of protoplasm-like material as opposed to gears, wheels, silicon, wires . . . (As we shall see in Volume 2, Searle (1980) comes close to adopting such a position, but adds one or two extra conditions.)

The weakness of this argument is that even if it is a necessary condition of an entity being alive that its structure consists of certain biological features, this is certainly not a sufficient condition from the point of view of those who wish to formulate conditions for being alive. It is quite possible that biological material may itself be synthesized and put into a mechanical entity, such as an android, in order to make the mechanical entity more 'life-like'. Thus, the structure of an entity cannot by itself determine whether an entity is alive or not. The formulator of the conditions for being alive needs to introduce some other factor which serves to distinguish categorically between entities that are alive and those that are not (Sayre, 1968).

What the above shows is that, at the end of the day, debate on the Argument from Informality of Behaviour may well centre around the simple question, 'Can machines be conscious?' So what is consciousness? Alas, before we can look at that question, we need to examine developments in philosophy of mind since the original Objection called 'The Argument from Consciousness' was described by Turing himself back in 1950. And that is in the next volume!

Let us summarize the main contribution that AI can make to semantics. It is clear that if AI is attacked on the grounds that to follow rules necessarily does not lead to understranding, then much of formal semantics will also be victim to this attack. That may be no bad thing, in the eyes of some philosophers, but what AI can demonstrate here is that it is not only AI that is subject to this criticism. In fact, generalizing the criticism, the confusion may well have to be that any attempt to provide a formal theory of understanding or meaning is doomed to failure. But, of course, even non-formal theories which can be formalized will also be subject to this criticism. The conclusion that no theorizing about understanding and meaning is possible may well not be far away, and such a sceptical position may not be what is desired, especially if it is only AI that is the target. But if AI goes on the basis of the 'Informality of Behaviour' argument, so does a lot of philosophy and even psychology, or any study of human intelligence which attempts to formulate rules for the domain being studied. The traditional way to escape from this conclusion in other areas is to make clear the claims being made for the 'reality' of the rules and their ontological status. For instance, we can be quick to point out that knowing how to swim does not imply knowing the various laws of physics that deal with buoyancy. Similarly, if a rock falls to the ground, there is no necessity, or possibility, of the rock needing to have knowledge of the laws of gravity before it falls. That is, there are already clear distinctions available for attributing psychological reality, or ontological status, to formalisms. AI's main contribution to the debate may well be to show that these distinctions are either well-founded, or misconceived, and in either case the logical basis for picking out an individual, be it human or computer, in the world and predicating a mental property of it needs examining in great detail. The problem of whether machines can think will not disappear if AI disappears, since we shall still be left with the central problem of how it is that we ascribe mental predicates to each other. At the very least, AI will provide a lower bound on what counts as correct, or appropriate, ascription, and what does not.

The problem arises with the way the whole question is debated: if computers have no choice but to follow rules, then they cannot be said to think or be intelligent, even if the rules concerned are called 'semantic' rules; we humans think and are intelligent, and therefore we do more than follow rules in that we have a choice. We shall now reformulate the question. 'Can machines think?' and the Argument from the Informality of Behaviour, from a semantic point of view: 'Is it the case that solely in virtue of running a computer program of the appropriate sort a machine can be said to think, or understand, or have experiences?' We shall carry forward this question to the next volume.

## REFERENCES

Baker, G. P. and Hacker, P. M. S. (1984) *Language, sense and nonsense.* Basil Blackwell.

Carnap, R. (1947) *Meaning and necessity.* University of Chicago Press.

Carr, B. (1987) *Metaphysics: an introduction.* Macmillan.

Dennett, C. (1981) *Brainstorms.* Harvester Press.

Dowty, D. R., Wall, R. E. and Peters, S. (1981) *Introduction to Montague semantics.* Reidel.

Frege, G. (1879) *Begriffsschrift.* Translated and republished in Geach, P. T. and Black, M. (eds) (1970) *Philosophy writings of Gottlob Frege,* (second edition), Basil Blackwell.

Galton, A. (1987) Temporal logic and computer science, in Galton, A. (ed.), *Temporal logic and its applications.* Academic Press.

Grayling, A. G. (1982) *An introduction to philosophical logic.* Harvester Press.

Hofstadter, D. R. (1982) The Turing test: a coffee house conversation, in Hofstadter, D. R. and Dennett, D. G. (eds) *The Mind's I.* Penguin.

Lewis, D. (1973) *Counterfactuals.* Harvard University Press.

McCarthy, J. (1979) Ascribing mental qualities to machines, in Ringle, M. (ed.) *Philosophical perspectives in artificial intelligence.* Harvester Press.

McCawley, D. (1981) *Everything that linquists have Always Wanted to Know about logic (but were ashamed to ask).* Basil Blackwell.

Montague, R. (1970) English as a formal language. Reprinted in Thomason, R. H. (ed.) *Formal Philosophy: Selected Papers of Richard Montague.* Yale University Press, 1974.

Prior, A. N. (1955) Diodoran modalities, *Philosophical Quarterly,* **5** 205–213.

Prior, A. N. (1967) *Past, present and future.* Clarendon Press.

Sayre, K. M. (1968) *Consciousness: a philosophical study of minds and machines.* Random House.

Stillings, N. A., Feinstein, M. H., Garfield, J. L., Rissland, E. L., Rosenbaum, D. A., Weisler, S. E. and Baker-Ward, L. (1987) *Cognitive science: an introduction.* MIT Press.

Strawson, P. F. (1959) *Individuals.* Methuen.

Tarski, A. (1935) The concept of truth in formalized languages, originally published in *Studia Philosopoohica,* **1**, 261–405. Translated in Tarski, A. (ed.) *Logic, semantics, and metamathematics.* Clarendon Press 1956.

Thomas, S. N. (1978) *The formal mechanics of mind.* Harvester Press.

Wittgenstein, L. (1921) *Tractatus logico-philosophicus* (translated by Pears, D. F. and McGuinness, B. F.). Routledge and Kegan Paul, 1969 (fourth impression).

# Appendix — Greek Alphabet

| small | capital | name |
|---|---|---|
| α | A | alpha |
| β | B | beta |
| γ | Γ | gamma |
| δ | Δ | delta |
| ε | E | epsilon |
| ζ | Z | zeta |
| η | H | eta |
| θ | Θ | theta |
| ι | I | iota |
| κ | K | kappa |
| λ | Λ | lambda |
| μ | M | mu |
| ν | N | nu |
| ξ | Ξ | xi |
| o | O | omicron |
| π | Π | pi |
| ρ | P | rho |
| σ | Σ | sigma |
| τ | T | tau |
| υ | Y | upsilon |
| φ | Φ | phi |
| χ | X | chi |
| ψ | Ψ | psi |
| ω | Ω | omega |

In order to aid exposition of formed material, the Greek alphabet is commonly used to increase the number of symbols (26) available in the Roman alphabet. It sometimes helps to be able to call Greek symbols by their names, and the above table is presented here for that purpose.

# Index